ArtScroll® Series

Rabbi Nosson Scherman / Rabbi Meir Zlotowitz

General Editors

Touched

Published by
Mesorah Publications, ltd

by a Story

Inspiring stories retold by a master teacher

RABBI YECHIEL SPERO

FIRST EDITION
First Impression ... September 2003
Second Impression ... November 2003
Third Impression ... December 2003
Fourth Impression ... December 2003
Fifth Impression ... November 2005
Sixth Impression ... August 2013

Published and Distributed by
MESORAH PUBLICATIONS, LTD.
4401 Second Avenue / Brooklyn, N.Y 11232

Distributed in Europe by
LEHMANNS
Unit E, Viking Industrial Park
Rolling Mill Road
Jarow, Tyne & Wear, NE32 3DP
England

Distributed in Australia and New Zealand by
GOLDS WORLDS OF JUDAICA
3-13 William Street
Balaclava, Melbourne 3183
Victoria, Australia

Distributed in Israel by
SIFRIATI / A. GITLER — BOOKS
6 Hayarkon Street
Bnei Brak 51127

Distributed in South Africa by
KOLLEL BOOKSHOP
Northfield Centre, 17 Northfield Avenue
Glenhazel 2192, Johannesburg, South Africa

ISBN 10: 1-57819-382-6 / ISBN 13: 978-1-57819-382-0

Typography by CompuScribe at ArtScroll Studios, Ltd.
Printed in the United States of America by Noble Book Press Corp.
Bound by Sefercraft, Quality Bookbinders, Ltd., Brooklyn N.Y. 11232

מכתב ברכה מאת הרב דוד קוויאט

ר"מ בישיבת מיר

ורב דאגודת ישראל סניף חפץ חיים

ב"ה

י"ג מנחם אב תשס"ג

מכתב ברכה

לכבוד ידידי הרב יחיאל ספירא שליט"א, רבי בישיבת הק'
חפץ חיים בבלטימור,

הנה בא לפני עלים מספרך אשר כתבת ושמו "נתרגש פון א
מעשה" הנה כשמו כן הוא כולו ספורים יקרים המביא
רגשות קודש להקוראים בו, מה שנחוץ זה למאוד לחזק
האמונה וללמוד איך להתנהג באמונה ובמדות טובות כמו
שעולה מהספורים. ולכן אברכהו שיצליח בספרו ושיהנו
הקוראים בו,והשם יתב' יברכהו להרבות תורה ומוסר
ויגדיל תורה ויאדיר.

ממני ידידו המברכו בכל לב

דוד קוויאט

Foreword

*L*et me tell you a story.

Whether you are a speaker at the podium or sitting in the audience, these words have an immediate impact. Listeners lean forward in anticipation, speakers' eyes light up with excitement. There is something so special about stories — an energy inherent in the telling and hearing. Within just a few minutes, we are engrossed in a setting, we are part of someone's life, embroiled in their struggles or joys. And at the end — the powerful resolution, the implied life lesson leaves us with something to think about, something to laugh or cry about, and maybe even something that will change us forever. How many of us cite a special story as the very moment when we made a decision to make ourselves better, different, kinder.

Young children lie in bed waiting in breathless anticipation for the nighttime tale — whether their parents speak of their own childhood, or read a story about another person — a simple Jew or a great, famous *gadol* — children gobble up the stories like candy. As long as it is a story, they are captivated. And they learn.

The Torah itself chooses the method of *sippur* to convey the lessons of *Yetzias Mitzrayim*, the foundation of our *emunah*. What better way to touch the very *neshamos* of *Bnei Yisrael* than through a dramatic, awe-inspiring story that they will tell and re-tell and discuss and study for thousands of years.

These timeless tales carry with them a special something that touches us in a way nothing else can. They inspire and entertain. Motivate and amuse. But most of all they teach. Almost with a life of their own, they can touch our *neshamos* and reach places within ourselves we did not even know were there. Such is the power of a story.

It elevates us and uplifts us to dream of levels we never thought achievable. It gives us a chance to identify with individuals who have touched immortality, not necessarily through open miracles, but by overcoming the inclinations of human nature, the conquest of soul over body. The triumph of the *pintele Yid*.

Many of the stories in this book are tales borne out of intense suffering and tragedy — tales of loss, of pain, of deepest sorrow. Others are tales of utter joy and celebration. All come from real people — none are fabricated. For this I am thankful to and humbled by the stories' originators, because being able to share a horrific tale from one's history, or the history of one's family, is overwhelmingly difficult, just as sharing a very personal moment of joy requires giving up something which one might not always wish to share.

For all the stories' originators, it was important that the lessons learned from these life experiences be shared with others. Because what happened to these people is more than an episode in their lives — it is an episode in Hashem's holy world, and it happened for a reason. We will never know the true reason, but at least we can, by reading these tales, peek into a moment of someone else's life and get a glimpse of greatness, of true heroism and of the wonders of the *Borei Olam*.

Many of our *gedolim*, dating back to the days of the *Rishonim*, have extolled the virtues of stories. The great Reb Moshe of Kobrin suggests that the word *sippur* is related to the word *sappir,* meaning "light," because stories enlighten the *nefesh* of a *Yid*. These selections have moved me and I pray that they inspire the reader as well.

Stories do not change the world, people do. This dictum captures the essence of what this book is all about. Moments of inspiration flash before us all. It is what we do with this spark that dictates whether the flicker will kindle a light inside our *neshamos* or sadly dwindle and die. It is my hope and prayer that those who read this book will truly be — touched by a story.

Acknowledgments

FIRST AND FOREMOST, I WOULD LIKE TO THANK THE *Ribbono Shel Olam* for making this happen. Throughout the process of writing the book there were countless times when I was privileged to see the *hashgachah* and the *Yad Hashem*. For that and for everything else with which He has provided me, I am humbled and eternally grateful.

The Hebrew Academy of Cleveland, under the leadership of **Rabbi N. W. Dessler,** was the foundation of my Torah *chinuch*. It is at the Hebrew Academy that I was taught the *aleph- beis* of what was to be the cornerstone of my education.

Rabbi Yitzchok Schwartz, my eighth-grade rebbi, was perhaps the one whose stories most inspired me and many of my friends in my years in Telshe Yeshivah. We will never forget the *"radiator* *meiselach"* that were simply too *moiredik* to relate while standing on the floor and had to be told while standing on the radiator.

Rabbi Anshel Hellman has been much more than a rebbi to me over the past twenty three years. He has been my confidant and my inspiration. To him I am indebted beyond words. **Rabbi Shlomo Eisenberger,** my *shadchan* and rebbi, has encouraged me and given me goals for which to strive. He has never stopped demanding from me and his warmth and concern are always with me.

In Eretz Yisrael I was privileged to learn in the **Mirrer Yeshivah** under **Rav Beinish Finkel** זצ"ל and יבלחט"ט **Rav Nosson Tzvi Finkel.** My rebbeim, **Rav Elya Boruch Finkel** and **Rav Asher Arieli,** helped me develop in my learning and grow as a *ben Torah.* **Rabbi and Mrs. Nosson Weisz** opened their home to me and treated me as a member of their family. I will always remember their kindness.

Lakewood's Beth Medrash Govoha was my family's home for five years. The years that I spent there helped form the way we live as a family. It was there that I first met **Rabbi Shalom Kamenetzky.** His creativity, warmth and brilliance have made a tremendous impact on my life. A kind principal, **Rabbi Yitzchok Charner,** gave me my first job as a rebbi in the **Torah School of Greater Washington.** Thank you for believing in me.

Rabbi Tzvi Teichman is the *menahel* in Yeshivas Chofetz Chaim Talmudical Academy of Baltimore, where I have been *zocheh* to serve as a rebbi for the past five years. It was his idea to gather all my stories into a book that prompted me to write this book in the first place. His input, critique, encouragement, and advice are immeasurable. Thank you.

Rabbi Yaakov Schwartz is the *menahel* of the Yeshivas Chofetz Chaim Middle School. His friendship and support have been invaluable. **Rabbi Shea Benstein,** the principal of G.I.F.T., where I teach in the afternoon, is a visionary and a good friend.

During the past ten years of my life I have been fortunate to spend my summers in Camp Ma-Na-Vu, where I now serve as the head counselor. **Rabbi Shloime Klein,** the owner and director, has provided a beautiful summer home for my family and afforded me the opportunity to share my stories with the camp on countless occasions. Thank you so much. **Rabbi Pinchos Wachsman,** my uncle, as well as the head learning director in the camp, has always been supportive, encouraging and helpful.

Rabbi Sruly Fuchs and **Rabbi Aaron Basch** are dear friends, and their advice and critique throughout has been much appreciated. An added note of gratitude is due to **Chaim Wealcatch.**

My dear parents, **Dr. Abba and Sarah Spero,** have guided me through life. They are unique and special not only to me but to all who are privileged to know them. Their assistance and support throughout this entire project have made it so much easier. Without you where would I be?

Rabbi Yehuda and Nussy Lefkovitz are my in-laws. But I am treated with the same unbridled love they bestow upon each of their children. Pillars of the Baltimore community, they are loved by all. Their suggestions and guidance have helped me not only through this book but throughout life. May they continue to have much *nachas* from all their children and grandchildren.

My grandmother, **Mrs. Elissa Spero,** is a regal woman. She is the matriarch of the Spero family and a queen of a human being. She has entertained and amused her children, grandchildren and great-grandchildren on her couch for many many decades. She is a link to the past and an inspiration to those who know her.

My wife's grandfather, **Rav Moshe "Papa" Lefkovitz,** is a man of shining character and sterling qualities. He exudes love and warmth to his *eineklach* and together with his wife יבלח"ט Mrs. **Gertrude Lefkovitz** were a role model for us all. My wife's grandparents, **Rabbi and Mrs. Yerachmiel Berger,** with their *aidelkeit* and integrity have always shown their love and support and given their children a stellar example of what a Yiddishe family should be.

Some of my grandparents are no longer with us. **Mr. Herbert I. Spero,** my **Grandpa Herb,** was a tower of strength for the Torah community in Cleveland. I am fortunate to have learned much about him from those who loved him most. My **Bubby and Zaidy, Rabbi Yehuda and Rebbitzen Chana Leah Moses,** lost everyone and everything they had in the war. But with undying faith and the help of Hashem rebuilt their lives and their families. It is an honor to be an *einekel.*

Rabbi Nosson Scherman and Rabbi Meir Zlotowitz are creative, imaginative and inventive. They believed in my work and in this book when it was nothing more than a collection of stories scattered in a few notebooks. Their trust and faith in me is something for which I cannot thank them enough. A special note of thanks goes to Rabbi Gedalia Zlotowitz.

Mrs. Susan Leibtag is an outstanding editor, but more important, an outstanding person. Her talent for editing and critique and daily insights have proved invaluable, not only for myself but for the many institutions to which she lends her time. She always seemed to have the correct word and the appropriate suggestion. Thank you is not enough.

It was the staff of ArtScroll/Mesorah that finally "made" this book. Reb Eli Kroen's cover design is a masterpiece. Mrs. Mindy Stern's comments and revisions were invaluable; and they were patiently typed by Mrs. Libby Brecher. Mrs. Faigy Weinbaum and Mrs. Tova Ovits proofread the book, which was typeset by Mrs. Tzini Fruchthandler, Mrs. Leah Weiner, and Devorah Scheiner. Avrohom Biderman coordinated the many facets of the work, and held my hand throughout it all. Their professionalism and know-how are unique and much appreciated.

For all those who have shared their stories with me, whether their own or ones they have come across, thank you. Regardless of whether I have included them in this selection or not, I am extremely grateful.

The following have contributed through the stories in the book and I thank them: Sefardic Press and Rabbi Heber for the Joseph Beyda story, Rabbi Yitzchok Dinovitzer, Rabbi Yitzchok Raskas, Rabbi Shmuel Kaufman, Rebbi Hill, Rabbi Aaron Gruman, Mike Lerman, Freddy Levitz, Rabbi Yaakov Bogart, Rabbi Moshe Kulik, Shaya Katz, Rabbi Ephraim Wachsman, Rabbi Chaim Kahan, Rabbi Avrohom Notis, Rabbi and Mrs. Aryeh, Rabbi Moshe Eisemann, Rabbi Mordechai Finkelman, Rabbi Laibel Scheinbaum, Rabbi Yitzchok Feldheim, Rabbi Naftoli Hexter, Rabbi Yehuda Goldfeder, Dov Chernitzky, Moshe and Yehudis Spero, Rabbi Armo Kuessous, Rabbi Rephoel Mendlowitz, Rabbi Betzalel Elazary, Mr. Shaul Annisfeld, Mr. Chaim Kreiger, Mr. Hirsch

Meilich Kuhnreich, Dovid and Sorala Lefkovitz, Rabbi Shragi Hershkowitz, Mrs. Hadassah Shapiro, Rabbi Simcha Shafran, and Aryeh Gross.

My siblings **Chaim and Rebecca Spero, Moshe and Gila Spero, Chavi and Chesky Shneider, Yehuda Spero, Yanky and Shana Lefkovitz, Sruly and Zahava Lefkovitz, Ezzy and Esti Feuer, Shuku and Chayala Lefkovitz, Efraim and Leah Blumenkrantz, and Eliyahu and Sivi Rokowski** have supported and encouraged me throughout this entire venture. They are proof that there really is nothing like family.

My **talmidim**, both in school and in camp, have listened as I've retold all of these stories and many more. I thank them for their patience and enthusiasm.

My children, Tzvi Aryeh, Avrohom Yosef, Efraim Shimon, Miriam Brocha and Shmuel Avigdor, have taken such pride in the book. But all that I do pales in comparison to the pride I take in you. May Hashem continue to grant us immeasurable *nachas*.

And, finally, my greatest appreciation, admiration and thanks is reserved for my wife **Chumi**. And it is to you that I dedicate this book.

Yechiel Spero

Baltimore, Maryland
Elul 5763

Table of Contents

Rebbeim and Talmidim / Teachers and Students

Harmless Scuds   20
Eternal Impressions   22
Dancing Like a Drunkard   24
Anything ... for a Talmid   25
Ponytails and Peshatim   27

Mitzvos

Fresh and Crisp   32
Right Guy, Wrong Time   33
For the Sake of a Mitzvah   36

Kiddush Hashem / Sanctifying Hashem's Name

Children Will Be Children   40
Memories at Soldier Field   43
An Unforgettable Flight   44

Faith

Reach for the Stars   48
Quality vs. Quantity   50
The Trip That Lasted a Lifetime   53
The Next Gadol Hador   57
Paderewski, Pianos and Prodigies   60
Red Light, Green Ligh,t One, Two, Three, 62
Kishinev Konnections   63
Thank You   65

Teshuvah / Repentance

Who Are You? 68
The Search for Truth 70
One Small Favor 73
The White Flag 77
Lose the Battle but Win the War 81

Mesiras Nefesh / Self-Sacrifice

The Greatest Hero 86
A Smile Through Sadness 89
The Holy Stockings 91
Never Ever 95
Shabbos All Week Long 98
Dollars and Sense 101
Magical Lights 105
Heiliga Hakafos 107
The Wedding Ring 110
Little Angels 113
No Strings Attached 116
Wagons and the World to Come 118

Hashgachah Pratis / Divine Providence

The Badgering Beggar 122
Switching Places 124
Hashem Has a Plan 126
For the Fighting Irish 129
Souled Shoes 131

D'veikus BaShem / Cleaving to Hashem

Pesach Preparations 136
Heavenly Cake 138
Who Wrote This? 139
Of Joy and Sadness 141
The Kohen Gadol 143

To Sing From the Heart   145
The Blind Cripple   147
Resilience and Resolve   149
Sleep Well   157
A Ticket to Gan Eden   154
Ayy Ayy   156
Always Together   160
Alive and Well   163
The Time Machine   165

Tefillah / Prayer

A Bubby's Tears   170
The Most Valuable Thing in the World   172
A Mother's Prayers   176
Tehillim and Tumults   178
The Mysterious Letter   179
A First Time for Everything   182
Babies and Bubble Gum   184

Torah

Hunger Pains   188
The Holy Sweater   191
Shortcuts and Shteiging   193
Just a Piece of Paper   194
The Strongest Rock in the World   194
Accusations and Incriminations   197
Happy Birthday   199
The Very Last One   200
The Delayed Breakfast   203
My One and Only Mitzvah   205
The Happiest Man Alive   207
In the Shadow of the Kremlin   209
For Now and Forever   213
For the Sake of a Gadol   215

Chesed / Kindness

Angelic Inmates ... 220
Looking for Direction ... 223
The Everlasting Friendship ... 225
What a Wedding ... 227
Stammering and Stumbling ... 229
All the King's Horses ... 231
Two Are Better Than One ... 233
Measure for Measure ... 234
Heiliga Hakafos (Part 2) ... 237
The Wedding Blessing ... 240
Caught in the Act ... 242
Caught in the Act (Part 2) ... 244
The Bidding War ... 246
The Sounds of Silence ... 249
Sleep, Snow and Siberia ... 252
The Torn Tallis ... 254
Tell Him Mo Called ... 256
Kaddish on Credit ... 258
Saved by a Favor ... 261
I Never Stopped Hearing Her Cry ... 264
A Picture Is Worth a Thousand Words ... 266
Ah Freilichen Purim ... 270

Gevurah / Courage

Sensitivity and Strength ... 274
The Broken Bus Driver ... 276
Of Hugs and Kisses ... 278
Last Moments ... 280
Friendly Fighting ... 283
A Little White Lie ... 288

Glossary ... 293

Rebbeim and Talmidim / Teachers and Students

Harmless Scuds

*T*HOSE WHO ARE PRIVILEGED TO KNOW THE ROSH YESHIVAH
of the Mirrer Yeshivah, Rav Nosson Tzvi Finkel, do not have
to be reminded of his greatness. He is a warm, caring individual who treats each disciple as if he is the only one — when in
fact the Mirrer Yeshivah has 4,000 students!

What makes Rav Nosson Tzvi even more amazing is that he has
many physical handicaps. He suffers from an advanced case of
Parkinson's disease and as a result his body shakes continually, and
he cannot walk on his own. But the schedule he maintains would
wear down a healthy man half his age, and his tireless devotion to
his students is evident in his every action.

In early 1991 Saddam Hussein posed a serious, deadly threat to
Israel — he had threatened over and over again to fire scud missiles
into Israel should the United States threaten Iraq. On January 15,
1991, the first scud missile attack was unleashed against the people

of Israel. Thousands, on hearing the sirens, rushed into their sealed rooms and put on gas masks.

The students in the yeshivah also ran into their sealed rooms and began the final taping of the windows, as they had been instructed. Although they tried to maintain their composure, the fear of the unknown gave rise to a palpable tension. A few of the young men took charge and helped others. A quick check of the hallways insured that all the students were now in sealed rooms. The doors were closed and the final taping was done. The radio announcer was giving instructions as to what should happen next. It had been three minutes since the alarm had gone off, and the fear of the impending possible chemical or biological attack was taking its toll on several of the young men. Some were saying *Tehillim* while others were too overwhelmed to do anything. Tears could be seen on some boys' faces; anxiety and uneasiness mixed with fear of the unknown.

Awaiting the crashing sounds of bombs and explosions, the boys were alarmed by the harsh knocking on the door. Menachem, the young man in charge, shouted through his mask, clearly agitated and nervous, "Who is it?!" and thought to himself, *Why couldn't this guy have made it into the room in time? Now we'll have to undo all the tape to open the door!*

"It's Nosson Finkel." The reply was soft, almost apologetic. Menachem wondered if it was some sort of a cruel, poor joke — someone impersonating the Rosh Yeshivah! This was not a time for practical jokes. "What did you say your name was?" Menachem was hoping to detect from the response who it really was, but just in case, he began peeling away the tape from the door.

Menachem opened the door and standing before him was none other than the Rosh Yeshivah himself. He was exhausted and breathing heavily. He held his gas mask in his hands. Menachem was mortified. He quickly assisted the Rosh Yeshivah into a seat and helped place his gas mask over his face. "Rebbi, why did you come? How did you get here?"

"I had arranged beforehand with a taxi driver to come pick me up in my home the moment that the first alarm went off. I just wanted to be with my boys."

The room was now silent. The students all gazed at their rebbi in amazement and awe. For a healthy man to do what he did would have been courageous and brave, but for someone in the Rosh Yeshivah's condition to come at this time was both mind-boggling and incredibly inspiring.

Eternal Impressions

YITZCHOK RASKAS HARDLY EVER WENT TO SHACHARIS, not during the years he spent learning in Telshe Yeshivah and not during his brief tenure so far in Ner Yisroel. A young, impressionable teenager, he had his own ideas abut what was important and what was not. He was a good student who really enjoyed learning. And learn he did. He spent much of his spare time in the *beis medrash* and never thought that davening with a *minyan* was worth "sacrificing" his night-owl schedule. And so he continued to learn till 1 or 2 o'clock in the morning and Shacharis remained the furthest thing from his mind.

At that time, the *mashgiach* in the yeshivah, Reb Dovid Kronglas, had created a tumult in the yeshivah by expelling six boys from the dormitory for improper behavior. Among other things, they had been negligent in their attendance of Shacharis. But Yitzchok, although as absent as ever, was spared the punishment the others had suffered. No one dared question the *mashgiach*. He was well known for his expertise in handling each one of his students according to his needs. He had that special intuition, and the young men loved him for it. Yitzchok felt lucky to have been spared, but still his attendance did not improve.

The yeshivah's new campus was not yet fully paved, and when it rained, the path which led from the dormitory to the *beis medrash* was especially muddy. On one such rainy day, some of the students shied away from leaving the warm, cozy confines of the dormitory to venture out into the heavy downpour and mud-spattered, filthy, unpaved pathways. Among those who remained in the dormitory was Yitzchok. He really had not even thought twice about it. It was rainy and muddy and he was tired. The combination of all these factors made his decision easy.

Although Yitzchok hardly ever attended Shacharis, he loved Reb Dovid's *shalosh seudos shmuessen*. They were filled with depth and meaning and Yitzchok, who sat right next to the *mashgiach*, drank in every word. After the usual in-depth analysis in the first part of the *shmuess*, Reb Dovid began to speak in more practical terms.

"You *bochurim* don't appreciate the importance of davening together with a *minyan*. I knew people who gave up their lives to daven with a *minyan*." Yitzchok listened intently to each and every word.

Reb Dovid continued, "If I knew it would make a difference, I would have lain down on the muddy roads and allowed the *bochurim* to walk on my back to get to the *beis medrash*." As he spoke, Yitzchok noticed a tear form in his rebbi's eye and slowly roll down his cheek. He was stunned by Reb Dovid's sincerity and found himself moved beyond words. At that moment he said to himself, "Raskas, tomorrow you're going to Shacharis."

The next morning Yitzchok was the first one in the *beis medrash*.

Forty-seven years later, Yitzchok emotionally recalls the tear that his rebbi shed. And it has been forty-seven years since he has missed a *minyan*!

Dancing Like a Drunkard

*T*HE YOUNG MAN WAS DISAPPOINTED BUT HE KNEW there was no way the *mashgiach* would be able to attend his wedding, which would take place in a few months. Although the *choson* was very close to his rebbi, Rav Avrohom Grodzenski *Hy"d,* the *mashgiach* of the Slobodka Yeshivah, the rebbi had explained that he just could not make it. The young man did not for a moment question his rebbi's devotion to him or to the other students.

Several months later, Reb Avrohom traveled to visit a man who needed his spirits lifted. Along the way, when the sky grew dim he pulled over to the side of the road and checked into an inn to spend the night. The inn, owned by a kind, accommodating gentile, consisted of a modest building with perhaps a dozen rooms, and Reb Avrohom felt fortunate to be able to find an empty room on such short notice. He thanked the innkeeper for his assistance and headed to his room on the second floor of the building, within earshot of the main lobby.

Approximately an hour later the sounds of a man singing and dancing issued from the room. The proprietor had seen this happen before — very often his customers would arrive at the inn after a long journey and "drown themselves" in a bottle of whiskey. He knew that it would be a short while until this particular customer exhausted himself and fell asleep. Until then he was willing to bear the noise and allow for the disturbance. Sure enough, in about a half-hour the sounds stopped completely.

The next morning the owner of the inn approached Reb Avrohom and asked, "Feeling better?"

"Pardon me?" Reb Avrohom did not understand the reference.

"Well, I know you 'relaxed' last night — I figure you had a nice bottle of whiskey and let yourself 'loosen up' after a hard day!" Reb Avrohom looked at the man and wondered how he could possibly have thought that he had been drinking.

"I heard singing and dancing coming from your room last night," said the owner, "and I figured that you probably got drunk."

Reb Avrohom smiled at the man and explained, "I am the spiritual guide in a school with many students and one of them got married last night. I felt terrible that I could not participate in the wedding so I decided to share in the joy by dancing in my own room."

The innkeeper stared in disbelief. The man was for real! He really had cared enough to dance and share in his student's joy on this special night. Shaking his head in disbelief, the innkeeper said not a word and quietly walked away.

Anything ... for a Talmid

IT WAS TO BE THE LAST SIMCHAS TORAH OF THE CHOFETZ Chaim's life. He was 92 years old and his strength was diminishing by the day. And for this Yom Tov his closest disciple, Reb Elchonon Wasserman, who himself was considered one of the *gedolei hador,* had come to Radin to be with his rebbi. The short distance to the *beis medrash* would normally never have deterred the Chofetz Chaim from attending *Hakafos,* but now he was weak and frail and could no longer manage the walk.

There was much cajoling and begging from those surrounding him, yet the aged sage would not be persuaded. It was then suggested that a few young men carry their rebbi on a chair into the *beis medrash.* They would not ask him to stand and dance but just to sit and lend his presence. Still the Chofetz Chaim refused to go.

Finally, Reb Elchonon spoke to his rebbi. The scene was unforgettable: Reb Elchonon, a towering figure, speaking to the Chofetz

Chaim, a spiritual giant but diminutive in appearance. As the Chofetz Chaim peered up at his *talmid,* Reb Elchonon spoke, his eyes and his voice suffused with love and devotion. The discussion between rebbi and *talmid* was brief and immediately the Chofetz Chaim agreed to attend the *Hakafos.*

What had Reb Elchonon said? What could have changed the Chofetz Chaim's mind?

The students lifted him up on a chair and carried him out of the house, down the street and into the *beis medrash.* The moment they brought him in, the entire room lit up with an excitement unlike anything anyone present had ever experienced. The electric atmosphere ignited the dancing, and circles formed around Reb Elchonon and his rebbi. The towering *talmid* danced in front of his mentor by first crouching as low as he could in front of him and then, as he came closer, rising up like a tidal wave to stand erect facing his saintly teacher. The Chofetz Chaim, frail and weak, sat almost motionless, a wan smile on his face. And then it was over. The memories of this unforgettable night remained etched in the minds of those who were privileged to see it.

Reb Elchonon, together with a select group of *talmidim,* carried their rebbi home. And as they brought him back into his humble house, their exhausted rebbi wished them a "Gut Yom Tov" and bid them well. Walking out the door, one of the younger students turned to Reb Elchonon, who now took on the appearance of the teacher he was and not the student he had just been. "Rebbi, how did you convince the Chofetz Chaim to come celebrate the *Hakafos* with us when none of us were able to do so?"

"I tried to persuade him like you did and nothing worked. But then I told him that the *talmidim* would be saddened if he did not come. When I mentioned their disappointment, he immediately changed his mind, because to the Chofetz Chaim *nothing* in the world was as important as a *talmid.*"

Ponytails and Peshatim

LARRY LEVINE SCANNED THE CLASSIFIED SECTION FOR A job, any job. Sure, he had some things working against him. Most of the businesses where he had interviewed had immediately turned him down because of his appearance. He wasn't a bad-looking fellow but his ponytailed "hippie" image, a bit unkempt and disheveled, made a bad impression. Unemployed for the past three months, he was on the verge of being evicted from his apartment — not that it was so beautiful to begin with, but a roof over your head was ... well ... a roof over your head.

When Larry entered a room, one could almost feel the unwelcome atmosphere. If he sat down next to someone, the person would usually scoot over to create a distance between himself and Larry. Wherever he went he felt unwelcome.

But it was not only his appearance. For one reason or another, Larry was not successful at his various places of employment. He had tried his hand at washing dishes, waitering, being a doorman and a chauffeur. In each instance the job had not lasted long. Larry was at his wit's end. Finally one ad caught his eye:

Wanted: Janitor to clean yeshivah study hall and building, good pay.

That was it. They had written the magic words — "good pay." Larry figured, "It's not as if my last job was so glamorous to begin with. What do I have to lose?" And so he dialed the number for Yeshivah Shaar Yoshuv. He arranged to meet with the plant manager the next day.

Larry traveled from his Brooklyn apartment to Far Rockaway for the interview. Wanting to make a decent impression, he put on a relatively fresh shirt and pulled his hair back neatly in a long ponytail. He desperately hoped that these were not people who judged a book by its cover.

The interview, oddly, was not with the head of maintenance, as he had expected. Surprisingly, it was the dean of the school who conducted the interview. He introduced himself as Rabbi Shlomo Freifeld. His warmth was immediately evident.

A few moments into the interview, Rabbi Freifeld asked Larry if he understood what type of a place a yeshivah was. Larry responded that he himself had once learned in a yeshivah — though perhaps his appearance suggested otherwise. The Rosh Yeshivah inquired as to why he had left. Larry told his story — how he had fought with his unsympathetic parents and how he had embarked on the wrong path of life. He explained that he been looking for redemption but had not been given the opportunity. Larry found it unusual to be pouring out his tale of woe to this rabbi, but there was something so genuine about him that Larry just felt comfortable talking about himself.

Finally Larry realized that he had babbled on and said more than he should have. He wondered why he always had to ruin every chance that came his way. Why couldn't he have just asked for the job without "spilling his guts" to the rabbi? He waited for the disappointing decision. He had heard it so many times before that it rang in his ears, "We're sorry but we just don't feel that you're the right person for the job."

"So you want a job?" the question snapped Larry out of his self-pitying reverie. Had he heard right? Was this man really interested? "Okay, I have a job for you as a rebbi beginning on Wednesday."

"As a what?!" Larry was shocked. "Can't you tell from the way I look that I'm not here interviewing for a rebbi job? I'm here for the janitorial position that you advertised in the paper." Larry could not help but wonder if this was some sort of joke the rabbi was playing on him. But what seemed really odd was that this rabbi seemed to be sincere about his offer.

"Didn't you tell me that you learned Gemara before? I have three boys who have hair longer than yours and I'm sure that you can relate to them much better than I can." Larry was waiting for the other shoe to drop. The man couldn't possibly be serious. "But, Rabbi, I'm not even religious. I haven't davened or worn *tzitzis* in years. How can I possibly be a rebbi?"

"Listen, if you don't want the job then I'll just have to give it to someone else. But this is the only job available at the present time." Larry thought of how cold it had been walking here. He knew that if he did not pay his rent this week his belongings would be dumped on the street outside his apartment building. He thought about it for a moment and finally agreed.

"Have you ever learned the first chapter of *Bava Metzia*?" Rabbi Freifeld asked. Larry vaguely remembered something about two people holding onto a garment, each one claiming that it was his. He told the rabbi that he had learned it many years before. Reb Shlomo informed him that if he needed help in preparing his classes he should feel free to come to him at any time. The two shook hands and just like that Larry had a job as a rebbi in Yeshivah Shaar Yoshuv. He could not believe his good fortune and was overwhelmed by the rabbi's sincerity. And what's more, the pay was twice that offered for the janitorial position.

That Wednesday Larry met his three students. He had actually enjoyed opening up the Gemara and preparing the *shiur* after so many years without doing anything remotely religious. Somehow it had all come back to him easily. He did not quite know where this was leading, but for now it felt pretty good — and after all, it was a job. After brief introductions, Larry, wearing a blue blazer and brown moccasins — the rabbi had given him an advance on his first check — taught the Mishnah to these young men. After successfully teaching the class, Larry mentioned to Reb Shlomo that he felt uncomfortable teaching without wearing a yarmulka and *tzitzis*. The Rosh Yeshivah suggested that he wear them for his own sake, so as not to feel uncomfortable, and even lent him *tzitzis* and a yarmulka.

Larry, or Levi as he was now called, blossomed in his new position. The yarmulka and *tzitzis* became permanent fixtures and his keen understanding of the Gemara and unusual insights into his students helped him to become quite a popular rebbi.

Thirty-five years later, Reb Levi Levine is a popular rebbi in a yeshivah in Eretz Yisrael. His wife Ruchi and their nine children are all fine young men and women following in the path of Torah. And they are forever grateful to a great and wise man who uncovered the spark of greatness hidden deep inside the soul of a lost fellow Jew.

Mitzvos

Fresh and Crisp

REB YIDDEL AIDELMAN IS NOT THE TYPE OF PERSON who spends his days doing household chores, going to the market or stopping by the bank. Generally the elderly *talmid chacham* spends his days and nights learning and being occupied with various aspects of kindness. His family has long ago shouldered the responsibilities of housework and the errands that need to be done. Some of the children pick up the groceries at the nearby market while others perform the tasks of paying the bills at the local *doar* (post office). But that's what made today's visit to the bank all the more peculiar.

It was Taanis Esther, the thirteenth day of Adar. It is a day when most people spend their time in the supermarket making last-minute preparations for *mishloach mannos*. But today Reb Yiddel was, uncharacteristically, in the bank. Those who recognized him wondered at this sight, but said nothing. Finally one of his friends,

Reb Leibel Ostrovitz, came up to him and asked him why he was, of all places, in the bank on, of all days, Taanis Esther.

"Tomorrow, as you know, is Purim and one of the mitzvos of Purim is that of *matanos l'evyonim,* distributing funds to the needy. I figured that one way I could beautify the mitzvah would be to give out fresh, crisp *shekalim* instead of the crumpled, creased bills that I had in my pocket."

Reb Leibel smiled and walked away. He could not help but marvel at the unusual consideration, sensitivity and love that his friend Reb Yiddel displayed for the mitzvah of *matanos l'evyonim* and for the poor unfortunates who would be receiving the money.

Right Guy, Wrong Time

SHAYA COHEN HAD GONE THROUGH THE SYSTEM BUT HE always felt that something was missing. It was not that he did not get along with his parents or other family members like so many other teens, but his experiences in yeshivah had caused him to drift away. At first he hopped from one yeshivah to the next, but each time the scenario would repeat itself: the promises for improved behavior, the misunderstandings, the threats, the "last chances" and finally the expulsions. At first it bothered Shaya, but eventually he would just shrug his shoulders and move on to the next situation.

And so it would go. On and on. From one yeshivah to the next until finally, after 11th grade, Shaya's yeshivah career had come to an end. The days of learning and davening were now over. It did not take long for the next phase to begin. Shabbos and *tefillin* soon fell by the wayside and Shaya slipped fast into the dark world of drugs and danger. He was no longer viewed as a "teen at risk"; rather he had already fallen too fast and too far. His parents cried and dav-ened for his *yeshuah;* even thinking about him was extremely pain-ful for them.

Shaya was involved in drugs not only as a recreational outlet for himself but also as a way of making money, by dealing and dis-tributing the drugs to others. Some of the drug sales proved to be quite profitable, not only here in America but abroad as well. Every two or three months Shaya would travel to Eretz Yisrael — but not for spiritual pursuits. Instead, he would spend his time there deal-ing with the lowest elements of society. On every trip he would earn a significant amount of money, sometimes up to $20,000!

The system worked like clockwork. A week or so before his trip to Israel he would contact his dealer and inform him how much he needed. Within the week he would arrange for a pickup, where he would be given the drugs in exchange for cash. He would then travel to Eretz Yisrael, where he quickly made the proper contact for the deal to be finalized. He had done this more than ten times, although he knew he ran the risk of getting caught and being thrown into jail. Perhaps it was the thrill, or maybe it was the money, but whatever it was, Shaya had worked it all out very care-fully — and he liked what he was doing.

Slowly, however, the gnawing feelings of guilt tugged at his conscience. He felt a little guilty about his rampant desecration of Shabbos and absolute disregard for the Torah and all that it stood for. He saw his parents' pain and felt their tears. He wanted to tell them that he still loved them and just needed to work things out, but the words would just get stuck in his throat and, instead of losing his composure in front of them, he opted to ignore the subject entirely.

The time had come for another of Shaya's trips to Israel, and on Thursday he put in a call to his supplier for sufficient drugs to earn enough money to support a small family for a year. He waited for his beeper to ring but nothing happened. Friday afternoon came and went and still there was no return call. Finally he put in one more call to the "middleman" and waited for the response — but none came. On Friday night at around 9 o' clock the call finally came. But instead of answering it, Shaya thought for a fleeting moment about the Shabbos from which he had grown so far apart, and he realized that he had not yet desecrated Shabbos on this Friday night. A feeling of hope overcame him and instead of answering the call he decided to wait until Shabbos was over. Then he could call back and get what he needed.

Shabbos was not exactly the most sublime experience of his life. He did not spend hours in shul davening and learning, nor did he sit down and eat a beautiful Shabbos meal replete with *zemiros* and words of Torah. But he had not violated it in any way, and he felt very good about that. About an hour after nightfall he picked up the phone and called his supplier. But it was too late; he was gone. Earlier that morning he had gone to Florida to do some business. The "window of opportunity" was lost. And with it went thousands and thousands of dollars.

Somewhat dejected, Shaya decided to go to Eretz Yisrael anyway. But this time he went without the usual stash of illegal contraband. Normally he was somewhat wary about the possibility of getting caught, but now for the first time, he was actually relaxed on the flight. Shaya checked in early and settled in for the nonstop El Al flight from JFK to Lod International Airport.

The flight was uneventful, and immediately after passing through customs Shaya moved toward the carousel to retrieve his luggage. But as soon as he grabbed his two suitcases, four security guards approached him and hustled him into an adjacent room.

"What do you want from me?" Shaya was confused. Clearly there was some sort of mistaken identity. Not one to panic, he calmly waited for the head of security to explain what the problem was.

"We know that you have drugs on you and we're going to search you and your belongings. Your face and eyes tell it all." The man spoke with the utmost seriousness as he and three other men began picking through Shaya's belongings.

Shaya burst out laughing. "I don't believe it. You got the right guy but the wrong time." Shaya explained to them that he had brought in drugs in the past and was planning to do so this time as well but it just hadn't worked out.

The annoyed and disappointed security officers did not believe a word he said. They assumed that he was covering up and continued to search through every nook and cranny of his luggage. Then they conducted a personal search, but found nothing. "I'm telling you. I ain't no saint but I don't have any drugs on me this time."

Shaya thought about it as they continued searching. Why didn't he have contraband this time? Only because after so many years he had decided not to desecrate Shabbos. The awesome realization that keeping Shabbos saved him from a long prison term for drug smuggling was shocking. "G-d is really looking out for me," Shaya thought and smiled broadly.

It was not long until Shaya became a complete *baal teshuvah*. Today he is married and has several children. And now he smiles as he thankfully recalls the one call that he refused to answer on Shabbos.

For the Sake of a Mitzvah

HEAVY-HEARTED AND DEJECTED, THE FELDMANS LEFT the fertility center in Jerusalem. Once again, the results of the tests were disappointing. For nineteen years, Moshe Leib, a handsome black-bearded, popular rebbi in Yeshivas Ohr Torah, and Chaya Rifka, a beloved teacher in the local Bais Yaakov, had desperately yearned for a baby. How their hearts ached. Maybe the doctors were right. Maybe they should just accept their fate. Perhaps their sad destiny was not to ...

No! They wouldn't just give up. They had to continue davening. Who was to tell which heartfelt prayer would be the one to break through. And so, with unyielding faith, they held strong.

Moshe Leib, meticulous in his mitzvah observance, was unusually careful about one particular mitzvah — *Kiddush Levanah*, sanctifying the new moon. As each month passed, Moshe Leib anticipated the special occasion of blessing the new moon. He could not help but think of his own painful predicament as he viewed the glowing moon that shone brightly and instilled hope amidst the gloom of night and dim of darkness. And from this he gained encouragement.

In the month of Teves 5755 rain fell continuously. Night after night the ceaseless rain and thick fog deterred Moshe Leib from performing the mitzvah of *Kiddush Levanah,* and he began to despair.

The night of the fourteenth of Teves, the last possible night on which to fulfill the mitzvah, drew near and the endless pitter-patter of raindrops on the misty windows proclaimed that this month the elusive mitzvah of *Kiddush Levanah* would just not be. Innovative ideas and halachic loopholes raced frantically through Moshe Leib's worried mind — but he was quickly running out of time.

That evening, Chaim Weinman, a dear friend of the family, stopped by the Feldmans' apartment. Mindful of the *Kiddush Levanah* situation, Chaim proposed that they contact the surrounding army posts to inquire regarding the projected forecasts in their respective areas. All out of options, Moshe Leib nervously picked up the phone and began dialing.

"Really?!" Moshe Leib excitedly called out. "Are you sure? Oh, thank you so much!" He could hardly believe the lieutenant's report. A short distance away, in the vicinity of the ancient city of Chevron, the forecast called for partly cloudy skies. Though it was a slim chance, it was still a possibility. A galvanized Moshe Leib set out down the perilous Beis Lechem Road, together with his devoted friend Chaim.

When they arrived in Beis Lechem they looked up and to their delight saw that the moon was shining brightly. They immediately got out of their car and began to say *Kiddush Levanah.* After they finished, they danced and sang, "*Tovim meoros shebara Elokeinu,*" then proceeded into Kever Rachel to daven at the burial place of Rachel Imeinu.

A group of Chassidim were in Beis Lechem at that time and they had been very moved by the way Moshe Leib said *Kiddush Levanah* and by his happiness in performing this mitzvah. Shyly, they approached him and asked that he tell them about himself.

After hearing of his plight, they each beseeched Hashem, "*Ribbono Shel Olam*, look at the sacrifice this Jew has shown for the mitzvah of *Kiddush Levanah*. Look at how precious this mitzvah is to him. *Mamma Rochel*, please cry for this couple who has gone through so much pain and suffering. Please cry and daven that they should be blessed with a child."

Miraculously, a little over nine months later, on the eleventh of Cheshvan, the *yahrtzeit* of Rachel Imeinu, this couple was blessed with twin girls.

Kiddush Hashem / Sanctifying Hashem's Name

Children Will Be Children

REB LEIZER, A WELL-RESPECTED ROSH YESHIVAH, HAD THE ideal life. His *shiurim* were magnificent in scope and depth, and young men flocked from all over to learn from him. His students maintained contact with him and turned to him for advice throughout their lives.

His family was considered the envy of all Jewish families. His home was open to all and his children were well-mannered and well-raised. The love and importance of Torah that they witnessed in their home was echoed in the manner in which they conducted their own lives.

But one day the serenity and beauty of their lives was shattered. It began with the need for Reb Leizer to stop more often than usual to catch his breath. His hectic schedule had apparently taken its toll on his health and he figured that by slowing down he would rectify the problem. But the problem ran much deeper than that. Medical tests revealed that a tumor had developed on the right side of his brain and needed to be operated upon immediately.

His family and students davened around the clock as they stormed the Heavens, beseeching the A-mighty on behalf of their father and rebbi. The operation, a delicate procedure, was relatively successful and the doctors predicted a complete, albeit slow, recovery. When his children first walked into the intensive care unit they were somewhat taken aback by the way their father looked. His head was bandaged and his eyes barely opened. He seemed to have lost movement on one side of his face but the doctor reassured them that this would clear up in a matter of weeks.

The recovery went slower than expected. In fact their father barely recognized them. He was confused as to who was who in the family and didn't recognize even his closest *talmidim*. But perhaps what was most painful was the fact that this outstanding Torah scholar remembered not a word of his Torah. He couldn't even read *aleph-beis* let alone understand a complicated *Tosafos*. He had been diminished to the level of a kindergarten child and was in need of a complete reeducation.

The family was devastated for their father and cried bitterly for him, although he was completely unaware that anything was amiss. He was amazed to see people performing even simple tasks; the ability of a young child to read *Chumash* made him express great wonder. He tried to recover all his knowledge immediately but everything seemed so foreign. One day his children, all grown adults, suggested to their father that perhaps he would like to attend a *cheder* for a short while. His reaction was astounding — he was thrilled with the idea. However, his children were apprehensive about the plan. How would it look for a Rosh Yeshivah who was a known Torah scholar to attend a kindergarten class? The idea seemed absurd but once they had mentioned it to their father, there was no turning back.

The day arrived, and their father began to attend school. The principal was skeptical at first about how the children would react. In walked Reb Leizer, fully attired in his long black coat and hat.

Some of the children giggled, but most of them just figured that one of the fathers was visiting the *cheder* that day. The schedule called for Reb Leizer to attend the school for two and a half hours in the morning and then for his children to pick him up and take him home.

The rebbi found it an uncomfortable challenge to teach *aleph-beis* and the weekly *parshah* to a man who was known as one of the greatest scholars in all of Yerushalayim. But the day went surprisingly well and Reb Leizer's enthusiasm in learning the basics all over again was admirable. However the initial excitement was tempered by an incident that took place during recess.

Reb Leizer's children arrived at recess time and saw their father playing ball with the children. The sight was pathetic. A fully grown man playing with children young enough to be his grandchildren was enough to bring his children to tears. It was just too much. They quickly ran over to their father and pulled him away. "Tatty, don't you remember who you are? You're a *gadol b'Torah*! You're not a little child! We beg you to try to remember who you are!"

His children cried as they pulled him away from the game and brought him back home. Tragically, he could not even understand what they were so upset about.

> *Reb Yitzchok Zilberstein used this powerful parable to describe how it must seem to the A-mighty when we do not act in a manner befitting our status as the Torah nation. It is as if we do not even remember who we are or why we are here. We have been given such gifts, and the ability to be so great, yet we act as if we do not remember even one word, playing children's games when we could be doing great things to make Hashem proud.*

Memories at Soldier Field

*T*HE FOOTBALL GAME HAD GONE AS MOST FOOTBALL games went at Soldier Field, especially of late. The game was nearing the end of the first quarter and the Bears were already down by two touchdowns. The Chicago football team had fallen on hard times and the glory days of yesteryear could not seem further away. The lull in the game provided Mark Stein with some time to make small talk with the man sitting next to him.

For this game Mark had gotten good seats in an area that was shielded from the wind. This way, even if the game was not so exciting, he would not have to freeze. Mark introduced himself to the fellow next to him, and his seatmate introduced himself as Jerry. Small talk revealed that they were both successful business-men who were involved in supplying nursing homes. Mark com-forted himself — even though the game was not exciting, perhaps he would make a new business contact.

They swapped business cards and exchanged e-mail address-es. But when Jerry glanced at Mark's business card he asked, "Are you Jewish?"

Mark answered that he was. "Why? Do you know any Jews in the Chicago area?"

"Only one. And it's not me — it's my wife who does. His name is Rabbi Soloveitchik. Do you know him?"

The look on Mark's face changed from one of pleasantness to sadness. "Well, of course I knew him. He was one of the greatest rabbis in the Chicago area, but I'm sorry to inform you that Rabbi Soloveitchik passed away last week."

"What? I don't believe it." A look of sadness and shock appeared on Jerry's face. Jerry immediately used his cell phone to call his wife.

"Lisa, it's me," Jerry said slowly. "Sit down, I have some terrible news to share with you. Rabbi Soloveitchik passed away last week." Jerry looked up at his new acquaintance and motioned that his wife was crying. "All right, I'll call you back soon just to make sure that you're okay."

Jerry turned to Mark and began to explain. "She has been a stewardess for the past few years on American Airlines. Every week Rabbi Soloveitchik would fly from Chicago to New York. He told my wife that he went there to teach ever since his brother passed away. He sat in first class. Most of the passengers in first class pretty much ignore the flight crew but the rabbi took a genuine interest in the welfare of my wife and the rest of the crew. He knew their families and all the important things that were happening in their lives. So my wife feels like she's lost someone special in her life."

Mark was humbled. Here he was sitting in Soldier Field, next to a gentile whose wife, a stewardess, was extremely saddened over the loss of Rav Soloveitchik. The Rav could have kept to himself on his flights. Everyone else did. But instead he had decided to make a difference, to make a *kiddush Hashem*.

Mark had come to the football game to get away and enjoy himself for the afternoon. Little did he know that he would learn a lesson about how a person should conduct himself at each and every moment of his life.

An Unforgettable Flight

THE LATE HOUR WORRIED HIM BUT REB CHAIM KAHAN, A bearded Orthodox Jew, had no choice. If he wanted to get home for Shabbos he would be forced to take the flight that arrived in Denver from San Fransisco a mere two hours before Shabbos. His friend Reb Yehudah Lefkovitz would pick him up at the airport and they hoped there would be no delays.

The flight departed on time and Reb Chaim's worry about being delayed for Shabbos dissipated. All seemed to be going fine as the weather appeared to be pleasant and the pilot announced that the planned arrival would be a few moments earlier than scheduled.

But suddenly everything changed. It is the fear of anyone who has ever been in an airplane. With about a half-hour left to the flight the captain made an announcement: "Attention, ladies and gentleman, this is your captain speaking. Please listen carefully. I regret to inform you that the plane's hydraulic system has failed. That means that we have no way to stop the plane. We need you to follow our instructions for your own safety. Remove all sharp objects from your pockets and lean forward. Place your head between your legs and brace for a crash landing. Oh, and one more thing — please pray."

At first no one moved or spoke. And then suddenly everyone began to cry softly. Reb Chaim could not believe this was happening. He followed the instructions and then began to reflect on his own life. He thought about what he had accomplished during his lifetime. What sort of a father had he been? What type of a husband? Had he really done all he could? He was a young man but he had learned what one is supposed to do during his last moments on this world. And so, softly, quietly, he started to recite *Vidui*.

After he finished tearfully reciting *Vidui* he tried to remain calm and began saying those chapters of *Tehillim* he knew by heart. The words came forth from his heart as he prepared to meet his Creator. And then, an hour after the first announcement had been issued, the plane began its final descent. But it did not descend the way a plane normally does. Instead it descended the way a helicopter does. And it touched the ground gently with just a slight bump.

Disbelievingly, the passengers sat up straight again and looked out the windows to convince themselves that they were indeed alive. And after they saw the many fire engines and ambulances rushing toward the plane they realized that indeed a miracle had taken place. In a brilliant move, the pilot had exhausted the fuel supply and the plane had been able to float to the ground safely. Cries of relief filled the cabin and cheers erupted from the thankful passengers.

Reb Chaim glanced at his watch and realized that it was now less than an hour until Shabbos. He hoped that his friend had given up waiting and gone home, and decided that he would find a taxi to take him home. He unfastened his seatbelt, opened the overhead cabinet, removed his attaché case and rushed toward the exit door. But just as he reached the door he was stopped by the steward and stewardess. "Rabbi, do you have a minute?"

Reb Chaim looked up at them and wondered what they could possibly want from him after the harrowing flight they had been through. "We want you to know something. During the entire last hour of the flight when we thought we were going to die, the passengers looked to us for strength. And, Rabbi, we looked to you!"

> *Reb Chaim recounted this story a few months later when he spoke at a dinner. He felt that the entire ordeal had happened because the A-mighty wants us to realize that the world is watching us and looking at how we behave. We must not let them down.*

Faith

Reach for the Stars

ERHAPS THE GREATEST VISIONARY OF OUR TIME WAS the legendary Ponovezher Rav, Rav Yosef Kahaneman. Many have wondered about his uncanny ability to build and grow in the face of adversity and tragedy. When asked about it, he responded by stating, "*Andere cholomen un shlufen, uber ich cholom un shlof nisht* — Others dream when they are sleeping but I dream and don't sleep."

One time the Rav was suffering from an intensely painful toothache. After some convincing he paid a visit to the dentist and was informed that the tooth had to be extracted. But the Rav refused to have the procedure done. The dentist could not understand why and insisted that if the Rav did not have the infected tooth removed the pain would intensify and he would suffer terribly.

But still he refused to have the tooth removed and explained to the confused dentist, "I am a Kohen. And one day soon Mashiach will come and the *Beis HaMikdash* will descend from heaven. I will want to perform the *avodah*, but I am afraid that the procedure may cause one of the imperfections that invalidate a Kohen from performing the *avodah*. Therefore, I'll suffer now if I must, as long as I remain a full-fledged Kohen."

Nazi General Erwin Rommel and his troops were poised on the doorstep of Palestine. Nothing seemed capable of blocking their ascent to Yerushalayim. Military experts predicted that capture of Eretz Yisrael was imminent, and that the future of its inhabitants was in jeopardy. At this time the Ponovezher Rav suffered a medical setback. Some feared a stroke, and under doctor's orders he was forbidden to speak. Confined to a hospital bed, he lay there virtually helpless as the medical staff and a few *talmidim* stood by, hoping to be of help in any way they could.

One of those in the room relayed the news of the looming attack on the country. The Rav, upon hearing the reports, sprung into action; a man who a moment ago had been lying listlessly in his bed knew he had little time to waste. He called over one of the *bochurim* and wrote the following three commands. "First of all, inform Rav Shmuel Rozovsky that I want him to become the Rosh Yeshivah of the Ponovezher Yeshivah in Eretz Yisrael. Second, there is a wealthy man who has offered the money to purchase a building. Tell him that I do want it and will repay him soon. And third, here is a list of ten *bochurim* I have spoken to regarding their attending the yeshivah. Tell them we begin the day after tomorrow."

The *bochur* understood that time was of the essence and hurried to carry out the urgent dispatches. Within a day he had delivered the messages and soon the yeshivah was up and running. History has told the rest of the story. Rommel never made it into Eretz Yisrael — he was defeated by British troops at the Battle of El Alamein. And Ponovezh Yeshivah, under the leadership and guidance of the Ponovezher Rav and Rav Shmuel Rozovsky, blossomed into one of the greatest yeshivos in the world.

Years later someone asked the Rav what made him decide to jump into action at that precise moment — when the future seemed so dim. The Rav answered in his most classic manner. "I decided that even if Eretz Yisrael was going to be attacked we had to have here a living memorial to the original Ponovezh Yeshivah."

At the time when most people were lamenting the imminent destruction of their homes (and possibly their lives) the Ponovezher Rav was laying the groundwork to build an edifice to shape the future!

Quality vs. Quantity

Reb Isser Zalman Meltzer, the Rosh Yeshivah of Yeshivas Etz Chaim in Yerushalayim, was married to his rebbetzin for over sixty years. The start of their relationship was an unusual act of dedication from a unique person.

ISSER ZALMAN LEARNED AND GREW IN THE FAMED Volozhiner Yeshivah for six memorable years. Afterwards he traveled to Radin and studied together with the son of the Chofetz Chaim, Reb Avrohom. It did not take long for Reb Isser Zalman to be regarded as one of the finest young men in the entire land. Many offers for marriage came and Reb Isser Zalman went to seek advice from his rebbi, Rav Chaim Soloveitchik. The name that intrigued him most was an orphaned girl from a small town near Kovno. Her father, Reb Shraga Feivel, had been a *talmid chacham* as well as a philanthropic Jew who had supported many institutions. On many occasions he had even hosted the great Reb Yisroel Salanter. In general his home was viewed as an open house to scholars and laymen alike. Unfortunately, he had passed away at a young age, leaving four daughters. Before his passing, he had set aside a large dowry for each of his daughters, so that each would be able to marry a *talmid chacham.*

Reb Isser Zalman received his rebbi's blessing, and the *shidduch* with Reb Shraga Feivel's daughter was completed. All those involved were very excited that the young orphan had found such an outstanding young man for a *choson*. But their happiness was short-lived.

Reb Isser Zalman soon fell ill with hepatitis — a disease which had proved fatal in many cases. Among those who had succumbed to the illness was the Chofetz Chaim's son, Reb Avrohom, Reb Isser Zalman's *chavrusa*. A debate took place in the *kallah's* hometown. Those who were close to the *kallah* and her family urged her to break the engagement. "You became a *yesomah* at such a young age, and you want to be a young *almanah* as well?" Although the words stung and she was devastated at the news, the logic behind it made sense. The *kallah* was tormented by the decision she had to make, and convinced her *choson* to see a top specialist in the field.

His *kallah* accompanying him, Reb Isser Zalman underwent a thorough examination. The doctor then gave his evaluation — the prognosis for a long life seemed doubtful at best. Privately the *kallah* spoke with the doctor and asked if he felt that Reb Isser Zalman would live out the coming year. After wavering for a moment the doctor stated that it was entirely possible, but added that he could not promise anything longer than that. The young lady had heard enough and she made up her mind. She was going to marry Reb Isser Zalman.

Many people continued to pressure her to break the *shidduch*. They felt she was acting irrationally, but she remained adamant. She was going to marry this *talmid chacham*. To her detractors, she declared, "If I can have the privilege of being married to this *tzaddik* for only a year it will be worth it to me, regardless of what might happen." The declaration was stated with such conviction that everyone knew there was no way to change her mind. She had decided and nothing would convince her otherwise.

Reb Isser Zalman and his wife did get married and were married for sixty years. Their daughter married Reb Aharon Kotler, one of the greatest disseminators of Torah in the 20th century.

❧ ❦

Rebbetzin Elyashiv's entire life revolved around her husband's learning. Early on in their marriage, she took it upon herself to wake up early each morning — at 4 a.m. — to prepare a cup of coffee for her husband as he learned. It was not that Rav Elyashiv was unable to make his own cup of coffee, nor that he asked her to do so. On the contrary, he had specifically asked her on many occasions not to get up and bother herself. But she insisted. It was her privilege. No, it was her *tafkid* in life and she cherished the opportunity.

And so it was. The rebbetzin served her husband in every way, always striving to alleviate his every burden so as to allow for the maximum Torah learning. But then one day she fell ill, and much to her disappointment she was no longer able to maintain the schedule. As her health deteriorated, she found it more and more difficult to serve her husband. Simple tasks became harder to perform as the end drew near.

It was not long until she became bedridden and her husband began to be the caretaker — a true role reversal for this husband and wife. He devotedly stayed by her side and tended to her needs. Reciting *Tehillim* and learning, Rav Elyashiv spent the bulk of his days helping when he could.

One morning, as he sat by his wife's bedside, she turned to him and asked him to go back to his regular learning in the other room. "They'll call you." Incredibly, even from her deathbed, the rebbetzin did not want her husband to do anything but learn.

And that is how she lived. From the very first moment of *Sheva Berachos* until the sad day that she left this world, Rebbetzin Elyashiv lived her life as a paradigm of a supportive wife and an *aishes chayil*.

The Trip That Lasted a Lifetime

JONATHAN FRIED, A HIGH SCHOOL SENIOR AT WOODBROOK High and a member of the Tennis Club, looked forward to graduation and to college life. He was a bright, insightful young man, but more than anything he loved his social life, his sports and his friends. Religion was important to him only in an abstract way, and did not have much bearing on his daily life. The rest of his family, however, was moving in a different direction. His sisters had somehow become involved with NCSY and were becoming more observant, and his parents followed suit. However, Jonathan was decidedly not following in the same direction. He wondered why his family was so "into" the traditional practices, which seemed to interfere so much with one's way of life. As for him, he was much too busy for "that stuff," and had no intention of altering his lifestyle one bit.

Jonathan's sister was concerned about his becoming distanced from the rest of the family, and decided to explain to him why she had made changes in her life, and why these changes had influenced other members of the family. They had a heart-to-heart talk about priorities, and she carefully explained how living a Torah life puts everything in perspective and gives a person higher goals to reach for than just a good set of tennis. Jonathan was touched by his sister's words and moved that she took the time to explain all this; he respected her, and she had somehow touched a nerve in him. His initial reaction was to resist any change, but he couldn't help thinking about what his sister had said. The next day he began to look around his high school classroom, and realized he was seeing everything in a different light. He could not help but wonder where he was heading. He loved his friends, but what his sister had said made him think: what were their priorities? None of them ever spoke about what was important to them outside of sports, parties and complaints about their parents. Did any of them have loftier thoughts? He suddenly realized that he understood, just a little, what his sister was talking about. It shocked and disturbed him that he was having doubts about the world in which he lived. Did he actually desire to live like his peers? Their lives suddenly seemed quite empty. Not that he was entirely sold on the other way of life — but he thought perhaps, just maybe, he would consider giving it a try.

Two days later, while he was still pondering all these issues, and wondering what, if anything, he would actually do about them, he happened upon a flyer from his public school regarding a trip to Eastern Europe. The trip, run by an Orthodox woman, involved a tour of the concentration camps, coupled with a visit to some of the synagogues that had been destroyed or vandalized during the war years. There was definitely going to be a good deal of Orthodox Jewish content, as well as historical content, in this trip. Jonathan read and was intrigued — he had always had a penchant for history, and loved to travel. And somehow what had happened to the Jews during World War II was a chapter in history that he thought about often. He also figured that it would be a good way for him to learn about religious life. After consulting with his parents, who were surprised at his eagerness, Jon booked his reservations and began making arrangements for the trip.

His neighbors from down the block, the Waldmans, an Orthodox family, were close to the Frieds. Recently the two families had enjoyed a Passover Seder together. Aaron Waldman, a robust fellow with a zest for life and a sharp sense of humor, led the Seder well and made the evening completely enjoyable.

The evening prior to Jon's departure, Aaron Waldman knocked on the Fried's door and Jon's mother invited him in. Jon was upstairs packing, stopping periodically as friends dropped by to wish him well. Jon came downstairs and shook Aaron's outstretched arm, as Aaron cracked a joke about Jon returning as an Orthodox Jew, wearing a big black hat. Jon chuckled and thanked him for his good wishes.

Just before he turned to go home, Aaron mentioned to Jon that he had a small gift for him to use on his journey. Shocked, Jon turned curiously toward his older friend and accepted the small package. He removed the wrapping paper and stared at the yarmulka and *siddur* that Aaron had purchased for him. He was truly touched and thanked Aaron for the gifts, though he doubted if he would use either one of them. Aaron turned toward the door and wished Jon well on his trip.

It really had been a memorable experience. Auschwitz. Birkeneau. Buchenwald. Sobibor. The sounds of silence were deafening. The ashes of the six million seemed to have been scattered over the entire landscape of Europe. Each city they passed had another story, one more tragic than the next. Women and children. Teachers and shoemakers. Yeshivos and shuls.

Jon had been moved beyond tears. He was emotionally drained; he had never felt this way before. He felt at the same moment intimately connected with those who had lived such pious, innocent lives and had been killed so brutally, and with those who had survived and managed to remain true to Torah values, even after experiencing such utter horror. For some reason, he kept thinking about the conversation with his sister as well.

Working through his emotions, he thought of the *siddur* that Aaron had given him. He retrieved it from his suitcase and held it in his hands. But the words seemed so distant, their message so cryptic. He yearned to unlock the secrets that it held yet he felt unable and unworthy of doing so.

Torn and tormented, Jon struggled to make sense of what was happening to him. Each day he tried to work through his emotions, some days faring better than others. His guides and friends on the trip provided few answers and Jon felt he needed to hear more. He had never felt so inept and incapable. Each time he tried to pray even a simple prayer for the dead or say a chapter of *Psalms,* the frustration would grow at his inability to express what was in his soul.

Toward the end of the journey, they stopped to visit one of the oldest shuls in all of Prague. Upon entering the building, one immediately was struck by the decorative walls and ceiling, faded from years of negligence and indifference. Lack of funding and dwindling numbers in the community added to the poor condition of the well-known synagogue. Jon looked around, wondering how many generations of people had prayed there before.

He gently touched the walls and caressed the worn benches, staring in awe at the old awe-inspiring ark and feeling more undeserving than ever. "Generations of Jews sacrificed their lives for their religion; and where is my sacrifice?" Jon thought guiltily.

Just then, an aged fellow with a wrinkled face slowly came up behind him. He placed his hand on Jon's shoulder and called for his attention. "Here," he said in a raspy voice in broken English, "take this." Jon looked down at a brown brittle *siddur* with torn yellow pages. He held the delicate relic in his hands as if clutching a rare jewel. He dared not turn its fragile pages too quickly lest they fall out of their age-old binding.

"I can't," Jon stammered, looking down at the *siddur*. " I ... just ... can't ... take ... this." Jon was uncertain why he had said it. Perhaps it was because he felt unworthy, but more likely because he just couldn't take a *siddur* that had held a place in this sanctuary for so long and now he did not know if it would be ever used again.

The old man looked intently at the young American tourist and held his young, strong hands in his old, frail ones while gazing intensely into his eyes. "You have to," he declared with conviction, "because if you don't then no one else will!"

Mesmerized, Jon took the *siddur* into his hands. His hands did not move, his lips did not speak. But for the first time in his life he understood what his very soul was saying.

A few moments later he dug into his backpack, removed the yarmulka that Aaron had given him, placed it on his head and began to pray, as he never had before. Suddenly, he knew who he was, why he existed and where he was going.

Twenty-five years later, Reb Yonoson Fried, an author of *sefarim* and a *rosh kollel,* wrote a heartfelt letter of thanks and appreciation to the Waldmans for the warmth, friendship and especially the small gift of a yarmulka and *siddur* given to a young teenager searching for meaning.

He also thanked in his heart the old man he had met in the ancient shul in Prague for changing his trip into one that lasted a lifetime.

The Next Gadol Hador

LITTLE DOV WATCHED FROM THE HALLWAY AS HIS MOTHER sat down on the rickety wooden chair and sighed deeply. It had become an all too common scene. Working hard at two different jobs, she had struggled just to earn enough money to pay for what was most important — hiring the very best *melamdim* in town to teach her precious 7-year-old boy. She had learned to live without luxuries, even forgoing some basic provisions. Her house was a simple two-room wooden home sparsely furnished with the barest necessities. But it was all about priorities — there was only one thing Dov's mother cared about, and that was her son's learning. Nothing else mattered.

This night, her heavy workload had taken its toll. Wiping the tears from her eyes, she tried, as she always did, to prevent her son from seeing her so exhausted and overwhelmed. It certainly wasn't his fault that his father had died so suddenly a year ago. That is what had been decreed and it was not for her to question. But she also refused to compromise her son's Torah learning and therefore pushed herself to her limit. And tonight the combination of the two had come to a head.

"Don't worry, Mama, everything will be all right," Little Dov comforted his mother. And although there really wasn't much that Dov could do to lessen her burden, she felt somewhat calmed by her son's assurance.

Day after day the routine had repeated itself. Rising early in the morning she would pack a lunch for Dov, and would then escort him to shul to daven and recite the *Kaddish*. After davening she would drop him off by Reb Yossel, the finest *melamed* in town, and proceed on to the first of her two jobs. During the course of the day she would finish one job and go to the next. Finally, towards evening, winding down her hectic day, she would leave her second job and rush to pick up her little *talmid chacham*. Whenever she felt inundated by her workload and responsibilities, her son would be there to encourage her with his unswerving reassurance, "Don't worry, Mama, everything will be all right."

This day had been a particularly difficult and exhausting one. But once again, by focusing on her son she had managed to survive. After stopping by the *melamed* to pick up Dov, mother and son walked down the street together, eager to relax after a long day. As they walked home, it had become their custom that Dov would share with his mother the highlights of his day and she would reciprocate. Suddenly, as they turned their corner the two looked up in horror — their home was engulfed in flames. The street was filled with crackling sounds of burning wood and billows of smoke drifted through the nighttime sky. Small crowds huddled to watch and whisper at the pitiful sight of a mother and her son who had lost everything but each other. A moment passed. She was in shock, realizing with complete clarity how devastating this was to them and wondering if they would ever recover. As she saw their little home being destroyed, she could barely handle the wave of emotions that overcame her. They had so little before — now they had nothing. What hurt the most, she realized, was that now nothing existed to connect them to their past.

Clutching her son tightly, she could hold her tears back no longer and she sobbed bitterly. Dov looked up at his mother and watched as she cried. "Don't worry, Mama, everything will be all right."

Suddenly aware of her son's presence she regained her composure and bent down to speak to him. She reminded herself that she had to remain calm for him, and took the opportunity to speak to him in a quiet and measured tone. "My dear Dov," she began, "I want you to know that I'm not crying for the reasons that you think. All through the past year, no matter how difficult the circumstances might have been, I always knew deep down that everything would work out. The reason I am crying is not for the loss of material matter. I know that Hashem will provide for us. He guards over all His children, especially the *yesomim* and *almanos.*" Dov listened intently as he stared at his mother's tear-filled eyes and he desperately hoped that the never-ending struggles would cease. "Each night," she continued, "I used to read to you from a book before you went to sleep. It was a *Sefer HaYuchsin,* a book of your ancestry. I wanted you to know where you came from and who your father, grandfather and great-grandfathers were. It provided you with a glimpse into the greatness you could achieve. And now that book is gone ... forever." Her words trailed off into the distance and a thick silence filled the air.

"Mama, please don't cry. Really, everything will be all right." She listened to her son's optimistic tone yet knew deep down that he was just too young to understand. "You don't have to cry over losing our *Sefer HaYuchsin.*"

"Didn't he understand?" she wondered. "It's not the book but what it represented." But she couldn't blame him. He was just a little boy.

Dov stared at his mother and declared, "Mama, we might have lost our old *Sefer HaYuchsin* but I am going to begin a new one. And my grandchildren are going to learn about me." Dov spoke with determination; he appeared to have matured instantly. "I'm going to become the next *gadol hador!*"

Shocked at his declaration, she looked into her son's piercing eyes. Reflected there she could see the image of their home going up in flames, but more importantly, she saw his determination, and prayed that he would indeed become the next *gadol hador.*

Dov's mother's perseverance paid off. Her *tefillos* and tears found their way to the Heavenly throne and little Dov fulfilled his promise. He grew up to become Reb Dov Ber of Mezritch, the Mezritcher Maggid, the most prized disciple of the Baal Shem Tov and, indeed, the next *gadol hador.*

Paderewski, Pianos and Prodigies

The following entertaining anecdote depicts how we are oblivious to the "siyata d'Shmaya" we are granted throughout all of our endeavors.

SALLY GOLDSTEIN WAS OVERJOYED WITH HER SON Adam's progress as a pianist. She had great aspirations for her little boy and when she discovered that the world-renowned pianist Paderewski was coming to New York and would be performing at the famous Metropolitan Opera House, she immediately purchased two orchestra seats for herself and her son.

Adam was not yet 5 years old and nearly all of Sally's relatives, most notably her husband, considered Adam too young and immature to attend the concert. Nonetheless, Sally insisted that her talented "prodigy in the making" would find the concert fascinating; and so, contrary to the opinion of most of her family, she elected to go.

Arriving early, Sally escorted her well-dressed youthful companion into the impressive, elegant concert hall. After the kind usher guided them to their seats, Sally spotted a former acquaintance and turned around to converse with her, momentarily disregarding her inquisitive child.

Adam slipped out of his comfortable seat, made his way down the aisle, and meandered toward the double doors labeled, "Do not enter — for employees only." A moment or two later, the lights dimmed as the much anticipated performance was about to begin. Sally had been so caught up in her own conversation that she had not noticed Adam's disappearance until now. Worriedly, she scanned her immediate surroundings, hopeful that he had not wandered too far. As she took her seat, she scanned the entire theater looking for Adam — or for an usher to help her find him.

The extensive stage provided an ample setting for the solitary instrument it displayed: a baby grand Steinway piano — Paderewski's very own. The crowd hushed and the curtains opened. Paderewski prepared to stage his grand entrance. The audience waited for his entry with bated breath. Shockingly, and to his mother's complete astonishment, out pranced little Adam, entirely unaware of the spectacle he had triggered.

The audience whispered, amused but puzzled, about the pint-sized vision on the stage. The whispers soon turned to expressions of amazement as Adam, with complete confidence and poise, settled onto the piano bench and began his finest rendition of "Twinkle Twinkle Little Star." Uncertain of what to expect, the crowd waited patiently.

Suddenly, Paderewski, bedecked in a long black tail coat, sauntered onto the stage and came up behind little Adam. Wrapping his skilled and proficient hands around Adam's novice fingers, Paderewski calmly whispered, "Just keep on playing, son. You're doing a beautiful job." Adam looked up at the face of the world-renowned musician, then turned his attention back to his little fingers which were still pounding the keys.

As Adam resumed his basic melody, Paderewski's fingers began to dance around the keys like a child in a playground, intricate harmonies weaving their way through the uncomplicated beauty of the child's simplistic tune, the contrast breathtaking in splendor. The intensity rose to a feverish pitch as Paderewski dazzled the crowd with an unforgettable finale, climaxing to a thunderous standing ovation.

Adam lowered himself down off the bench and onto the stage as he now stood side by side with the greatest pianist of his generation. Soaking in the audience's applause, Adam was proud of his performance. And so was Paderewski.

Every day of our lives we face overwhelming challenges. Yet, we step onto the stage named "life." The A-mighty "wraps His arms around ours" and whispers encouragingly, "Just keep on playing. You're doing a beautiful job." We then struggle to do our best and amazingly ... we succeed.

Red Light, Green Light, One, Two, Three

*R' Sholom Schwadron, the master of all storytellers,
would often use incidents from everyday life as parables
to drive home meaningful lessons. The following
humorous episode is one such instance.*

EVERY DAY THOUSANDS OF PEOPLE COMMUTE BACK AND
forth from Jerusalem to Tel Aviv via the country's busiest
highway, Kvish Tel Aviv. At the end of the thoroughfare, right
before the entrance to Jerusalem, hangs a traffic light. Likewise,
each day, alongside that same road wanders a very interesting individual, known to all who travel this route — Yaakov, a self-pro-
claimed rush-hour traffic conductor. As cars race by at sometimes
dangerous speeds, this 40-year-old man waves his hands wildly,
gesturing to the oblivious cars to move forward while simultaneously shouting frantically, "*Zuz, zuz. Maher, maher.* Move, move.
Faster, faster."

Each time the light turns red and the approaching cars slow down
and crawl to a complete stop, the conductor, as if orchestrating a clas-
sical symphony, raises his hands and extends them forward. He
thinks to himself, "It is a good thing that I am here coordinating the
flow of traffic. Otherwise the results could be catastrophic."

The light proceeds to switch back to green and Yaakov lowers his
hands, relieved that he has prevented countless accidents by pre-
venting oncoming cars from colliding with one another. He never
abandons his post; he remains until the conclusion of rush hour.

*Reb Sholom smiles as he glances over the crowd. "How
many of us are different from that meshugena? We, too,
imagine that we are controlling the traffic of our hectic*

lives, juggling our countless obligations with myriad conflicting responsibilities. And when it all works out, do we pat ourselves on the back or do we thank the One Who really deserves all the credit?"

Kishinev Konnections

Rabbi Moshe Eisemann wrote a series of articles in the Baltimore monthly magazine "Where, What and When" about his experiences in kiruv rechokim in Russia. I thank him for allowing me to share these experiences.

WHY KISHINEV? WHY WOULD THE A-MIGHTY LEAD Jews to establish a yeshivah in Kishinev, Moldova, to most Jews some remote town in a forgotten area of the world? The odds of a yeshivah being in this exact location out of the entire vast landscape of Russia seem immense.

In the late 1980's Rabbi Moshe Eisemann, *mashgiach* of Yeshivas Ner Yisroel of Baltimore, set out on a personal mission to spread Torah across the Soviet Union. During the first few years, he and his group organized informational seminars in order to make contact with young Jews who were brave enough to let their Jewishness come out into the open. One of these seminars was held in a small town outside of Kishinev. Everyone was surprised at the large turnout which, it became apparent, was because many Jews from Kishinev were interested in meeting Jews from America. From an initial informational meeting with a group of curious Jews came another, and another, which led to discussions about setting up a yeshivah. Eventually, after much hard work and devotion, a yeshivah was established in Kishinev.

But is that it? Is that all there is to say about the flourishing yeshivah for Russian boys that now is located in Kishinev? We know not Hashem's real reason for doing what He does, but Rabbi Eisemann suggested a possibility.

There was a Jew whom we know very little about. He may have been a "paragon of virtue," a "mover and shaker" or a drunken vagrant. But one thing we do know. One day many years ago he touched greatness.

The Nazis had gathered the townspeople of the Kishinev ghetto to the town center where machine guns had been set up. This Jew was aware of his fate but had one last thing to do. He asked the Nazi devil if he would be permitted to go across the road and say good-bye to someone. Wonder of wonders, the monster agreed. And this Jew, together with a small group, entered the *beis medrash* and said a bitter, tearful good-bye for one last time to their Father, the A-mighty Himself. In Rabbi Eisemann's powerfully moving words, "They entered, they davened, they left and they died."

There is a story about the Chofetz Chaim which begs to be told at this point. When the Chofetz Chaim was yet a young man he visited a small town. On the first day of *Selichos,* he, together with the town's Rav, in whose house he was staying, passed by a home. They heard bitter crying coming from within and upon checking discovered that the man inside had just been released from thirty-five years of service in the Czar's army. This former soldier had known only harsh army life for the past thirty-five years, and had never had any sort of Jewish education. He had just learned that Rosh Hashanah was coming, and was crying because, although he wanted to pray, he could not even read the *aleph-beis.*

Years later the Chofetz Chaim returned to that same town and asked to be shown the house where he had met that tragic figure.

The house no longer stood. But in its place had blossomed a flourishing *beis medrash* where people learned and davened all day long. The Chofetz Chaim smiled in satisfaction knowing that *Yiddishe treren* never go unanswered. Hashem had taken the tears that had been shed on this spot and used them to water the seeds that produced this edifice of *kedushah*.

On that fateful day, as they entered their synagogue for the last time, the Jews of Kishinev cried bitterly, knowing the fate that awaited them. And today, in that exact place, stands a lasting memorial of that final act of *mesiras nefesh* — the Yeshivah of Kishinev, Moldova.

Thank You

THE CROWD OF FAMILY AND FRIENDS THAT HAD GATHERED in the shul in Baltimore listened as Yehoyada Aryeh delivered his Bar Mitzvah *derashah*.

The Bar Mitzvah boy was known by his rebbeim and peers as a lively, engaging young man. Those privileged to watch him learning in the Ner Yisroel *beis medrash* witnessed a young man who energetically reflected his excitement with whatever he was learning — he would move about quickly, wave his arms and gesticulate with great energy. It was a pleasure to watch. Today at his Bar Mitzvah, the topic for his speech was anything but typical — the laws of a *gideim,* one who is physically handicapped, donning *tefillin.* The discourse was intricately woven, a beautiful piece of Torah befitting a budding *talmid chacham.*

Yehoyada performed admirably and impressed the crowd, his parents and his teachers. After his speech many people in the audience approached him and gave him a hearty *yasher koach* for the beautiful job he had done.

A bit later, the Bar Mitzvah boy's father, Rabbi Aryeh, who served as Rav of the Iranian shul Ohr HaMizrach where the event was taking place, began to address the guests. His remarks began with traditional words of thanks and congratulations. But his next words of appreciation were somewhat unusual. He paused, looked for a moment at his son, then at the guests, and stated that he wanted to thank Hashem publicly for giving his son arms that are long enough to place *tefillin* on.

As only the close family members knew, both Yehoyadah and his sister were born with deformities. His arms are not as long as those of a healthy person. Neither are his sister's. This is enough of a trauma to send any child into despair. However, for a religious young boy, the deformity had even graver consequences — one's arms have to be a certain length in order to have *tefillin* placed on them. As a young boy anticipating the day he would put on *tefillin* for the first time, Yehoyada found out only recently that, by a measurement of a few centimeters, he would indeed be able to fulfill the mitzvah of *tefillin*. And for that "*berachah*" his father expressed thanks to Hashem.

The initial reaction of the crowd was a blend of both numbness and inspiration, and the guests began murmuring to each other, feeling great awe and respect for this unusual family. All who watched this Bar Mitzvah boy, who had already impressed them with his learning, felt inspired by the entire family's love and courage.

Teshuvah / Repentance

Who Are You?

MOSHE LOPIAN HAD NOT FELT WELL OF LATE. The headaches were increasing and he constantly felt dizzy. Resting did not seem to help him and finally he went to the doctor together with his parents, Rabbi and Rebbetzin Elya Lopian. Extensive testing revealed a cancerous growth in the young boy's brain that had already progressed rapidly.

Reb Elya tried his best to support his child during this trying period. He constantly encouraged him and spent countless hours by his bedside. Every day his brothers and sisters would come by and converse with Moshe. In an attempt to get his mind off the dreaded disease they would play games with him and read his favorite books to him. The laughing and playing was a pleasant break from the constant needles and prodding that were routine. In fact, the time he spent with his family was the highlight of his gloomy day. But shortly, all of that changed.

The headaches had begun to increase as had the dizzy spells. Moshe's personality was not the same. He had been upbeat throughout his painful illness but now his resistance was weakening. His friends and family redoubled their efforts and tried to visit him even more often than they had earlier. Reb Elya himself remained by his son's bedside. Unfortunately none of this was able to reverse or stop the spread of the disease.

Tragically he no longer knew his friends; it was as if he had never seen them before. His best friends were now total and complete strangers. When Reb Elya saw what was happening, he feared the worst: His son was dying.

Several weeks passed, and Moshe's friends, who up until now had come daily, began visiting less frequently. It was now only his siblings and parents whom he could identify. The treatments were continued, but to no avail; slowly he was losing touch even with those closest to him.

When his siblings came to visit him, and he looked around the room, he wondered who these people were. Sadly, he did not recognize any of them. Reb Elya and his wife cried at the sight of their sick child. The illness had robbed him of his ability to recognize those who loved him most. Each day was now a battle that Moshe was losing. Finally the painful day arrived when Reb Elya and his rebbetzin walked through the door and looked at their son. And though he looked back at them, the expression on his face told the tragic story. He was no longer able to recognize even his own mother and father. A few weeks later the young boy's pain was no more and he ascended to Heaven.

Perhaps what is most amazing is that Reb Elya was able to look back on this tragic episode in his life and derive a lesson in mussar from it. He viewed this painful period as a message that can be learned regarding the sanctity one maintains in his life. As long as one's mind and soul remain untainted and free of outside impure influences one can clearly identify who his Father is. But once the "infection," the impurity, enters his mind, then he is no longer capable of knowing who his very own Father is.

The Search for Truth

A NUMBER OF YEARS AGO, LAKEWOOD YESHIVAH began to send *yungerleit* to teach Jews from the surrounding tri-state area who were eager to learn more about their heritage. Some groups headed out to college campuses like Rutgers and Princeton. Other groups traveled to Twin Rivers and Freehold, New Jersey and New Rochelle, New York. Depending on the background of the students in the class, a broad range of topics was covered, ranging from *aleph-beis* to advanced classes in Gemara. Each group was run in whatever way the students preferred; some liked traditional classroom settings while others preferred *chavrusa*-style learning.

One small group of *yungerleit* set out to establish a group in Scarsdale, New York. Unsure of what to expect, they assumed that it would be wise to arrange for a few individual study partners for those with more background, while the others were offered a class on the weekly Torah portion. Their assumption was on the mark. Immediately, they could tell that the knowledge gap was quite wide. Part of the group wanted to set up advanced Gemara *chavrusas* and the rest was divided into two or three smaller groups that would learn various subjects. The vast majority chose *Chumash* and the weekly Torah portion while a few of the others didn't quite make any choice, but waited to be approached by one of the *kollel* fellows for a special one on one learning opportunity.

Mike Gindig was one of those who was waiting. A totally unaffiliated middle-aged Jew, he felt a spiritual curiosity tugging at him and had heard from a friend about the program and figured that he would try it out. He was not aware that an Orthodox group would be running it. Yehoshua Ottensoser approached Mike and asked him if he would like to learn. Mike immediately sensed Yehoshua's warmth and agreed to give it a try.

After discussing the matter for a few moments they decided to study *siddur.* Aleph-beis would be picked up along the way as

Mike was not a fluent reader by any stretch of the imagination. They began with *Ashrei*. Yehoshua, realizing that Mike was not satisfied with just the basic text, prepared "extras" through a meaningful book entitled *The Art of Jewish Prayer* by Rabbi Yitzchok Kirzner.

The weekly *chavrusa* time went well and each week their relationship grew. Mike really looked forward to the learning on Tuesday nights and week after week became more proficient in his reading. He worked hard at it and was proud to report his progress to his "teacher" every week. Finally, after a few months, Yehoshua felt it would be a nice gesture to buy him a gift. He decided on an ArtScroll *Siddur*. The bookstore wrapped the present nicely and Yehoshua was excited to give it to his friend. That week Yehoshua waited anxiously for his *chavrusa* to come, but he never showed up.

He was surprised. Not only had Mike said that he enjoyed their study session but he had even mentioned that it was the highlight of his week. Why had he not come? Yehoshua reviewed the last week's meeting in his mind just to ensure that he had not said anything to anger or insult Mike. Satisfied that indeed he hadn't, Yehoshua was confused and disappointed. That night the hour and forty minute return trip to Lakewood seemed to take longer than usual. The customary excitement in the car was somewhat tempered by the fact that Mike had not shown.

The following day Yehoshua approached the other members of the group. He appeared distraught as he told them the bad news. After many tries, he had found out why Mike had not shown. Mike had cancer. Actually, a cancer that he had suffered with twenty years earlier had returned. The doctor had told him that further testing would be necessary but it seemed the illness had moved aggressively. The group was shocked. Though they were only acquaintances, they felt closer to him than to anyone else in the Scarsdale crowd, largely because he was the one upon whom they had had the greatest impact.

The next week there was palpable apprehension in the car. Uncertain as to what they should expect, they each approached Mike and told him how they felt. Yehoshua sat down with him and listened as Mike spoke. He told Yehoshua about his past ordeals with this dreaded disease and wondered aloud how he could handle it again. He wasn't sure how much longer he would live and he wanted to make the most of the time he had left. They spoke about the mitzvah of *tefillin* and Mike committed to putting them on daily. Yehoshua was awed by Mike's drive and humbled by his resilience. Right before his very eyes he was witnessing the transformation of *a baal teshuvah.* It was incredible!

Toward the end of the evening, Yehoshua presented Mike with the *siddur* he had purchased earlier. Mike was touched beyond words. They all wished Mike well and told him that they hoped to see him soon. Mike left that night a different man than when he had arrived. The group discussed plans for a combined present to give to Mike. Suggestions for different options were given by each member. Finally they decided that since prayer had made such an impact on Mike's life, an ArtScroll *Tehillim* would be the appropriate choice.

The next week they made the presentation to an emotional Mike. His words were choked with tears of thanks. The moment was bittersweet. They knew he had "arrived" but they also knew that he was dying. The disease had spread and now it was noticeable on him. His face was pale and thin and his demeanor was slow and calculated. It had been a challenge to come that evening but he had made it. The time he spent with his *chavrusa* was now more precious than ever.

Mike's attendances became less frequent. Yehoshua went to visit him in the hospital and encouraged him. He tried to cheer him up but the pain visible on Mike's face did not allow for any joking around. When they said good-bye to each other, Yehoshua had a premonition that this might be the last time they would meet.

A week later the phone call came. It was from Mike's daughter. Mike had passed away earlier that day and she wanted to inform Yehoshua. She told him that no words can describe the transformation her father had undergone over the past three months and the impact it had on his life. Though she was not religious she knew that he put on *tefillin* every day. She also wanted to tell him one last thing. When he died there were three things that he had on his nightstand: *The Art of Jewish Prayer,* an ArtScroll *Siddur* and a *Tehillim.*

> *Our rabbis mention that there are those few who have merited to acquire a portion in the World to Come instantaneously. We pray that Mike Gindig was one of those.*

One Small Favor

EB CHATZKEL HAD NOT BEEN FEELING WELL FOR A while. It seemed his chest pains were more than just that. Walking up and down the stairs left him short of breath. Following the urging of his wife, he decided to take a complete physical — blood work, x-rays and all. It had been three years since his last one and back then Dr. Weiner had pronounced him as healthy a 65-year-old as he had ever seen. So he expected nothing different this time around. However, this time things did not go so smoothly.

"I'm afraid that we have a small problem," Dr. Weiner announced, holding up one of the chest x-rays to the light. "We're going to have to perform surgery immediately. You're going to need a triple bypass. It's a good thing you came in now because in another week or so I don't know if you would have been able to walk in on your own two legs."

Chatzkel could not believe what he was hearing. His wife stood close by, wondering just how serious this was. The doctor had seemed terribly concerned. She walked out into the hallway and called her three sons, Yankel, Yisroel and Reuven, or Robert as he was now known.

The Morgensterns had raised three wonderful sons — loving, respectful and caring. Yankel and Yisroel's families were involved in every aspect of the community's needs and their children were all well-respected, fine members of their communities. However, Robert, now a successful businessman, had chosen as a teenager not to be religious. He lived far away, in Phoenix, Arizona. It had been over ten years since he had kept Shabbos and this had caused his parents a great deal of aggravation and pain.

The three boys came as quickly as they could; Robert had taken the first possible flight out. Within several hours they stood around their father's bedside hoping they had not spoken to him for the last time. Unfortunately the surgery had not gone as well as had been expected. Chatzkel's chest pains had increased and his breathing was more laborious than ever. Suddenly, he opened his eyes and called his three sons closer.

One by one he gave over his responsibilities to his children, appointing Yankel to assume the position of shul *gabbai* and Yisroel as interim president of the yeshivah. Ignoring their pleas to stop, Chatzkel sensed that his end was near.

"And Reuven, I have a special favor to ask of you," Chatzkel spoke slowly, short on breath.

"Anything, Father. Anything. Whatever you ask me to do, I promise to do it." Robert begged his father to entrust him with a mission as had done for his two brothers.

"But you have to promise me –" Chatzkel's weak hands reached out for his son's.

"I do, father, I do," Robert reached out, sensing it was the last time he would be able to hold his father's hands. His heart was pounding, and he stared intensely into his father's sad, old eyes.

"Reuven, promise me that after I die ..."

"Yes, Father. Speak. Anything. I promise."

"Promise me that after I die, until you mend your ways, you ... won't ... say ... *Kaddish* ... for ... me."

For a moment, Robert could not move or speak. He stared at the father he loved so dearly, at once pained for himself and for the elderly man. There was nothing he could say but — "I ... I ... promise."

Silence.

Shock and sadness permeated the room. They had all heard their father's last requests, and had witnessed him taking his last breath.

The *chevrah kadisha* was called and arrangements were made for the funeral to take place early the next morning. The boys stood with their mother, hugged her and each other, and turned to go home to their families. Robert had barely said a word. He had hugged his mother but felt, in many ways, inconsolable.

He took time to ponder his father's request; never once, since he had given up being a *shomer mitzvos,* had he considered that he would not be able to say *Kaddish* for his father. He knew that his parents were displeased with his life choice, but they had always been so loving, so caring about him. With this one, final request, his father had declared a judgment on Robert and made it clear — you may not participate in this final mitzvah to honor me until your life changes. Robert was truly stunned, shocked, and — finally — angry.

It was his right, he felt, to say *Kaddish* for his father, and no one could take that away from him. Religion aside, he had always been very respectful toward his parents. His lack of performance in regard to the Torah was his own personal decision, not an outgrowth of hatred he had toward his parents. And if he chose now to observe the custom of *Kaddish* then he should be allowed to do so.

All of the arguments swirled inside his head, but he kept coming back to that moment that would forever be etched in his memory — his father's intense stare, his cold but firm hands and his strong words. A promise was a promise and Robert knew he had to keep his word. He felt utterly confused and lost, but he had no choice.

The next day, eulogies were given by many of the respected members of the community. All the brothers sat next to each other but Robert could not have felt further removed from his family. Finally the eulogies came to a close and the procession proceeded to the cemetery where Chatzkel was buried in a plot he had recently purchased, a few rows in front of his mother.

It was a bitter cold day and the gusting wind cut into their faces, freezing their tears against their cheeks. After the final shovelful of earth was thrown onto Chatzkel's grave the Rav motioned to the brothers to say the *Kaddish.* Yankel and Yisroel stood next to each other and slowly began to recite, *"Yisgadel veyiskadesh shemei rabba."*

The words sliced through Robert's heart and for the first time he broke down, crying uncontrollably. His heart longed to join with his brothers and speak the words that had been designated millennia before as a comfort to one's soul.

"Please, Father, how could you have done this to me?" Robert thought as, together with his mother, he watched his brothers finish the *Kaddish*. The friends and family watching wondered why Robert did not say the *Kaddish* for his father, and Robert could almost feel their stares and hear their whispers.

All through the *shivah* the scene repeated itself again and again. The brothers would recite the *Kaddish* and Robert would quietly watch and answer together with the rest of the *minyan*.

Shivah finally ended. Robert bid farewell to his mother and brothers and returned to Phoenix to resume his life. The colleagues in his law firm noticed that he was acting differently than before and understandably attributed it to the loss of his father. However, Robert could accomplish very little at work or at home. And although he did miss his father that was not the main reason for his pain.

His insides twisted and turned. His wife tried to console him but nothing seemed to help. His lack of sleep was beginning to affect his health and so he decided to take a few days off from work. His partners would surely understand.

That afternoon his wife came home and found Robert crying softly on the couch. She sat down next to him and tried to comfort him. Suddenly he turned to her, his face contorted in grief, and cried out, "I can't take it anymore! I *have* to say *Kaddish* for my father! Everything feels wrong now!" He turned to his wife and looked into her kind, understanding eyes, declaring, "If this means that we have to change the way we live — then so be it." His wife saw the fire in his eyes, and felt the pain in his soul; she knew at that moment that their lives were about to change.

Robert, or Reuven, as he was now called, and his wife returned for his father's *yahrtzeit* and together with his brothers made a *siyum* in memory of his father. As the last Mishnah was read aloud, the *hadran* was recited and together with his brothers Reuven declared in a strong clear voice, *"Yisgadel veyiskadesh shemei rabba!"* His mother and brothers looked on proudly, amazed at the wisdom and holiness that their husband and father had shown in making his final request. Reuven's wife was beaming and felt a great love for her father-in-law who, at the last moment of his life, had done something which brought such meaning and happiness into their lives.

And we can be most certain that his father looked down from Heaven and smiled.

The White Flag

Rabbi Yitzchak Feldheim is a rabbi in the growing community of Yardley, Pennsylvania. A few years ago an older gentleman approached him days before the Yamim Noraim and shared with him a story that he felt captured the essence of these days of awe.

THE TRAIN WAS ABOUT TO LEAVE. IT WAS A TWO-AND-A-half-hour ride from Port Authority to Harrisburg, Pennsylvania and almost every seat was full. Jack Eastman, a successful lawyer and an impressive looking gentleman, hopped on and settled in on the last remaining seat. Jack was sharply dressed in his black pinstripe Giorgio Armani suit, off-white Valentino shirt with an arc spread collar, and split toe Mezlan shoes. He placed his raincoat in the small compartment above his seat and pulled out a state-of-the-art laptop from his sleek leather attaché case. Satisfied with his preparations, he settled in for the trip.

As the doors were about to close, in dashed Jason Gross, a disheveled looking 19-year-old boy, his hair unkempt, his clothing wrinkled and messy. With no seats available, Jason reached up to grab hold of the plastic hook next to his head. Just then the doors of the Amtrak train closed and the train sped off.

Jack had been working studiously on his laptop when he noticed the boy standing above him. How sad, he thought. The young man appeared to be totally lost, with nowhere to go. "Excuse me, would you like to sit down next to me?" A seat had opened up next to Jack and he offered it to Jason.

"Nah, it's okay. I'm just gonna stand here." Jason hadn't even made eye contact with him. He just stared straight ahead.

A half hour passed and once again Jack offered the seat. He could not get back to his work, wondering why this boy seemed so troubled. Jack had two kids: a boy of 15 and a girl of 12. He tried not to imagine his children ending up this way, but if they did he would want an older, caring person to help them.

Once again Jason refused the offer. He obviously wanted to be left alone. Another half hour passed and finally Jason's weary feet convinced him to accept the seat. He was happy to finally be able to rest. He muttered a meek word of thanks and rested his head against the cold window. Although his head bobbed back and forth from the vibrations of the train, the cool feel of the window against his cheek was refreshing.

"Do you want to talk? It looks like something's bugging you." Jack tried to recall some of the teenage jargon he heard around the house but his mind came up empty. Jason continued to stare blankly out the window.

"If I want to talk I'll let you know." For the very first time Jack made eye contact with this troubled young man. He had once heard that if you look into someone's eyes you can see what's in his soul. What he had seen in this boy's eyes was pure sadness. Just by looking at him you could see he was lonely and lost. Jack tried a few more times to extract from Jason what was troubling him, and how he could help, and finally Jason relented.

"It all started when I was around 15," Jason began to bare his soul as Jack sat back and listened carefully. "I was the type of kid who was into electronics and was generally viewed as a recluse. My parents constantly encouraged me to get together with friends and they would always bother me. I would tell them to let me run my own life but they kept sticking their noses into my business.

"Well, one of the advantages of being an electronics 'nerd' is the ability to create and invent different things. And that is precisely what I did. I created my very own invention and made a mint off of it. I became a millionaire overnight. By then I was 17 years old. Sure enough I became popular. My parents tried to warn me about the 'groupies' who wanted to get close to me because I was rich. But I had had enough of their advice; I told them once and for all that they should stay out of my life. They pleaded with me and begged me but the last time we spoke I hung up on them, insisting that they never call me again."

By now Jack was hanging onto every word of Jason's tale of woe. He watched closely as Jason shifted uneasily in his seat. He felt Jason's parents' pain yet sympathized with Jason as well; he wondered how much suffering this boy had endured.

"Money helped me find a wife and we got married immediately, with neither of our parents present at the wedding. Nine months later we had our first child. Life seemed to be perfect. There we were — a young couple living in a beautiful high-rise Manhattan apartment with a precious little baby. Then one day a shady character, one that in hindsight I should have stayed away from, offered me the 'chance of a lifetime' — an investment that would allow me to retire. I invested the millions that I had made and waited for a phone call that never came. The entire thing was a scam. Just like that, I was poor again.

"When my wife discovered what happened she left me and took our child. I was evicted from the apartment and suddenly had no friends to turn to. My entire world had crumbled. Less than two months earlier I had been sitting on top of the world and now I was penniless, homeless and lonelier than I had ever been. I scrounged around like a beggar going from restaurant to restaurant pleading for food. Doors were slammed in my face; the humiliation was unbearable. Finally, starved and ashamed, I stretched out on a park bench, closed my eyes and went to sleep, thinking, 'This is where I'm going to die.'

"I don't know how long I had been sleeping but a man tapped me on the shoulder. I had never seen him before and he didn't know who I was, but he sat down next to me and listened to my story. He cared about me and encouraged me to come back to his home, change my clothing and contact the only people that still cared for me — my parents.

"I thought to myself, 'How could I use them like this?' For as long as I could remember I had treated them more like my worst enemy than my parents. I showed them no respect and refused to include them in any part of my life. And now that I needed them I should use them?! I felt remorseful and ashamed about my entire existence. But left with no other choice, I decided to write them a letter.

"I sat down and tried to write. Tears blinded my vision and stained my words. I poured out my soul to them and related the entire chain of events that had transpired since we last spoke. I imagined them reading the letter, and even though I knew they loved me, I was uncertain what their reaction would be. After all, I'm sure I had caused them great pain and frustration. I told them that I needed them in the worst way but that I did not have the courage to ask them in person to take me back. What if they refused to have anything to do with me? I knew it was cowardly of me but I had no choice. This was my last resort.

"So instead I asked them for a favor. I informed them of the train ride that would be bringing me back home on the third of June at 7:30 in the evening. Approximately fifty yards from the train stop there is a large oak tree. If they found it within themselves to forgive me for my past sins they should hang a small white flag on one of the branches of the tree. And if not … then I'll just stay on the train and continue on to the next stop."

Jason was spent. He had just bared his soul to this complete and total stranger but he had no choice because the stop was just ahead and he didn't have the courage to look and see if the flag was there. Jack held what was now a little scared boy close to him. He had cried throughout the story and was anxious to do what he could.

The train slowed and the stop was near. Jason put his head between his knees and was nearly shaking with fear and apprehension.

One hundred yards.

Seventy-five.

Fifty.

Jack looked out the window. The train had almost stopped completely. The sound of its screeching wheels was growing louder. Jason looked up, his eyes red, his face white. "So tell me ... what did you see?"

Jack stared at Jason and smiled. "The ... entire ... tree ... was ... covered ... in ... white ... cloth!!" Jason stood up, hugged his friend and walked toward the exit of the train. Standing there with tears in their eyes were his loving parents. At first he hesitated, but then ran into his parents' arms and held them closer than he ever had before. His mother and father too held their broken son close and whispered into his ears, "Welcome home, son, welcome home."

Lose the Battle but Win the War

ROSH HASHANAH HAD ARRIVED AND MEIR GOLDBAUM, A 17-year-old yeshivah *bochur* learning in a yeshivah in Ofakim, Israel, was disappointed. He had worked hard to improve in his *yiras Hashem* — both his davening and learning — but he did not feel that he had progressed sufficiently for the upcoming Day of Judgment.

As a disciple of Reb Shimshon Pincus *zt"l*, Meir had begun to understand what the awe of the High Holy Days meant. Reb Shimshon's inspiring *shmuessen* had made a distinct impression

on him and resulted time and time again in commitments and res-
olutions to improve in his *avodas Hashem*; and time and again Meir
failed to put his commitments into action. As a result, he felt like a
complete and absolute failure.

Rosh Hashanah morning, Reb Shimshon stepped outside the
beis medrash for a moment during the *chazzan's* repetition of the
Shemoneh Esrei and spotted his student in the corner of the hallway sitting on a low chair with his head between his knees. Reb
Shimshon, with his warm and caring demeanor, approached
Meir, placed a hand on his shoulder and asked him why he
seemed so depressed.

Meir looked up into his rebbi's gentle eyes and poured out his
frustration. He told him how hard he had tried during this past Elul
to improve and how each time his efforts had fallen short. In
essence he perceived himself as a complete and total failure. He
had pledged that this Rosh Hashanah would be different and he
would rise to the occasion — yet he had not. Meir cried bitterly and
hung his head in shame.

Reb Shimshon sat down next to the boy and related the following incident:

"It was during the Yom Kippur War and I was sitting in the
Emergency Room in the Shaarei Tzedek hospital waiting for one of
my children to be seen by a doctor for a cut that apparently needed stitches when I noticed a commotion taking place. Many doctors
had converged in front of the Emergency Room doors and
appeared to be discussing an important matter.

"I inquired as to what had happened and was told that a soldier had been shot and had been brought to the hospital. The bullet was lodged in his leg and needed to be taken out. After the
doctor had removed the bullet he notified the soldier, who had
been awake during the entire procedure, that the surgery was
complete and he was free to go home. The young man, no older
than 19 years, grimaced in pain as he struggled to slide off the
operating table. Beads of sweat formed on his forehead and he
looked curiously at the doctor.

"'Home? You think I'm heading home? True, I was shot and lost
this battle, but there's a war raging out there and my fellow soldiers

need me back on the battlefield.' The brave young man hobbled out of the room and headed back toward the front lines."

Reb Shimshon concluded the inspiring story and looked into the eyes of the vulnerable young man. "Meir, I'm not going to convince you that you have not stumbled. But just because you've fallen does not mean you can't get back up. Losing a battle does not mean that you've lost the war. We're fighting a war in there and I don't want to head back in without you. We need you to fight alongside the rest of us!"

A shy smile formed on Meir's face and he thanked his rebbi for his warm words of encouragement. Reb Shimshon placed his arm around Meir's shoulder and together they walked back into the *beis medrash* to "fight" alongside one another.

Mesiras Nefesh / Self-Sacrifice

The Greatest Hero

IN 1962, ADOLF EICHMANN, THE MOST WANTED NAZI fugitive, was captured on his way to work in his village in Argentina. In a brilliant display of strategy, the Israeli Mossad carefully planned the kidnaping by observing his every move for months beforehand. The details of what happened have been recorded in the annals of history. The Israeli government then put him on trial. But they wanted more than just an isolated trial. Rather, they hoped to place the entire Holocaust on trial and thus called countless witnesses to detail the horrors they had experienced. For this monumental event they built a special building to house the trial and wanted to construct in front of it a representation depicting the greatest heroes of the Holocaust.

The leaders of the operation met to decide what form this depiction should take. Different people expressed their opinions as to who served as the greatest symbol of heroism during the war.

The first and obvious suggestion was to portray the leaders of the Warsaw ghetto uprising. The icon of a gun-toting resistance fighter, it was suggested, represented the courage of the Jewish people. But someone brought up an important issue. Would that mean that all those innocent men, women and children who had died with *Shema Yisrael* on their lips were not heroic? Surely that was not true!

And so the elusive search for the most heroic figure of the Holocaust continued. One suggested it was the little orphaned boy who would climb over the ghetto walls to find food for his starving family. Some nodded their heads in agreement. There was certainly no denying the heroic nature of that boy.

Another suggested the doctor who traveled from door to door risking his life to aid the sick and injured without so much as a stethoscope. Though limited in supplies and medicine, he risked life and limb to save as many as he could. Again there was no disagreement as to the valiant courage this man displayed in the ghetto and beyond.

Then someone proposed that the *Yiddishe mamma*, who used her motherly love and care to will her family to live when she had no food to give them, personified the superhuman efforts of the Jews during the Holocaust. And again they all nodded their heads in agreement. Surely no one would dare argue with such a premise.

But before the final votes were cast a thin yet strong voice piped up and suggested something unlike any of the previous suggestions. "The most valiant members of the ghetto were a group of mysterious young men. They were not the freedom fighters who armed themselves with artillery and machine guns. They showed their defiance in a different manner — by refusing to bend to the German codes of conduct. If the Nazis insisted that they cut their *payos* and shave their beards these young men refused. If sacrificing their meager rations of bread was the cost then so be it. But only the A-mighty was to dictate what their standards of behavior would be. These men were known as 'Matisovitzen,' after their leader, a Gerrer Chassid by the name of Matis Gelman. He was a young man with a scraggly beard who appeared out of nowhere to encourage those in need. Though still a young man, he brought hope to countless souls. But perhaps what was most amazing was the schedule that these young men kept. Their daily schedule remained for the most part uninterrupted, and with it their steadfast commitment to the learning of Torah. It was these courageous young men, the 'Matisovitzen,' who epitomized the spirit of the heroes during the Holocaust."

Naftali and Falk were two of these Matisovitzen. And they, along with their friends, spent months hidden in the cellars and attics of apartment buildings in the ghetto. They spent their days and nights learning Torah, risking their lives for what was most important to them and to the rest of the Jewish people. In a certain respect it was they who were fighting the battle on the front lines. Their rations of food and water were forfeited to enable them to remain out of sight and to allow them to retain the appearance of a Chassidic Jew. But tragically one day these "secret agents," Naftali and Falk, were caught.

The soldiers who seized them immediately separated these young men so as not to allow these "dangerous infiltrators" to collaborate and endanger the Third Reich. They were tortured and beaten to force information out of them. One cold winter night they were each led down a dimly lit corridor to an unknown location. They hurt badly but the defiance in their eyes spoke of the spirit alive in their hearts.

And as they approached each other, with each having had his beard ripped off and with the bruises on their bodies witness to the barbaric beatings they had suffered, two armed guards flanked each of these "dangers to society." They came closer to one another and as they passed in the hallway, Naftali turned to Falk and whispered, "Falk, don't forget. Tomorrow night, we start saying *Vesein tal umatar livrachah.*"

Falk nodded, his heart swelled. Message received.

A Smile Through Sadness

THE FIRST GERRER REBBE, REB YITZCHOK MEIR ALTER, THE Chiddushei HaRim, together with his rebbetzin, brought sixteen children into this world. Tragically, fourteen died at a young age. Only two reached adulthood and one of those two, Reb Avrohom Mordechai, married and bore the Rebbe a grandson. Sadly, Reb Avrohom Mordechai died at the very young age of 38. After Reb Avrohom Mordechai's tragic passing, his son was raised by his grandfather and became the famous Sfas Emes.

As Reb Yitzchok Meir was sitting *shivah* for his fourteenth child, amidst the crying, a small smile appeared on his face. The Chassidim surrounding the Rebbe wondered what could have possibly brought a smile to his face. The Chiddushei HaRim gave an incredible answer. "One day it is possible that a family will suffer the tragedy of losing a child. Maybe, G-d forbid, they will lose two. But they will always be able to point to our family as a source of inspiration for the tragedies that we suffered through and were able to survive."

> *The Rebbe realized that although the tragedy that he and his wife had gone through was indescribable, if that suffering could indirectly bring comfort to another suffering family, that in itself was a source of nechamah.*

The Second World War had taken its toll on almost every family in Europe. Among those who had suffered the losses of large families was the Imrei Emes, the Gerrer Rebbe. Almost all of his children and grandchildren had been wiped out and only one grandson, Noach Yoskovitz, had survived. After the war, Reb Noach made his way to Eretz Yisrael to greet his grandfather. After a long journey he finally reached the house where his grandfather lived.

Overjoyed to see his grandson, the Imrei Emes hugged him and kissed him and then told him the following:

"It says in the *pasuk*, '*Vayisha'er ach Noach*,' after the Flood only Noach remained." The Rebbe looked at his grandson and asked him, "Why do you think that Hashem saved Noach from the Great Flood which destroyed the world?" He paused and then looked his grandson in the eye, "The answer is because Noach had to build!" Leaning in even closer, he charged his grandson with the same responsibility. "Build, Noach! That is why Hashem allowed you to survive — because He wanted you to rebuild what was destroyed over the last six years! Think of how much has been lost. Millions! But not only that. Think of how much precious time *you yourself* have lost. How many hours of learning have been taken away from you? My dear Noach, go to the *beis medrash* and rebuild that which has been taken away from us!"

The tears that were shed years before by the Chiddushei HaRim were not shed in vain. The strength to rebuild was embedded in his grandchildren and they were able to rebuild Gerrer Chassidus into the thriving dynasty that continues to blossom.

Rav Chaim Kanievsky and his rebbetzin have fourteen children. Incredibly, they managed to raise them in a cramped two-bedroom apartment. On one occasion a group of wealthy supporters of Torah were made aware of the difficult living accommodations Reb Chaim and his rebbetzin endured. They decided to raise the funds necessary to help purchase an apartment that would be able to accommodate a family of the Kanievsky's size.

However, one of the problems that arose was how they would present the money to Reb Chaim. They knew that he wouldn't want to accept the money from outside sources so they decided to give the money to Reb Chaim's mother, wife of the Steipler Gaon.

There seemed to be no logical reason for her to refuse the money for her children and grandchildren. After all, no one could possibly imagine how much maneuvering was done on any single night to put all the children to sleep. Surely she would be thrilled to accept the gift on behalf of her children and present them with the money for a brand new large apartment located near their present one.

However, her reaction showed that great people look beyond their own needs and concerns. When the donors presented her with the money she thanked them for their thoughtfulness but refused to accept it on behalf of her children. She explained her decision with the following sensitive reasoning. "As long as my Chaim and his family live in cramped quarters, then other families with a few less children in the same sort of living conditions can always look at them and rationalize that if the Kanievskys can manage with their large family then we can certainly manage with ours. But if my Chaim moves to more comfortable quarters then many other families will begin to feel more uncomfortable in their own houses … and that's not fair to them."

The humbled group of benefactors who had generously given from their own pockets walked away from their conversation with the Steipler's rebbetzin humbled as well as enlightened as to how far one can go when thinking of another Jew.

The Holy Stockings

HAVING GROWN UP IN THE HEART OF THE MEAH Shearim neighborhood in Yerushalayim, Reb Zecharyah Greenwald, a scholarly and pious young man, was well sought after as soon as he came of marriageable age. Soon after he turned 20 Zecharyah married a fine young woman, Chanah Lipman. They moved into a small two-bedroom apartment, sparsely furnished with just the basics. And although it was a simple apartment it suited their needs well, especially considering that they were located a mere five-minute walk from both his and her parents. After learning for a few years, Zecharyah decided to open a small grocery store to help support his family, which had grown to five with the birth of three daughters. But in the early 1940's it was quite difficult to support a family. The business venture did not go smoothly. Every day was a struggle, and it was a challenge just to put food on the table. Some days they were fortunate to have a real meal, and other days they would make do with much less.

The main reason for Zecharyah's business problems was that he allowed an enormous amount of credit. Many of his customers piled up bills that would remain unpaid for months on end. And finally, when Zecharyah would go to ask for the money and would witness the grinding poverty in which these families lived, he would become overwhelmed with emotion. He couldn't help himself — he would usually just forgive the entire debt.

After a few years he realized that running a grocery store was not his forte and he looked elsewhere for employment. One day he was approached by an old friend with a suggestion — to become a rebbi. For some reason something so obvious had never occurred to him; he simply had never thought of himself as being capable.

Zecharyah decided to make the move and when he did, he found it very satisfying to return to what he was most comfortable doing — learning and teaching Hashem's Torah. There was only one problem — the ongoing struggle to support his family. His wife, a kind and giving woman, did her best never to complain but when the children lacked sufficient food, her motherly compassion would overwhelm her and she would complain to her husband. Zecharyah always felt terrible at these times, and vowed that he would do whatever it took so that his family would not go hungry.

Several months later, Zecharyah began feeling sharp pains in his chest, and after a few weeks, he realized that he could no longer put off seeing a doctor. Without telling his wife that anything was amiss, he set up an appointment.

Dr. Wallach, a kind, elderly man, had a knack for diagnosing correctly. He might not have been the most up-to-date medically but his experience had taught him more than modern medicine could have. After listening to Zecharyah's chest for few moments he decided to do more extensive testing and told Zecharyah to come back in a few days.

Zecharyah did not like the look on the doctor's face. He knew that Dr. Wallach was not the worrying type and yet he had seemed more concerned than usual. As Zecharyah went home that night he promised himself that no matter how severe the pain was, he was not going to cause his family unnecessary worry.

Zecharyah returned to the hospital a few days later and without Dr. Wallach saying a word, he knew that things were serious. The doctor spoke with tears brimming in his eyes and informed Zecharyah that he was suffering from a terminal illness and there was not much to be done. For Zecharyah, being told that he was dying was a strange experience. Fear and anxiety were not the first things that hit him, rather he immediately thought of his family. Who would care for them? Who would support his little girls? Who would help his wife?

The answer, he knew, was the A-mighty. He and only He would care for them. Zecharyah had never placed his trust in anyone else. On his way home his mind wandered and he thought of how to break the news to his wife. He pictured her crying and imagined the sadness and sense of futility that would pervade their home. He decided not to say anything yet. He would try to live the rest of the time he had without worrying and saddening his family. But all the same he knew that he would have to prepare some important things for his children.

The way home seemed longer than usual. He stopped to pick up a few basic items for supper and as he turned to go up his block he noticed that the clothing store was still open. He thought of his little girls (he now had four daughters) and went into the store. He had but a few pennies left and did not know when he would receive his next check from the yeshivah. But this was important. He asked for four pairs of stockings for his daughters. Normally his girls could not afford a luxury like stockings but Zecharyah felt he had to prepare for his departure.

Arriving home later than usual, Zecharyah found his wife worried about where he had been. He placed the bread on the table and next to it a bag with the stockings. He called in his daughters, and the four little girls sat around their father at the table. Their dresses were frayed and their cheeks sunken. Zecharyah told them that he had bought them a treat. He pulled four pairs of stockings out of the bag. He tried to keep his composure as he hugged each child and gave her a pair of stockings. The girls' sad eyes lit up as they hugged their father. His wife, who knew — despite his best efforts at hiding his pain — that he was not feeling well, watched him carefully and began to sense that something was terribly wrong.

Zecharya looked tenderly at his daughters and then spoke from the heart. "My dear little girls, we never know how long Hashem will allow us to be here and so we must always prepare for the future. Where tomorrow's bread will come from, I don't necessarily know. But I do know that Hashem will provide us with our most basic living necessities. It is my job to ensure that my girls are going to dress in a modest manner and therefore I have bought you these pairs of stockings."

He could not speak any further. He wanted to but the words did not come. His daughters, oblivious to their father's emotions, jumped off their chairs and ran back to continue what they had been doing. But his wife had a strong sense of foreboding.

Later that week Zecharayah told his wife the terrible news, and just a few weeks later he returned his soul to his Maker. There was no prolonged illness. It had happened just the way he had hoped it would. He had a chance to say good-bye to his wife and daughters and the stockings he had presented to them bespoke an eternal message of modesty and the responsibility that came with it. They knew what was important to their father and they promised to heed his dying wish. Many years later these girls found wonderful husbands with whom they would share their lives. Their *shidduchim* and the families that they raised are a credit to the parents who were willing to give up everything for the *chinuch* of their children.

Never Ever

The Shuvu school system for Russian children was founded by Rav Pam and has done wonders for the Torah education of these children. Many have gone on to study at yeshivos of higher learning. Every week the children are allowed a few moments to express any feelings or stories they would like to share with their classmates and teachers concerning their incredible sacrifice for Torah and everything for which it stands. The following is one such inspiring story.

YURI WAS ALL EXCITED. HIS PARENTS, WHO HAD RECENTLY arrived in Israel from Russia, decided to send him to Shuvu. Although their religious affiliation was minimal and they had entertained the thought of sending their son to the public school system, they were impressed by the warmth and sincerity of the Shuvu family.

Every day the 11-year-old would come home with new information and he seemed to just soak it all up. The excitement of davening and learning outweighed all his other interests. He still enjoyed doing all the things that 11-year-olds do, but clearly Shuvu was making its mark. And the one mitzvah that meant more than anything to Yuri was the observance of Shabbos.

At first his parents were amused by his fervor and joy regarding this mitzvah. However, when the Shabbos restrictions began to cramp their lifestyles, they felt resentment toward the school and their son's obsession with keeping the "strange customs" he was learning about. They could not understand why it should be forbidden to turn a light on and off and had difficulty comprehending what was wrong with writing a letter. But out of their love for their son they went along with it and allowed him to adhere to the laws of Shabbos.

That tolerance was short lived. The inconvenience and expense of kosher food and the restriction of not turning on the television on Shabbos were just two examples of a long string of nuisances that slowly wore away at their patience. One evening after Yuri had gone to bed, his parents discussed the conflict that was going on in their home. They decided that the family was being troubled too much by Yuri's desire to keep Shabbos and they were no longer willing to compromise. It had only been a few months and they were fairly certain that they would be able to undo all the "damage" that had been done. They would simply inform him that he would no longer be attending the Shuvu school. Although they knew that he enjoyed it very much, they assumed he would quickly get over the disappointment and make new friends in the public school that was located less than a five-minute walk away. But they were wrong.

They waited until Friday after school to inform him of their decision that would take effect at the end of the semester in two weeks. Yuri did not take the news well at all. He badgered his parents with questions as to why he was being removed from a school that he liked so much. At first they focused on the fact that it was a convenience issue, but at Yuri's persistence they finally blurted out that his religious lifestyle was hindering their family life. At that point Yuri grew angry and began to shout and insist that he remain in Shuvu. The argument went full scale and the screaming escalated to a point where Yuri's younger siblings covered their ears and began crying.

The initial fight lasted about a half hour, though the matter was far from settled. Yuri had gone off to his room — angry, hurt and confused — and stared out the window. The sun was setting and that meant that Shabbos was fast approaching. He could not help but think of what type of Shabbos it would be. What fights would his mother pick with him? What forbidden things would they ask him to do? He wanted to pick up the phone and call his rebbi who had been so warm to him, but he knew that it was already too late to do that.

After another hour Yuri came downstairs and walked into the living room where the television was blaring. There was tremendous tension in the air. He wanted to just eat his Shabbos meal and go back up to his room to sleep. The day had been long enough and he did not want to fight any further. But his mother, a stubborn woman, could not let go that easily. She looked up from the show she was watching and asked him if he had finished the report that was due that coming Monday.

"It's not due until Monday and anyway I can't do it on Shabbos, Mommy. You know that." Yuri did not want to argue about this any further but sensed that his mother was not about to let go.

His mother stood up and stared at her son. She wondered if she should walk away but decided instead to put her foot down. "Yuri, you are going to finish that report right now. I've had enough disrespect out of you today. We are not going to wait until it gets hectic on Sunday to complete your assignment." She glared at her son and declared, "You'll complete it now!"

"Mommy, I can't! It's Shabbos!" Yuri's eyes filled with tears and his heart with pride for the Shabbos.

"Yuri! You better listen to me!" She was now screaming and yelling as she picked up a pen and held it in her hand for him to take and begin his report.

"No!" Yuri ran over to the door and placed his hand between the door and the frame. With all his might he swung the door forcefully and smashed his hand. The blood dripping from his hand and the bruise marks that appeared bore testament to his broken fingers. He was crying but his eyes were burning brightly with pride. "Are you happy now? I can no longer write on Shabbos because my fingers are broken!"

Yuri's mother was horrified at what she had caused, and filled with regret over her insistence that her son desecrate what was so important to him. He had only wanted to observe the Shabbos. And he wanted it so badly that he was willing to hurt himself to make sure he could do it. After all, what was so wrong with keeping the Shabbos? She pulled her son close to her and held him tightly. "It's all right. I'm sorry. I'm so sorry."

Yuri's brave defiance and dedication for the Shabbos won over his parents and they decided to allow him to stay in Shuvu. And now, together, as an entire family, they've begun to keep the Shabbos.

Shabbos All Week Long

YANKEL ROSENGARTEN, A THIRD-GENERATION JEW FROM Yerushalayim, was apprehensive about his trip to America. He had never been there before but now he had no choice. His school, part of an orphanage for young girls, needed funds desperately and he had exhausted all other financial options. He had therefore resolved to make the long journey himself.

This was not the first time that Yankel had left Eretz Yisrael. He had been to England twice before and he had also traveled to Zurich, Switzerland once. But those cities were more *heimish* than your typical American town. Yankel was worried about communicating with the English speaking Jews in America. In Europe almost everybody was fluent in Yiddish, but outside of New York City, most Jews just spoke English. Part of his success in fundraising stemmed from his knack for connecting with people, but with a language barrier he was worried about how he would communicate.

A good friend had given him a list of people he could call in cities throughout the United States in case he needed a place to stay. Yankel was thankful, though he really hoped he would not have to use his "just in case" list.

The nonstop El Al flight was uneventful. Yankel's itinerary was set. He would spend the first few days in New York and then move his way westward to the Midwestern cities of Cleveland, Detroit and Chicago. He would conclude his fundraising trip with a flight to Los Angeles, where he had a few wealthy supporters who had pledged generously to the orphanage.

The first portion of the trip was quite successful. He stayed with a cousin with whom he was close, and who helped him with logistics. Satisfied that he had met his goal in New York, he sat down that evening with his cousin Reb Leib to discuss the next leg of his trip, starting in Detroit. His cousin added a new name to the list of potential contributors, Reb Berel Gross, an influential member of the Detroit community who would assist him and perhaps offer him a place to stay. Grateful for his cousin's help, Yankel felt a little more confident.

As soon as he landed in Detroit he called Reb Berel Gross, introduced himself and was touched that Reb Berel graciously offered to send a cab to pick him up at the airport. Reb Berel was even upset that he had not been contacted earlier so that he could have arranged for Yankel to be picked up on time. He also invited Yankel to stay in his home while fundraising in Detroit. Yankel thanked him for his kind offer. Thirty minutes later the taxi arrived, and before long they reached Reb Berel's house. Yankel paid the driver and removed his small attaché bag from the back seat.

He knocked on the door and Reb Berel, a short, stocky man with a grey trimmed beard, answered the door and invited him in. Yankel conversed with Berel for a while, discussing the school's dire financial situation and then sharing some thoughts of Torah learning. Yankel was pleasantly surprised that Berel was a scholarly individual who was well versed in every Torah topic they discussed. Berel was sympathetic and understanding of the school's needs and wrote out a generous check. Yankel was pleased with the donation but even more satisfied that he would be able to stay with such a fine family for the next few days. However, one comment caught Yankel off guard.

Berel had mentioned something about the standard of kashrus in his home perhaps not being up to Yankel's standards. Yankel was confused. This was a man who was well versed in Torah learning and appeared to be a strictly observant Jew. Yankel felt he could control himself no longer and asked Berel what the problem could possibly be.

"I'm not sure if my Shabbos observance was always what it should have been," Berel answered, while averting Yankel's gaze, but he knew that an explanation was necessary. Yankel sat back, quite puzzled, and listened closely to every word Berel said.

"Many years ago I lived in a small *shtetl* in Poland. The poverty was extreme and although my parents tried, supporting the family was very difficult. I tried to help out as much as I could but as a young boy of 12, I was limited. Finally my father decided to send me to my uncle who lived in America. There, he figured, things would be better. America was the land where they had 'streets lined with gold.' My father felt that this would be my only chance to break free of my impoverished life.

"The trip by boat took several weeks and finally I arrived. My uncle came to greet me at the dock but his appearance startled me. Instead of the long beard that I had expected to see he sported a trimmed goatee. As a replacement for the long black coat my father wore he dressed in a stylish double-breasted herringbone grey sports jacket. But perhaps what startled me most was the fact that he walked around with his head uncovered. I tried to hide my shock, though the contrast between what I was expecting to see and the reality was overwhelming.

"He quickly used his connections to find me a job and I enjoyed being a carpenter's apprentice. However, when I did not show up for work on Shabbos morning I was immediately fired. This happened for three consecutive weeks. Each time, my uncle would lecture me on responsibility and each time I would defiantly refuse to go to work. I couldn't believe that my uncle had forsaken his heritage. He entirely dismissed the notion that Shabbos was non-negotiable, rationalizing that during the era of the depression 'making a living' was not something that could be taken for granted.

"On my fourth Sunday morning I was warned by my uncle to guarantee my boss that I would show up for work on the following Saturday. The pressure was so great and I was a lonely 12-year-old with no family other than an uncle who was urging me to give up the most sacred tradition I had known, and so I gave in. When I showed up for work, I told the boss that I would work on Shabbos.

"He kept on asking me throughout the week if I would come to work on Saturday and I answered him that I would, sincerely believing that I was in fact prepared to sacrifice the holy Shabbos for the security of my job. Finally, on Shabbos morning I tearfully left the house with every intention of going to work. Instead of taking the train as I normally had, I walked toward my place of employment, crying the entire time. But as I walked up the steps and stood on the threshold of the shirt factory where I worked, the image of my father flashed before my eyes and I heard him warning me in his soft, loving tone, 'Guard the Shabbos, Berel. Guard the Shabbos.'

"Suddenly I stopped. What was I thinking? How could I have even thought of desecrating the holy Shabbos? I turned around and ran as fast as I could, though I had no idea where I was going. I finally reached a park bench and begged Hashem for forgiveness. I knew I could never return to my uncle's house — but I had made a choice about what was dearest to me."

Berel looked up with red eyes at his guest and painfully recalled the event of which he was so ashamed. "I did not work that Shabbos. But every day of the preceding week I had planned to work on Shabbos, to desecrate its holiness. Shabbos isn't one day a week. You have to prepare a whole week for Shabbos and in that respect — I had failed. So if you want to eat in my house, that is your choice."

Yankel stared at his host for a long while, overcome by the holiness of this man who had suffered for so many years not because he actually desecrated the Shabbos, but because he had planned to. He gently embraced his new friend and realized that, aside from the financial benefit of meeting him, he had gained in many more important ways from being in the home of Reb Berel Gross.

Dollars and Sense

IT HADN'T BEEN EASY. FOR THE THIRD WEEK IN A ROW, Moshe dejectedly returned home on Sunday morning without a job. He had promised his boss that he would compensate for the lost time that accrued from his absence on Saturday, but it was too little too late. His insensitive supervisor threatened to fire him for his unexcused absence. Over the years he had labored as a carpenter, as a textile factory employee, and subsequently as an assembly line worker at the local bottling company. That's the way it was in New York City in the early 1900's in America, which was supposed to be the land of golden opportunity.

Many came home crushed, lamenting their fates with the adage, *"Es iz shver tzu zein ah Yid — It is difficult to be a Jew."* Others succumbed to their need for money and desecrated the sacred Shabbos by working on that holy day.

But Moshe was included among those few whose unwavering faith could not be broken. He had arrived two years earlier with a commitment to never violate the Shabbos and he was determined to adhere to that hallowed pledge.

Moshe stared at the manila envelope lying on the floor of his Lower East Side apartment. Though he had been dreading its arrival, he had anticipated its coming — after all, he was overdue on his last three rental payments. Moshe cautiously opened the small envelope. Though he could not read English well, his minimal comprehension of the language confirmed his worst fears. Their eviction would take effect the first of the month.

Moshe immediately arranged a meeting with Mr. Wells, the landlord of his apartment building, and pleaded for a one-month extension. Mr. Wells, a compassionate man, nonetheless would not bend. "I'm sorry, Goldman, but the bills got to be paid."

After Moshe made a desperate plea, he and Mr. Wells negotiated a compromise, buying the Goldman family some additional time. They were allowed to remain in the building, although they would have to leave their relatively pleasant apartment and move into the dark, damp cellar. Their new apartment was actually the building's coal room; thick black soot permeated the entire room and with it their meager belongings. Soot was everywhere, on everything, always.

One day, Mark Bookman, a local businessman and philanthropist, was driving through Moshe's neighborhood and glanced out of his car window to see an amazing sight — two black boys wearing yarmulkas. Impossible, he thought.

Bookman instructed his driver to pull over to the side of the road as he called aside the two "black" boys to inquire about their origin. Upon closer examination he discovered that they were two fair colored young Jewish boys who were covered in black soot.

"What happened to you?" Mr. Bookman inquired. The young boys described their heartbreaking living conditions, the grimy coal room, and their resulting bizarre appearance.

"Would you boys be able to show me where you live?" Mr. Bookman requested. And before he could offer them a ride, the anxious boys eagerly scampered down the street.

The chauffeured car pulled up in front of the apartment building. Mr. Bookman got out of the car, followed the energetic boys down the staircase into the cellar and waited patiently by the doorway to their "apartment."

"Mommy, we have a guest," the boys shouted. Mrs. Ettel Goldman, a middle-aged European woman, adjusted her hair-covering, turned around and did a poor job of hiding her shame as she quickly "tidied up" her immediate surroundings. "Welcome ... how can I help you?" Mrs. Goldman stammered to her prestigious looking guest.

"I just wanted to introduce myself — Mark Bookman." Sparing Mrs. Goldman further embarrassment, Mr. Bookman tried not to stare disbelievingly at the furnishings of the "apartment," wondering how in the world anybody could possibly live here.

Overcome with compassion, Mr. Bookman removed his checkbook, put pen to paper and wrote out a check for $5,000, an enormous sum of money — sufficient income to support an entire family for more than a year.

Mrs. Goldman, moved beyond words, silently accepted the much-needed funds as Mr. Bookman excused himself and hastily departed. She could hardly believe her good fortune. Her exhausted husband would be thrilled with this incredible sequence of events. What *hashgachah pratis*! She just knew that the A-mighty had answered her prayers.

Later that day, Moshe arrived home, crushed by the burden of another futile job interview. How much more could he take? How much longer could his family survive under these trying circumstances?

He glanced at his wife and noticed that she seemed to be in an unusually joyful mood. He then stared down in amazement at the check that lay before him. "Where did this come from?" he asked incredulously.

"Earlier this afternoon some goodhearted person unexpectedly walked in and presented us with it," she replied, sensing skepticism in her husband's tone of voice.

"Well, we can't accept it." Moshe quietly declared.

"Why not? Mr. Bookman gave it wholeheartedly!" Ettel pleaded, the frustration mounting in her voice.

"Ettel, I know who Mark Bookman is. The man is a *mechallel Shabbos*! We haven't sacrificed for the last two years to observe Shabbos only to be rescued financially by one who desecrates the Shabbos!"

Early the next morning Reb Moshe paid a visit to Bookman's sweater factory. After some informal introductions, Reb Moshe plainly announced that although he was extremely grateful, he could not accept the money.

"Please, Goldman, I know you're a proud man. Who isn't? But you have to think about your family. Their living conditions are abominable." Bookman sincerely wanted to help and couldn't figure out what was troubling Goldman.

"It's not about pride. It's about the Shabbos. We refuse to take money from someone who doesn't close his factory on Shabbos. Really, Mr. Bookman, I'm sorry, but it's not up for negotiation." Moshe Goldman abruptly turned and walked out the door.

That night a subdued Mark Bookman entered his home. His wife immediately recognized that something serious was troubling her husband and tried to get him to talk about it, as she had never seen him so distraught. "I can't believe he turned it down," Mark, dumbfounded, declared as he proceeded to relay the entire episode to his wife.

Mark was painfully aware of the tears brimming in his eyes as he spoke slowly and deliberately. "We used to be like that. Don't you remember? We also treasured the Shabbos ... until one week when business was awful. We were short on money and we promised to leave the store open ... just this one time." Tears streamed down his cheeks as he agonizingly recalled that dreaded day. "And that was ten years ago ..."

"Come in, the door's open," called Moshe as he skimmed through the classified section in the rear of the coal room.

Mark Bookman entered the room wearing a broad smile. "Hello, Moshe. I just wanted to bring this by." Mark placed a check on the table and turned to walk away.

"I thought I already told you that ..."

"Last week," Mark interrupted, "when you returned the check, I thought deeply about what you had said and it stirred memories that had been trapped inside of me for the past ten years. You see, my wife and I were also once *shomer Shabbos*.

"This past week, an hour before sunset, we entered the factory and proudly announced that the factory would be closed until Sunday morning. When I arrived home on Friday afternoon and watched my wife light the Shabbos candles for the first time in ten years, I felt as if I had returned home from a long, lonely journey.

"Moshe, thank you for bringing me home!"

As Moshe appreciatively accepted Mark's generous gift he understood better than ever that even more than a Jew watches over the Shabbos, the Shabbos watches over the Jew.

Magical Lights

REFUSNIKS. THE MERE MENTION OF THE WORD BRINGS to mind images of Eliyahu Essas, Anatoly Sharansky and other heroic figures who withstood the persecution of the Soviet Union's secret police, the dreaded K.G.B. Nothing came easily, as they had to constantly look over their collective shoulders to ensure that no one was watching every move they made.

One of the most famous *refusniks*, Yosef Mendelovitch, had been thrown into prison for "spreading false propaganda" — whatever that meant. Mendelovitch had been on the K.G.B.'s list for many years and now that they finally had manufactured enough evidence to jail him, they intended to drill him for all the information he had. But the harder they pressed the more stubborn he became. The authorities used all their persuasive measures but none seemed to work. Finally, frustrated and at wit's end, they threw him into solitary confinement.

The process was simple. Not only would his food rations be limited but also he would not be allowed to see the light of day; they assumed that as his resistance was lowered, his spirit would break. But that was easier said than done. Yosef's defiant nature made their job even harder, for each torture method fortified his resolve. Instead of weakening him, the different tactics implemented against him actually made him stronger.

Incredibly, Yosef was able to calculate when the Jewish holidays were, and based on his estimation, Chanukah was coming. The lights of the menorah precisely symbolized his own battle against the forces of evil that he was fighting. How he longed to light the menorah and bask in its glow. But how would he be able to do so?

He thought long and hard about it and finally came up with a plan. He somehow managed to obtain a match from one of the guards. Now all he needed was a wick and a small container of oil.

Creating a wick was simple. Yosef pulled at the threads of his prison clothing and wove a few of them together. However, obtaining oil was a problem. All alone in his cell, Yosef pondered the problem of getting hold of the elusive menorah he wanted so badly. Chanukah was only a few days away and the few moments he spent out of his cell were not enough for him to make the necessary arrangements.

The day before Chanukah Yosef sat in his cell, sadly lamenting the reality that he would not be able to perform the mitzvah for which he longed. He desperately hoped for a miracle. As evening drew near Yosef was about to concede defeat when he was struck by an idea. Perhaps he would not be able to fulfill the mitzvah in its fullest sense, but he would try his best and do what he could.

Yosef picked up a jagged rock and walked over to the wall and began to chisel out the form of a menorah: a base and eight stems. He took the one precious wick he had and wedged it firmly into a crack in the wall where he had carved out the form of the first light.

He then removed the match he had held onto for the past few weeks and struck it against the concrete wall. Yosef then proudly recited the blessings of the Chanukah lights and touched the fire to the wick. The improvised wick caught fire, and Yosef gazed at the small flickering flame that lit up the cell.

It did not burn long, perhaps only a few seconds, but it had ignited. The sparkling fire had illuminated that dark Siberian cell for but a moment, lending hope and promise to a bold and brave Jew in a cold, lonely chamber.

And long after that flame had been extinguished it continued to burn strongly inside the soul of a young, courageous *refusnik*.

Years later, when Yosef recounted his fascinating tale, a teenage girl asked him why he had continued to perform the mitzvos amidst all the difficult circumstances. Yosef responded matter of factly, "Can you tell a tree not to grow?"

A Jew's innate nature is to develop and grow, increasing our level of holiness by each act that we perform. The greater the difficulty, the more opportunity to grow and become all we can be!

Heiliga Hakafos

SHEMINI ATZERES WAS FAST APPROACHING AND REB Yekusiel Yehudah Halberstam, the Klausenburger Rebbe, had targeted that day as one in which he could spend time alone with his Creator. He was not going to let the Nazis ruin this one day as they had ruined so much else. "Let those barbaric animals do what they may, but I will not work on that day," he said. And so arrangements began to provide the Rebbe with a work furlough for the upcoming Yom Tov.

Mehldorf, the forced labor camp where they now resided, had never seemed more distant from Klausenburg, where Simchas Torah had been celebrated as an auspicious day which many anticipated the entire year. Dedicated Chassidim would gather from far and wide to behold the Rebbe's devotion to the A-mighty and His Torah. Fathers would hoist their young children up onto their shoulders to catch a glimpse of the Rebbe's fervent dancing as young chassidic *bochurim* would dance enthusiastically, adding additional links to the chain stretching from Mount Sinai.

However, those were the glorious days of yesteryear. The *shtetl* of Klausenburg was no longer. Now a distant memory, it had been destroyed, set afire by the cursed Germans. The Jews who had lived there had been brutally driven into the gas chambers and crematoria. Individuals sent to the forced labor camp of Mehldorf were ironically thought of as fortunate, though from the welts and bruises on their skeletal bodies one would never have guessed it.

All the forced laborers harbored distant memories of the festive aura of *zeman simchaseinu* (the time of our Happiness — Succos) that had permeated the narrow streets of Klausenburg: one *succah* more beautifully adorned than the next; men grandly marching through the streets with their own "weapons of battle": the fragrant *esrog* accompanying the regal *lulav*, its stalwart companion. These beautiful, inspiring and comforting visions and sounds had now been replaced by the goose-stepping, thunderous stomping of Hitler's executioners in their bloodthirsty rage.

Shemini Atzeres was unique among the Yamim Tovim. It is the day when Jews unite, merging together with Hashem and His Torah. From that unification, the Rebbe would not — could not — be excluded.

Dr. Greenbaum, the Jewish camp doctor, also agreed that the Rebbe should not work on Shemini Atzeres. He examined the Rebbe and diagnosed him as too feeble and frail for heavy labor, and thus exempt from working. Sufficient bribes were administered to the appropriate officers and with the onset of Hoshana Rabbah, the Rebbe found himself on his way to the infirmary. However, Moishe Einhorn, one of the Rebbe's well-informed Chassidim, became aware that the infamous Nazi physician, Dr. Fluken, together with the Camp Oberfuhrer, would be conducting a *selektsia,* a weeding out of all those who are too weak to work; those "selected" would be sent to their deaths. Their first stop was the infirmary.

Moishe, grasping the urgency of the situation, immediately reacted by pleading with Dr. Greenbaum to revoke his diagnosis and release the Rebbe. The confused doctor, now aware of the impending inspection by the Nazis, retracted his diagnosis and sent the Rebbe back to his barracks.

Undaunted, the Rebbe strengthened his resolve to refrain from any physical labor, choosing instead to spend the day with his Creator. During roll-call his absence was noted instantly as infuriated guards were dispatched to inspect the barracks. The S.S. men stormed in and found the "Rabbiner" praying.

They angrily seized the Rebbe, threw him down onto the cold floor and dragged him mercilessly outside. They proceeded to strike him repeatedly, at first lashing out with truncheons and then kicking him with their metal tipped boots. Lying there in a pool of blood and unable to move, the Rebbe was lifted by a few distraught inmates and carried to the infirmary.

Those who witnessed the brutal incident, and knew of the impending *selektsia,* worried that perhaps they had seen the last of their beloved Rebbe. Reluctantly, the downcast group set out for their work, despondent and fearful of what they would find upon their return. They worked diligently, eager to get back and check on their Rebbe. The shrill sound of the siren ended the long workday and the Chassidim anxiously lined up to return to their quarters.

A number of brave inmates took a detour off the regular path and rushed toward the dilapidated medical building to inquire about their Rebbe. Stealthily they moved about the hallway, peeking inside the poorly maintained rooms. Fear mounted as they began to entertain the possibility that their mentor had not survived. Suddenly they stopped.

They had reached the room where the Rebbe was being detained, and as they peered through the broken window, they could not believe their eyes. Situated in the center of the dank room stood a rickety stool masquerading as a *bimah.* On top of it lay torn remnants of a *Mishnayos Moed.* And hobbling around, his face aglow, radiating sheer, unadulterated joy, was their Rebbe — celebrating *Hakafos*.

There were no fathers hoisting their children up onto their shoulders to catch a glimpse of the Rebbe. And there were no young chassidic *bochurim* to dance enthusiastically. But perhaps as never before the Rebbe had united with his Creator with the understanding that indeed, *"Ein ... od ... milvado!* — There is nothing and no one besides Him!"

The Wedding Ring

*L*AIBEL GROSSMAN WAITED FOR HIS WIFE TO COME HOME from grocery shopping. The Lakewood *yungerman* had just balanced his checkbook — or at least he had tried to. It was simply becoming too difficult. They had proudly struggled to learn in *kollel* for as long as possible, but now it was time for him to get a job. He was a bright fellow and his good friend had recently told him that there was a job waiting for him as soon as he was ready. Now he just had to tell his wife.

Chani, his wife, pulled up in their station wagon and beeped the horn. Not that she had to. Recently their Taurus wagon had sounded more like an eighteen-wheeler. It needed a new muffler and the belts required tightening. The squealing sound was becoming too much to bear.

Running out to help her with the groceries, he asked her how she had paid for them, hoping it was cash and not a check. He shuddered at the thought of it bouncing. Their savings were now depleted and he was uncertain if there was enough money left in their checking account.

Later that night, after things had calmed down in their household, homework had been done and the children put to bed, Laibel sat down with his wife to have a serious discussion. He detailed how fortunate they had been to have had the opportunity to learn in *kollel* for seven years and told her that he felt the time had come for him to get a job.

Chani was quiet at first and only after a few moments did she speak. "I would like you to try to sell my diamond ring. That money should help us for at least another month or two."

Laibel was shocked. "Absolutely not! I could never do that. Tomorrow I'm going to work for my friend Dovid Langer. He has a job lined up for me." Laibel was certain that the time had come. He would hear nothing of his wife's absurd suggestion.

"What do you mean 'You could never do that'?! Don't I have a say in this decision as well? I beg you. Please." Chani spoke with tears in her eyes. She could barely get the words out as she choked up and caught her breath.

Up until this moment he had never realized how incredibly important his learning was to her. He wondered with awe how many women were prepared to make such a sacrifice.

"Okay, I'll try. I promise. Tomorrow I'll go to the diamond district in Manhattan and see how much they'll give us for the ring." Although Laibel's heart wasn't in it, he had to try as best he could.

Early the next morning, Laibel hopped onto a Jersey Transit bus to Port Authority. After catching the appropriate connections, he found himself as far away from Beth Medrash Govoha as he could ever have imagined. The blaring horns and flashing lights had replaced the *kolos uverakim* — thunder and lightning — inherent in the sounds of learning in the Lakewood *beis medrash*.

Walking into the first shop he saw, Laibel was relieved to see that it was owned by a Jew, Shmeel Yankel Rosenbaum, a Satmar Chassid, who immediately offered his hand and wished Laibel, "Sholom Aleichem." Laibel and Shmeel spoke for a minute or so and then Shmeel asked how he could be of assistance.

Reaching into his pocket, Laibel pulled out his wife's diamond ring and asked Shmeel how much he thought it was worth. Surprised, Shmeel held the ring between his fingers and excused himself as he walked toward the back of his store to examine the ring with his loupe. Returning a moment later, he told Laibel that he would give him $1,000 for the ring but suggested that he show it to his brother who had a store down the street. His brother, who had a bigger business, would probably be able to give him a better price. Laibel thanked him for his time and headed down the street to Shmeel's brother.

Immediately after Laibel headed out the door, Shmeel picked up the phone and dialed his brother Chaim. "Listen, Chaim, in a minute a 30-year-old guy is going to come into your store looking to sell his wife's ring. Find out what the story is."

Sure enough, a moment later Laibel entered Chaim's shop and showed him the diamond. Chaim followed through on the same procedure as his brother. After carefully examining the diamond, Chaim cleared his throat and began, "Before I tell you how much I'll pay, tell me why you are selling the ring."

Laibel recounted the entire story, relating his desire to go to work and his wife's objections. "So you see, that is why I'm here trying to sell it."

Chaim could not believe what he had just heard. What this fellow had just described was legendary *mesiras nefesh*. Clearly, this was not just an ordinary woman. "I think I can do a little better on the price than my brother did," Chaim announced. He removed his checkbook, wrote out a check and handed it to Laibel.

Walking toward the door Laibel thanked Chaim as he peeked at the check. He looked at it again carefully. "I think you made a mistake. You wrote it out for $10,000!"

"There's no mistake, Laibel. I know exactly how much I made it out for. What your wife was prepared to sacrifice was indeed unusual and I would like to have a share in your learning as well." Laibel thanked him and humbly turned toward the door to leave.

"Wait. You forgot one more thing." Laibel looked back. Chaim smiled as he held out a small jewelry box ... with the diamond ring inside.

Little Angels

*I*T HAD ALL HAPPENED SO QUICKLY.

That last image was burned into Leon's memory: his mother holding him by his shoulders, her eyes burning with love and fear, tears streaming down her cheeks, begging him to watch over his siblings.

Leon, 12 years old, was the oldest of the Saplinsky brothers. The three boys had always been so close, and now they would need each other more than ever. The evil Nazi army had invaded their small Polish town and their first priority had been to break up families. Babies were wrenched from their mothers, siblings from one another. Leon knew that, most of all, his mother wanted them to stay together.

The shouting of the soldiers was too much for the young Saplinsky children. Jan, Leon's youngest brother, was merely 4 years old and he put his tiny hands over his ears to block out the deafening sounds of gunshots. Leon, mature beyond his years, tried to shield his brothers from the bloodshed a few meters from them.

Herded toward the center of the town, Leon was at a loss how to explain to the other children why they should feel fortunate not to have been led out to the forest. He just kept reminding them, "Whatever happens, stay together, just stay together!" They grasped each others' hands and shook with fear.

The entire group of a few hundred souls marched forward. One could pay with his life if he stopped for but a moment's rest. Leon prodded his brothers on, urging them to ignore their desire for food, drink and rest. "We'll be stopping soon," he deceitfully encouraged them, in truth having no idea when they would indeed see their next morsel of food.

Not far off in the distance, Leon noticed train tracks, and the whistling sound of an oncoming train confirmed what he already knew. They would be loaded onto the cattle cars. He had heard the rumors of trains, camps and unspeakable persecution. His little brothers had no idea and he was not about to tell them, opting instead to convince them that the train was there to ease their trek so that they could continue on their journey.

Jan was happy to climb onto the train, though the foul odor bothered him. Leon placed his arm around the boys' shoulders and sadly thought, "If you only knew what lies ahead, my dear brothers." A small tear formed in his eyes as he stopped for a moment to reflect on the fate of his parents, wondering if he would ever see them again.

Leon was jarred from his distant thoughts by the sudden jerking of the train's wheels. The compartment was crammed with 130 people of all ages. Leon wondered why certain people were chosen to live and others were not. Near the door stood an elderly couple whose care and concern for each other was evident. Situated directly next to him and his brothers were an infant child and his mother. How they had survived was beyond comprehension. Perhaps she had concealed him under her shawl. Regardless, she desperately tried to calm her hungry baby as the train sped forward.

The train had been traveling for hours, the stench of waste filling the oppressive boxcar. With no room to move, many attempted to rest their weary bodies on the shoulders of those next to them. Leon tried to transform himself into a comfortable headrest for his little brothers but it was to no avail. The hunger pains gnawing inside his stomach, coupled with the lack of air, prevented anyone from resting.

Thirst was fast becoming an issue. Jan's parched lips begged for a few droplets of water but none was to be had. Leon felt the anguish of helplessness — he had promised his mother to look after his brothers but now he could not help them.

Leon peeked out through the small barred window and noticed that snow had begun to fall and was accumulating on the window ledge. An idea flashed through his mind. If he could somehow manage to squeeze his hand through the narrow iron bars he could try to gather some snow in his hand, melt it and feed it to his thirsty brother. An hour or so passed and the buildup of snow on the ledge was now significant enough to collect.

Initially Leon attempted to squeeze his hand through the small opening between the bars. Though his hand wasn't big, it still would not fit. Jan watched the entire episode and then looked away with disappointment. Once again Leon struggled to maneuver his hand through the cold iron bars. This time it worked! Scraping his bloody hand alongside the rods, he gathered a fistful of snow and pulled it back inside the train. The price had been costly; his hand had lost a layer of skin and was now bleeding. But it had been well worth it. Jan stared at the priceless treasure and could hardly wait to wet his parched mouth. Leon proudly turned to his brother. He hadn't let his mother down after all.

At that instant, Leon became acutely aware of the young mother holding her infant nearby. The starving baby had been crying continually for the past three hours. Leon had been too focused on his own crisis to have worried about anyone else's. But now the young mother's listless eyes craved the droplets of water trickling from Leon's hand. Leon looked from his own hand to his brother's face, then to the mother and her baby. He knew what he had to do.

Tearfully, Leon stretched out his hand and offered the snow to the thankful young woman. She placed it inside the baby's parched lips and soothed the infant for the first time in hours. Leon slowly moved his gaze to his brother's little face, looked down at Jan, held him close and apologized for not having given him the drink he so desperately wanted.

Hiding his own tears of disappointment, Jan squeezed his brother tightly, buried his head against his older brother's protective body and bravely responded, "It's okay, Leon, I wasn't thirsty anyway."

Leon closed his eyes and wept. He wept for many things — what they had lost, what was to come, the hunger, the thirst ... Yet he knew, in the depths of his heart, that his mother would be proud of her children at this moment, and a small, weak smile passed across his face.

Mi k'amcha Yisrael!

No Strings Attached

URI HAD NOT BEEN FEELING WELL. FOR THE PAST TWO weeks the energetic 11-year-old had been experiencing stomach pains, and the pain was intensifying. Eating, running, even sleeping had become increasingly more difficult. Concerned, Uri's parents scheduled an appointment with one of the top gastrointestinal specialists in all of Eretz Yisrael, Dr. Benny Hofner.

Comprehensive testing revealed an awful scenario. A tumor was rapidly developing in little Uri's stomach. It would have to be removed immediately. Uri's parents, though terrified and distraught, knew that they needed to remain strong for their ailing son. That day they broke the sad news to him. Perhaps not fully understanding the ramifications of what he was about to endure, he reacted well to the doctor's bleak report.

The extensive surgery went well and was followed by several weeks of recuperation. Uri's recovery was progressing nicely and Dr. Hofner elected to move forward with the next stage of treatment, radiation.

Uri arrived together with his parents early that Tuesday morning, nervous and slightly apprehensive. After his mother filled out numerous forms, they were led into the dimly lit treatment room, furnished with several huge machines and an array of buttons, switches and lights, none of which made any sense to Uri. Looking around he felt intimidated and overwhelmed. He had been through so much already, and had handled it so well, but somehow these machines truly frightened him.

Uri sat on the table awaiting further instructions when a kind nurse entered the room and asked him to remove all his clothing and don the flimsy blue robe which would be worn throughout the entire procedure.

Returning moments later with Uri's medical records in hand, the nurse moved toward the large machine and set the controls for a boy of Uri's size and weight. Prepared to begin, she noticed that Uri had removed everything except for a small pair of *tzitzis* that he continued to wear. She reminded him that he was still partially dressed, and Uri's small face contorted in a determined expression as he responded by declaring that under no circumstances would he remove his *tzitzis*.

Uri gathered up his courage and began to explain to the nurse in a mature, measured voice, "You see, removing my *tzitzis* is like ... like, well like a soldier removing his armor before a big battle. My *tzitzis* protect me and I can't take them off, I just can't; I need them to help me get better and to protect me when I get the radiation!!" Though the woman was highly impressed with the young boy's conviction, she nevertheless insisted once again that he remove the *tzitzis* and Uri once again refused. Highly frustrated, she stormed out of the examination room, warning him that she would return shortly together with a physician, although she really did not know why that should make the boy change his mind.

Uri was proud of himself. His rebbi had taught him that nothing can protect you like a mitzvah and he firmly believed it. Moments later, Dr. Hofner entered the room sporting a white doctor's coat, a stethoscope dangling around his shoulders and a broad smile on his face. "So, what's this I hear about you not wanting to remove your *tzitzis*?" Dr. Hofner inquired, suppressing the smirk on his face, thus pretending to sympathize with the aggravated nurse.

"Well, the nurse told me that I had to remove my *tzitzis* and I told her that I wouldn't," Uri answered matter of factly. "And I'm not taking them off no matter what you or anyone else says," Uri concluded with defiance and resolve in his young but unyielding voice.

Dr. Hofner had not realized what a tough customer he had on his hands, and he explained to Uri in a calm manner that the treatment could not be administered as long as he was wearing any piece of clothing other than the hospital gown. The treatment would simply not be as effective, since the clothing would interfere with the administration of the radiation.

While Dr. Hofner was explaining all this to Uri he walked about, drifting beyond the dense glass partition to check the dials and ensure that they were set properly. A moment later he emerged, his face pale white. The nurse — in a nearly tragic error — had incorrectly adjusted the knobs for a person twice Uri's size. The magnitude of such a treatment could have proved fatal.

A shaken Dr. Hofner turned toward Uri and described the miracle that had just happened. The *tzitzis* had truly saved Uri's life. Uri didn't quite understand the magnitude of what might have happened to him, but he perceived that what his rebbi always told him was indeed true — nothing can protect you like a mitzvah.

Wagons and the World to Come

*L*ACKING EMPLOYMENT AS A TEACHER IN HIS OWN TOWN, Reb Moshe Ashkenazi, a disciple of the Vilna Gaon, was forced to become a rebbi in a village quite a distance away. He stayed away most of the year, as he could not afford more frequent trips to visit his family. For the Yamim Tovim, however, he would scrape together enough money to come home and bring with him whatever extra funds he had to share with his poor family.

Reb Moshe was an unusual man. Besides his scrupulous observance of all the mitzvos, there was one mitzvah about which he was especially careful, and that was the mitzvah of *tzitzis*. As far back as he could remember, Reb Moshe had never gone anywhere or even walked less than four cubits without donning his *tzitzis*.

The respect and reverence which he felt for *tzitzis* was something that he imparted to his young, impressionable students.

Prior to one Yom Tov, Reb Moshe boarded the wagon for the journey to his hometown. But midway through the trip, Reb Moshe's *tzitzis* somehow got caught inside one of the spokes of the wheels and tore in half. Immediately Reb Moshe asked the driver to stop the wagon so that he could check the *tzitzis*. Possibly they could be fixed, but certainly not here in the middle of a road miles away from the closest village. Reb Moshe offered to pay the driver if he would return to the village from where they had come and bring him another pair of *tzitzis,* but the driver refused. Finally, after much negotiation, Reb Moshe agreed to give the driver *all* the money he had made over the last few months. It was an incredible sum to pay for *tzitzis* but Reb Moshe felt he had no choice. With mixed emotions he sent the driver off and waited by the side of the road for him to return. But he never came back.

Now Reb Moshe had a dilemma. He had given away all his money and had received nothing in return. But while he was disappointed that the driver had tricked him, he felt elated that he had been willing to sacrifice so much for this mitzvah which he held so dear. He waited at the side of the road until a wagon came along a few hours later and the driver kindly agreed to go to the next town and obtain a pair of *tzitzis* for Reb Moshe.

A few months later, Reb Moshe was in middle of teaching his young students when a messenger burst into the room. The messenger informed Reb Moshe that his brother, Reb Yitzchak, the pious author of the *sefer Bris Olam*, had suffered a stroke and Reb Moshe was needed at his brother's side during his last moments on this world. Reb Moshe came immediately and as he arrived at his brother's bedside he asked that everyone leave the room. The small crowd exited but after they closed the door they peered through the cracks to see what was happening.

Reb Moshe was standing over his brother's still body and whispering words of *Tehillim* when suddenly he removed his *tzitzis* and spread them over his brother's body. "Master of the World, not only have I dedicated my life to performing your commandments, but I have sacrificed all my money for the sake of *tzitzis*. Now I am prepared to give up all my reward if You restore my brother's health."

He then donned his *tzitzis* and walked out of the room.

His brother miraculously lived for another five years.

Rav Aryeh Levin related this story and explained that we see how far one must go to save a brother's life. Not only must one sacrifice his body and his money but he is required to even forfeit his portion in the World to Come. And we are, indeed, all brothers.

Hashgachah Pratis / Divine Providence

The Badgering Beggar

*E*VERYTHING HAD GONE PERFECTLY FOR THE PAST TWO months. Yanky and his *kallah* had met and almost immediately decided to get engaged. The arrangements for the wedding were underway and as they drove down the highway together Yanky couldn't have been happier.

The wind picked up on I-95 and his compact car began to swerve back and forth. Controlling the car was becoming more and more difficult and Yanky felt slightly apprehensive behind the wheel. Driving alongside him was an eighteen-wheeler, and the driver was also struggling to control his vehicle. Suddenly the gusts of wind increased and Yanky's little car collided with the eighteen-wheeler. The last thing Yanky remembered hearing was the driver of the eighteen-wheeler calling the police, "Yes, we need an ambulance on the scene immediately. It looks like we have one fatality and one seriously injured."

∽ා ಌ

Arych Gross was visiting Eretz Yisrael. He planned to spend some time learning at the yeshivah which he had previously attended, daven at some of the sacred sites in the country and visit some of his relatives. On the day that he arrived he took a taxi to the Kosel. He hadn't been there in a while and was excited to return.

Immediately after he arrived at the Kosel, Aryeh was approached by some *meshulachim* for *tzedakah*. There was an old man who was jiggling change in his hand and an elderly woman holding onto a shopping cart. Each one's story was sadder than the next, but since Arye had forgotten his money back in the apartment where he was staying, he apologized to each of them and reassured them that he would bring money the next time he came to the Kosel. They nodded one by one. They had become accustomed to this response.

But one of the beggars would not let go. He insisted that Aryeh check his pockets once more, all the while urging him to give, "*Tzedakah tatzil mimaves*! — Charity will save from certain death."

"I'm sorry. I really don't have any money." Aryeh pleaded with him to let go but the man insisted that he continue to check his pockets. Finally Aryeh emptied his pockets and was surprised to find $1. He gladly handed it over to the collector.

"Thank you! Thank you! *Tzedakah tatzil mimaves*! Thank you! Thank you!"

Aryeh was relieved to have given away the *tzedakah* money that he had received before leaving America.

Later on that week Aryeh received a phone call from a friend. He was horrified to learn that his good friend Yanky and his *kallah* had been in a serious accident. Immediately he ran back to the Kosel to daven for them. Once again he was approached by the same beggar. And now a shiver ran up his spine, for he realized that he had given *tzedakah* to the persistent collector approximately 15 minutes before Yanky's accident had occurred — in another part of the world. And the dollar bill he had dug out of his pocket was the one that had been given to him — by Yanky!

B"H, Yanky and his kallah were married on Sunday, March 16, the twelfth day of Adar. Although the road to a complete recovery has been a long one, they are forever grateful to Hashem for their second lease on life. Aryeh Wald told this unusual story the day before the wedding, at the Aufruf. He thinks back to the dollar bill, the beggar and the endless badgering of "Tzedakah tatzil mimaves," and with tears in his eyes, he smiles: how true it is.

Switching Places

AS PART OF AN ARMY GROUP, THE ISRAELI *CHAYALIM* took turns performing *shemirah* as they kept guard over the settlements in the *shtachim* (West Bank and Gaza). The guard who was appointed to be the watchman for the evening generally was required to stay alert and watch for any unusual disturbances. If he noticed anything out of the ordinary he would call for backup, which would arrive in minutes.

Avi Cohen, who had served *shemirah* the previous night, was supposed to have the night off. He was tired and looked forward to an evening of relaxation back on the base. However, his friend Yosi Tabor, whose rotation had fallen on this particular evening, had asked Avi if he would switch with him. Avi, an easygoing fellow, agreed and figured he would just push off his night of relaxation one more evening. Soldiers in the army were used to pushing themselves to the limit and, after all, what difference would one more night make?

Avi drove his jeep the short distance from headquarters down the narrow, winding road to his assigned outpost. The evening air was pleasant and quiet, and Avi was thankful for that. But suddenly the sharp sound of machine-gun fire cut through the air. He was being ambushed! Avi immediately radioed for help. Completely surrounded by the enemy, he fought valiantly but by the time his friends arrived on the scene Avi had been murdered.

Yosi was awoken by the shrill sound of the alarm at the base. He loaded his backpack and gear, grabbed his Uzi and ran out as fast as he could. But by the time he arrived at the scene of ambush, he realized that Avi had been attacked by terrorists. Although he tried as hard as he could to revive his dear friend, it was too late. Yosi turned pale with shock — this should have been him! He was frightened as never before, yet remained on the road and refused to leave Avi's body. He cried bitterly and poured out his apologies to his friend for having switched assignments.

The *levayah* was unfortunately all too familiar. The devastated parents and grandparents sobbed and mourned for their unbearable loss. The siblings held onto one another and stared in disbelief. Avi had just been home for Shabbos — how could he be gone? Yosi attended the *levayah* but kept his distance and carefully watched Avi's parents. He could not help but imagine his own parents mourning for him this way. After all, this should have been him. If it were not for Avi's kind offer and easygoing nature, he would have died and not Avi.

The *levayah* ended and Avi's father recited *Kaddish* amid his own sobbing as well as the wailing of Avi's mother. Yosi could not bear to listen and muffled his own cries so as not to call attention to himself. The crowd dispersed and Yosi and his friends returned to the base. On the third day of *shivah*, Avi's friends gathered to go to the Cohen house. This was the moment that Yosi had dreaded. He was certain that Avi's parents had heard the story of how he had switched nights and was convinced that they questioned why their son had to be on duty the night that he was supposed to be off. Their child should be alive now and someone else's parents should be grieving.

The *chayalim* entered the Cohen apartment together and left their guns by the door. Dressed in army uniforms, they filed in and sat down on the chairs that surrounded the inconsolable parents. Yosi, the last of the group to enter the home, took a seat by the door and did his best to remain inconspicuous. Avi's father spoke first and mentioned how soft hearted and kind Avi was. Yosi squirmed in his seat, recalling their conversation from less than a week ago regarding switching places in the *shemirah* rotation.

As if he were reading Yosi's mind, Avi's father asked which one of the soldiers had switched places with Avi on that fateful night. Yosi managed a meek affirmation that it was him. He would have done anything to disappear just then. No one dared to speak.

A thick silence filled the room. Avi's father had not spoken for more than two minutes, all the while staring at Yosi. And then he stood up and slowly walked from one end of the room to the other. All eyes in the apartment were focused on this dramatic confrontation. Avi's father stood right next to Yosi and looked him straight in the eyes. Yosi's eyes were red and filled with tears and remorse. Mr. Cohen then leaned over, lovingly placed his hands on Yosi's face and kissed him on the forehead.

He then reached into his pocket and removed a *kippah,* the same one Avi had worn the night he was killed. He unfolded the precious reminder of his son and placed it gently onto Yosi's head and spoke softly, "We want you to know that what happened to our son had nothing to do with you. We firmly believe that *hashgachah* dictated what was to happen to him. Please don't ever think that you were the cause." As he ended his brief, courageous speech he hugged Yosi tightly. Yosi held onto his friend's father and hoped that this incredible family would be able to find the *nechamah* they deserved.

Hashem Has a Plan

THE CALL CAME EARLY THURSDAY MORNING. HIS FATHER had passed away. Aaron Kurman had expected the news, as his father had been sick for the past few months. Mr. Eliyahu Kurman, a beloved member of the Deal community, had moved to Flatbush ten years earlier to live closer to his two sons and their families.

Aaron expected that there would be a large crowd at the *levayah*. After all, everyone loved his father. His pleasant personality and good-natured character endeared him to all who had known him. But perhaps one trait stood out among all the rest. Nothing fazed Mr. Kurman. No matter what the dilemma, he always would optimistically state his ultimate belief in Hashem's help: "*Hashem yaazor, Hashem yaazor* — Hashem will help.*"*

A small crowd attended the *levayah*. True, there was only short notice but the undersized gathering troubled Aaron. After a few eulogies extolling the virtues of Mr. Kurman, the *levayah* continued to Kennedy Airport, from where Mr. Kurman was going to be taken to Eretz Yisrael. By now it was Thursday afternoon and time was of the essence as Shabbos was just thirty hours away.

"I really envisioned it different for Dad. He deserved better." Aaron could not help but express his disappointment to his brother as they entered the cargo area of the airport. But as their limousine pulled up, a sea of black hats greeted them. Aaron could not understand what was happening. As he and his wife stepped out of the car, they heard scores of people calling out their names.

Many in the large crowd recognized them, because simultaneously the *levayah* for Rabbi Goldberger, a good friend of the family, was in progress as well. Immediately Aaron felt comforted and relieved that the *levayah* and accompaniment that his father warranted was now realized. And incredibly it all turned out all right. His father was right, "*Hashem yaazor!*"

The flight to Eretz Yisrael, though long, was uneventful. And although the plane was as comfortable as could be expected, there was a certain tension as the hour was late. Midday was approaching and Shabbos was only seven hours away, plenty of time as long as everything ran smoothly. But it didn't.

For the first time in memory, the *chevrah kadisha* van broke down. Here they were, on Kvish Tel Aviv (the Tel Aviv highway), and the driver was informed that another van could not be there for two hours. Aaron and his brother Reuven were both disappointed. Not only was it disrespectful to their father, but in addition, Rav Rabinovitch, a *mekubal* in Yerushalayim who was close with Aaron's brother, was scheduled to deliver the *hesped* at 1 p.m.

After a few moments, Reuven smiled and turned to Aaron. He climbed out of the van and walked toward the back. "I know who can help us." He opened the back of the van, gazed at his father's *aron* for a moment and began to say *Tehillim*. He explained to Aaron that their father was never fazed when a crisis arose. He always had faith that things would work out for the best. And so they both moved to the back of the van and davened in front of their father's *aron*.

Down the road came a flatbed truck with nothing on it. It had not been 10 minutes since their van had broken down and not more than three minutes since they recalled their father's mission statement, "*Hashem yaazor.*" A disheveled-looking man with a long mane of blond hair pulled over his vehicle and announced that he was heading in the direction of the Shamgar funeral home and would be honored to participate in the mitzvah of *levayat hameit*. It seemed all too unreal. It was as if he had appeared from nowhere.

The van was hauled onto the flatbed truck and within the hour they arrived at the funeral home. Aaron and Reuven ran over to Rav Rabinovitch and apologized for the inconvenience. But they were relieved that the *levayah* would finally begin just a few short hours before Shabbos.

Rav Rabinovitch stood before the deceased and began to explain what had transpired. "We all know what faith your father possessed. He was confident that Hashem would take care of any and all problems that arose. Had your van not broken down and the funeral begun on time, then the Kabbalistic concept of *chibbut hakever*, a painful experience for the deceased, would have affected him. However, the Arizal (a 16th-century Kabbalist) explains that if a deceased is buried within four hours of when Shabbos is to begin then he is released from the retribution of *chibbut hakever*." The rabbi then wished the family comfort and only future happiness; for Aaron and his brother Reuven the pain of their father's death had already been somewhat diminished. Their father was right, "*Hashem yaazor!*"

For the Fighting Irish

South Bend, Indiana. The name evokes images of the Four Horsemen, the great Knute Rockne, Paul Hornung and other legendary football players who have played for the team known as the "Fighting Irish." The mere mention of the town instills a sense of awe in all college football fans. Young children are imbued with the fundamentals of life: G-d, family and football — not necessarily in that order. It is simply the college football mecca of the world.

So how, you might ask, did this town become the location of a *yeshivah gedolah,* a beautiful Torah community and a *mikveh?*

It all began in the town of Rock Island, Illinois. Young Nathan Lerman attended Rock Island High School and played on the varsity football team. He was one of the few Jewish boys in the school and the only one on its football team. One night the team from Rock Island High played a game against a high school from Chicago, a team almost completely comprised of Jewish boys.

Normally, a team will spend weeks preparing its codes and symbols for the captains of the offense and defense to signal to their teammates so they can know what they are supposed to do and where a specific play is going. However, this team from Chicago figured that instead of motioning and risking misinterpretation by their team members, why not just call out the plays in Yiddish? After all, everybody on their team spoke Yiddish fluently and nobody on the other team did — or at least so they thought. This way they could spell out the plays clearly. When they called a pass play, the wide-receiver would know it was coming to him; and when they set up a running play, the running back would know to expect the ball. On defense they would call out a "corner blitz" or a "cover two-zone" without the code name that was attached to it.

Little did they know that Lerman played for Rock Island High. Every play that was designed by the offense was defended masterfully by the defense. Lerman was all over the field. Every pass thrown his way was either deflected or intercepted. All told,

Lerman intercepted five passes that evening and disrupted the opponent's entire offensive game plan. He was simply masterful.

Sitting in the stands, unbeknown to Lerman, was a scout for the Notre Dame football program. He had been in attendance scouting a player from the opposing team. Immediately following the game he approached Lerman to tell him how impressed he was with his abilities. He was particularly astounded by his keen insight and astute football knowledge. And so he offered him an incentive-laden four-year scholarship to the University of Notre Dame. Lerman was shocked and quite flattered. He could not believe that he would be treading on the field where so many football greats had walked. He had not planned on a football career but was not about to refuse a scholarship to such a prestigious university. And so he gratefully accepted the invitation.

For the team's first practice, Lerman — suited up — trotted out onto the field. Although he was a small fellow, perhaps five foot six and 165 pounds, his enthusiasm and zest for the game showed up some of the more gifted players on the team. The coach, disappointed in his varsity team, reprimanded them for their poor effort. As a result the upstaged players targeted Lerman, and a few plays later he hurt his knee and had to be carried off the field. Just like that, his promising career was over. He recovered from the injury but was never able to play for the team again. However, since he was already attending Notre Dame on a four-year scholarship, he spent the next four years of his life in South Bend.

Along the path of life, Nathan Lerman slowly began to grow in his Judaism, and by the time he passed away at the age of 61, he was fully *shomer Shabbos*. He was a person with tremendous drive and desire, and in addition to growing in his personal life, he sought to become a high-level businessman. Before long, he had established one of the largest privately owned steel factories in all of North America.

A high school football game, an opposing team calling plays in Yiddish, a scholarship, a wounded knee – all led to one individual settling in South Bend, building a business, becoming a *shomer Shabbos*. Today South Bend, Indiana boasts a day-school, a yeshivah, a *mikveh* and a shul; and Mr. Lerman's sons continue to follow in their father's footsteps as lay leaders and supporters of their Torah community's institutions.

"Rabbos machshavos belev ish — " Man has his own plans regarding where he's heading but ultimately "atzas Hashem hee Sakum," the Almighty designates what our future will be.

Souled Shoes

*I*T HAD BEEN AN EXCEPTIONALLY GRUELING WEEK FOR RONI and his fellow *chayalim*. The situation in Israel necessitated a call for heightened security — meaning double shifts for his entire contingent — and Roni was totally exhausted. His weekend off could not have come at a better time. He had not been able to visit his parents in Beer Sheva for the past two months; they would most certainly appreciate his company. So Roni set out for the *tachanah mercazit* (central bus station) to catch a ride to his hometown.

Clad in his army fatigues, Roni's effort to hitchhike had fallen flat. Hauling around his heavy knapsack in the middle of a heat wave was beginning to take its toll on him and, sweaty and exhausted, he entertained the unpleasant thought of turning back to the base for the weekend.

Just then, a yellow Subaru pulled up alongside the curb, and Avraham Garfinkel, a stocky, black-bearded fellow, rolled down his window and called out in fluent Hebrew, "Where are you heading?"

"Beer Sheva," Roni responded, sincerely hoping that it was this fellow's destination as well.

"*Selichah adoni,* forgive me, sir, but I'm on my way to Netanya, though you're more than welcome to come along. We'd love to have you as our guest for Shabbos." The hour was getting late and Shabbos was fast approaching.

Roni hesitated. He genuinely did not want to "waste" this weekend on a new experience. He had never observed Shabbos before and had no desire to begin now. It wasn't that he was opposed to it, he simply had not been raised in a religious home and thus had minimal knowledge and exposure to the holy day. However, one quick glance at his watch confirmed that only a small amount of time remained until sundown, when the likelihood of catching a ride would be greatly diminished.

"All right, *lamah lo?*" Roni consented, as he opened the back door and placed his knapsack on the floor. Roni and Avraham settled in for the short journey.

Conversation flowed easily as Roni and Avraham spoke about their families, politics and daily occupations. Both delicately skirted any discussion of religion, Roni because he did not want to offend this kind man in any way, and Avraham because he knew that, come sundown, "the Shabbos will speak for itself."

Running late, they arrived only one half-hour before candle-lighting. Avraham showed Roni to a room in their humble three-bedroom apartment and quickly prepared for Shabbos.

Avraham took Roni to shul, and as the davening progressed Roni was surprised to find himself thoroughly enjoying the experience. The tasty Shabbos meals were enhanced through delightful performances by each of Avraham's four adorable children. Sweet sounds of Shabbos *zemiros* intermingled with thought-provoking words of Torah stirred Roni's emotions. Avraham explained several Torah concepts, most of which Roni had never heard of before.

The remainder of Shabbos progressed in a similar vein, with Roni becoming increasingly more enchanted. *Havdalah's* onset generated sincere disappointment in Roni, not because he was forced to return to his base, but rather because he realized that this Shabbos and these individuals were truly unique, and he desperately wanted to capture the moment and hold onto it forever.

Avraham, intuitively sensing Roni's feelings, spoke gently to him about the possibility of adopting some religious observance, just to try it out. He suggested that Roni select one principle to which to adhere. Roni was keen on the suggestion but was at a loss in determining which one to choose. Avraham proposed a plan: They would randomly open a *Kitzur Shulchan Aruch* (an abridged version of the Code of Jewish Law) and whichever precept they would point to would be the one he would observe.

Avraham removed the volume from his extensive library and directed Roni to open the well-used book. Roni closed his eyes and pointed to an apparently trivial rule. "When one puts on his shoes in the morning, he is required to initially don his right shoe, then his left, tie his left, then his right." It seemed awfully strange to Roni. But a deal was a deal.

Roni thanked his hosts sincerely, exchanged phone numbers and addresses and headed back to his base.

Two months later, the attack alarm sounded at Roni's base. Already on high alert, all battle-ready soldiers rushed toward the jeeps, which would transport them to the battlefield. Prepared for the confrontation, all Roni had to do was slip on his shoes and leap into the vehicle.

But while all Roni's friends made it into the first jeep, he required an extra moment to put on his shoes in the manner which he had been taught. Right shoe, left shoe, tie left and tie right. On countless occasions his buddies had mocked him, but to Roni a commitment, no matter how strange he believed it to be, was a commitment.

As the first van pulled off, Roni waited impatiently for the second's imminent arrival. Seconds later it arrived and Roni hopped in. Speeding down the dirt path, a sudden explosion sent Roni and his companions hurling through the air. Covered with blood and debris but miraculously relatively uninjured, Roni looked up and witnessed disbelievingly the carnage fifty meters down the road. His friends, all of them, had been killed by a strategically hidden mine. In a horrifying moment of *hashgachah*, Roni's life had been saved by a "trivial" halachah.

D'veikus BaShem / Cleaving to Hashem

Pesach Preparations

YESHIVAH HAD JUST ENDED AND I WALKED HOME CARRYING my laptop, briefcase and some interesting Haggados that I had shown to some of the boys in my class. The day had gone well but with Pesach cleaning and all that comes with it, I was slightly tired and looked forward to a restful lunch break. My wife had prepared an onion cheese omelet and I was eager to eat, as I had skipped breakfast that morning. I walked through the door and spoke for a few moments with my wife before we sat down to eat lunch together.

I had noticed that a *meshulach* was coming out of one of the neighbors' houses and knew that he was coming my way. I recognized him, as he had probably called at my house for several years in a row. Sure enough, a few minutes after I sat down to eat the doorbell rang. I got up and went to answer the door. I invited the man in and offered him a seat and something to drink.

He was collecting for Machon Rus, a fine institution for physically disabled children. His brochure included heartrending pictures of little boys and girls who were struggling to walk or even sit on their own. Some were tragically unable to feed themselves. Each photograph told the story of another challenge, another struggle. I opened my checkbook and wrote out a check. As I handed it to him he began sharing a *vort* on the Haggadah with me. He struck me as the type of person who had a wealth of Torah thoughts at the tip of his tongue. I listened although honestly I was itching to get back to my omelet. He finished his thought, placed the check in his pocket and wished me well.

We were still sitting by my dining room table, when he turned to me and said, "*Im yirtzeh Hashem,* we will see you soon in Yerushalayim." I nodded, smiled and mumbled that I hoped to see ,him as well. However he persisted. "You know that Mashiach is coming soon." Again I nodded, expressing the wish that I had for him to finally come.

At this point the elderly Jew held onto my hand with a firm grip. He stared deeply into my eyes and did not say a word. Finally after a moment of silence he declared, "You know, last week I went down to a farm in Komemiyus and bought a sheep for a *korban pesach* (paschal sacrifice)." I waited for the smile to appear on his face but none came. I went numb.

Did I hear correctly? I asked him if he really had a sheep walking around his courtyard and he promised me he did. It was incredible! Many people have spoken about Mashiach but this man went and did something to prove his faith. Trying to relate, I asked him if I could participate together with my family in his *chaburah* for the *korban pesach*. He looked down at his fingers and began to count as if he were calculating if he could in fact afford to take on an extra family. He then looked up, "How many *gedolim* (adults) and how many *ketanim* (children)? The adults I can promise a *kezayis* but the children are only partaking because of *chinuch* purposes and for that they don't need to receive a *kezayis*."

Again, I waited for the smile. But for this fellow the subject was no laughing matter. Walking him to the door, I wished him a kosher Pesach. He responded that he looked forward to seeing me in Yerushalayim soon.

For some reason I felt that it would not be too much longer until we would indeed meet in Yerushalayim.

Heavenly Cake

*T*HROUGHOUT THE 1800'S THE RUSSIAN CZAR DID everything in his power to prevent Jewish children from receiving any form of Jewish education. The Russian authorities did not lower themselves to actually openly kidnaping the Jewish children, but did manage to seize the children by various means. The most common way was to abduct the children for the Czar's army. These children were forcibly removed from their homes at a very young age and taken far away to serve an uninterrupted term of twenty-five years in the army. By the time they would leave the army, it was assumed that they would remember nothing about their previous lives. They would not even know that they were Jewish. And this is how thousands of innocent children were led away from their roots.

One day a search was conducted in a village to "recruit" and remove all children under the age of 9. Before they knew what was happening, almost all of the children in the village were seized and taken to the local seaport to be loaded onto ships and placed into training facilities to become soldiers in the Czar's army. Amid all the commotion, shoving and fighting, one little 5-year-old boy was trampled to death. A kind man picked up the little boy's body and brought it back to his mother's home. The funeral was quickly arranged and, as his parents wailed, the child was immediately laid to rest in the local cemetery.

The awful sounds of bitter crying filled the small village's roads. It is difficult to imagine a town where all the children have been removed: the deafening sounds of silence; no children to run around outside and play; no brothers and sisters to fight with each other; no little boys to chase after each other. All of that was gone. The only sounds that could be heard in the town were the sobbing of the parents who had lost their little boys. It was almost impossible to bear. During this terrible day, one of the grieving mothers heard a knock at her door. Standing by the entranceway was a boy holding a freshly baked cake.

The mother looked at him — *he* had obviously had enough time to hide and avoid being captured. He explained that his little brother had been trampled earlier that day in the crush of children running through the streets. "My mother sent this cake for you," he said. "She says that she was *privileged* to have her little child die as a Jew and that you shouldn't worry. G-d willing, yours will too."

The young mother held the cake in her hands. She could not believe what she had just heard. This mother's little boy had just died. And she came home after her son's funeral and baked a cake to comfort another woman whose child had not been "fortunate" enough to have died. The sensitivity for another person and absolute faith in Hashem was overwhelming. And incredibly enough, this young woman began to feel a little better. She cried and hoped that indeed the A-mighty would watch over her young boy as well and that one day hopefully he too would be *privileged* to die as a Jew.

Who Wrote This?

I T WAS THE FIRST YOM KIPPUR IN ALMOST SEVEN YEARS FOR some of them. Almost all assembled in Feldafing had lost everything. Their families were all but gone and only very few had the privilege of knowing where their loved ones were buried. At the helm of this assembly of survivors was Rav Yekusiel Yehudah Halberstam, the Klausenburger Rebbe. A famous Rebbe, he was dressed not in fine clothing, but in the same tattered garments that everyone else wore.

The tent that served as a makeshift shul housed this assembly in the displaced persons camp. Many could not help but think back to the previous year when they dared not gather publicly for *Kol Nidrei*. Now, they could indeed gather, but there was no *bircas habanim* because there were either no parents or no children. And no one was more painfully aware of that than the Klausenburger Rebbe, who had lost his wife and all of his eleven children.

There he stood in front of this gathering, the *She'eiris HaPleitah*, the remnants of a glorious people. What message of repentance could he possibly give? How would he speak to their fragile hearts without breaking them? He began *Vidui*:

"*Ashamnu*? We are guilty? Of what? Of receiving torturous treatment over the past years?

"*Bagadnu*? We have betrayed? The decree against performing any single commandment other than the ones administered by the Nazi guards was certain death! How could we have betrayed?!

"*Gazalnu*? Who had anything to steal? Was it forbidden to steal from the barbaric Germans? They stole everything from us! Our families. Our children. We're surely not guilty of that! Who wrote this? We did none of what is written here!"

And so the list went on. At each phrase of *Vidui* the Rebbe would explain why the assembly that was gathered there was in fact innocent of all guilt. The assembly was surprised and somewhat confused. But they listened intently and hung onto every word. Finally the Rebbe finished the list and concluded, " But we are guilty of one thing.

"There were those in Auschwitz that were guilty and in Mathausen they are responsible as well. In Dachau they are blameworthy and in Treblinka they are accountable. We are all guilty of the same sin. How many of us gave up hope? How many wished with all their soul that when they went to sleep their *neshamah* would be taken from them forever? Did we begrudgingly mumble the words of *Modeh Ani* because we no longer wanted to be among the living? For that we are guilty. For that we must repent. And we must promise never to lose faith again. We must commit to rebuilding our lives and creating new families with a renewed commitment to G-d. And for that today we must bow our heads, confess and ask the A-mighty for His forgiveness."

As they prayed with tears in their eyes and broken hearts, their muffled cries could be heard shattering the gates of heaven.

Of Joy and Sadness

THE LITTLE GIRL'S ILLNESS HAD LEFT THE DOCTORS dumbfounded. They could not figure out the cause of her high fever. But her condition worsened by the day and with the High Holy Days approaching, Reb Meir of Premishlan, the famed Rebbe, needed no further motivation for his prayers than his very own daughter's poor health.

His disciples as well as the other members of the community poured out their heartfelt *tefillos* but the little girl's condition continued to deteriorate. Nothing seemed to help. But while some members of her immediate family and even the local doctor began to despair, Reb Meir's faith held strong. His unbending trust in her complete recovery was a source of strength for the rest of the family.

Reb Meir was a unique individual. His pious behavior was well known and many came from far and wide for his *berachos*. But what stood out most was the way he prayed as he spoke to the A-mighty. When one witnessed his utter devotion and concentration during davening, there was no question about to Whom he was speaking.

Rosh Hashanah came and the doctor's grim prognosis caused Reb Meir to hesitate regarding where he should daven. But he decided to go to shul and plea to Hashem on his daughter's behalf. He blew the shofar there and his congregation was able to sense how critical his daughter's condition was. The situation led to an outpouring of emotion and heartfelt entreaties from the entire congregation.

On Yom Kippur, with no visible improvement yet no deterioration in the little girl's condition, Reb Meir again went to daven in the shul. On a day when the books of life and death were being sealed, the precarious state of his daughter's health was at the forefront of his and many others' minds. Succos was just around the corner and one could feel that with each passing day, the sick little girl's chances lessened. Her life was ebbing away and nearly all hope was lost.

Every day of Succos the challenge grew. Many marveled at the sight of Reb Meir leading his students in their performance of the various mitzvos the Yom Tov brought with it. But the feeling of dread that the Rebbe's daughter was dying had cast a dark cloud over the entire community. And as Shemini Atzeres arrived it was difficult to imagine Succos as the *zeman simchaseinu,* time of our happiness, in the current frame of mind.

Reb Meir was preparing to go to the *beis medrash* to pray when he stopped by to wish his daughter a "Gut Yom Tov." The room was small with nothing inside it other than a bed, a small table, a glass of water, various medications and a chair by her bedside that was usually occupied by her mother reciting *Tehillim.* Reb Meir looked at his daughter and was overcome with emotion. Finally, he cried out, "*Heiliga Bashefer*, You asked from Your Meir'l to go to shul on Rosh Hashanah and blow shofar, and he fulfilled Your request. You requested that he pray in shul on Yom Kippur and he heeded Your call. You even expected that in the face of his little girl's illness he celebrate the Yom Tov of Succos with joy, and with great difficulty he did that as well. But our Rabbis inform us that 'One must bless on the bad news one receives in the same manner as he reacts to good news,' explaining that one is required to react with joy. But now, as my daughter's life is slipping away, You ask Meir'l to react with joy. How can I? *Ein me'arvin simchah besimchah!* One is not permitted to combine two moments of happiness! How can I combine the joy of Yom Tov with the joy of accepting Your decree?!"

As he left the room the emotions ran high. *Hakafos* were celebrated with unusual joy. The Chassidim rallied around their Rebbe and he inspired them to dance with joy. Upon returning home he was greeted with the news that his daughter – for the first time in months – had shown some improvement. And for that Reb Meir'l was eternally grateful.

The Kohen Gadol

LIVING IN CHICAGO, REB AARON SOLOVEITCHIK SPENT most of his life out of the limelight — and that's the way he liked it. A modest man, Reb Aaron shied away from attention. Those who knew him, however, also knew that as mild mannered as he was, he was equally steadfast in his refusal to compromise in his Torah observance. His unbending allegiance to the letter of the law was yet another link in the chain of the Soloveitchik dynasty.

A few years prior to his passing, when Reb Aaron was well on in years, he suffered a debilitating stroke, one that paralyzed most of his body. Things that he always took for granted were now a far-off dream to this weak old man. He couldn't walk and could barely speak properly.

The enormous frustration would have set most people back. Here was a man who had the ability to express himself masterfully, to dissect and analyze the slightest nuances in the Talmudic text, to explore and navigate his way through seeming difficulties in the *Rambam*. And now he had trouble asking for a drink of water. The sight was sad if not pitiful. But Reb Aaron's determination could not be diminished.

As soon as was medically possible he insisted on beginning rehabilitation. Both the doctors and nurses were amazed at this rabbi's demeanor. Each moment spent in the company of non-Jews was an opportunity for Reb Aaron to sanctify G-d's Name. In fact, on one occasion a young gentile girl, selling decorative mugs, knocked on the door of his hospital room. While those attending to the Rosh Yeshivah dismissed the solicitation, Reb Aaron quickly invited her in. He asked her about the coffee cups she had decorated and took a genuine interest in them, even purchasing one. To Reb Aaron she was not a nuisance but an opportunity to sanctify Hashem's Name, and that was something to be treasured.

When the doctors gave the go-ahead for rehab to begin, they instructed those who would be helping Reb Aaron that it would be a long, arduous and painful process. It was not unusual for elderly patients in this position to give up. The doctors warned of possible infections and cautioned that the patient must not be pushed too hard too fast. They administered the appropriate regimen for a man Reb Aaron's age, and all was set to begin.

Periodically, *talmidim* would come to visit their rebbi. When they were there they would assist Reb Aaron with anything he needed. And on the day that Reb Aaron was beginning his treatment, his *talmid* Reb Dovid Green was privileged to be the one who was with him.

He helped Reb Aaron into his wheelchair and wheeled him from his hospital room down the hallway toward the rehabilitation area of the hospital. The stroke had rendered Reb Aaron unable to walk even one step, so he was now beginning to re-learn the basic skill of walking. He was placed between two parallel bars and was supported from behind, and one could see from the strain on his face that the task of taking a few small steps was a momentous undertaking. Each grueling movement required Reb Aaron to muster every ounce of strength in his frail body. After the first step, his *talmid,* seeing the effort that was required, asked his rebbi if he would like to stop.

Refusing his disciple's offer, he moved forward again. This time Reb Dovid noticed that his rebbi was muttering something under his breath. Another step and again Reb Aaron mumbled some words. Reb Dovid leaned closer and then he was able to hear, "*Achas. Achas ve'achas.*" Another step. "*Achas u'shtayim.*" And so on and so forth. Repeating the words that the Kohen Gadol recites when he sprinkles blood during the Yom Kippur service, Reb Aaron was counting and marking each step with tremendous concentration and effort.

Reb Dovid realized that his rebbi viewed the stroke and his difficult rehabilitation as his own personal *avodah,* which, when measured and worked on intensely, would help him to heal and gain strength.

To Sing From the Heart

FOR THOSE WHO HAVE BEEN PRIVILEGED TO EXPERIENCE it firsthand, it is an unusual pleasure. The Shabbos meal in the Machlis home located in an apartment in Maalot Dafna is unique and uplifting. Mrs. Machlis prepares delicious meals for the fifty to seventy guests they entertain at each meal! Her vegetable order is enormous, enough to literally feed a small army. Twenty-kilo packages of potatoes and onions are consumed as easily as most families finish a small package. They can easily consume twenty to thirty chickens a Shabbos. All told, it is a gargantuan task to feed the crowds.

But that is not the only reason they come. True the food is tasty, but the pull that this amazing family has on strangers runs much deeper than that. The crowd they attract ranges in age from young children who arrive accompanied by a parent or grandparent, to college kids who have never experienced a real Shabbos meal. Sometimes yeshivah boys with nowhere else to eat will stop by as well. And there are the "regulars" — people who come week after week, and who have nowhere else to call home.

The crowd was overflowing this Friday night. The small living room/dining room area was filled to capacity. Rabbi Machlis finally managed to quiet the crowd and announced that he was prepared to recite the *Kiddush*. He asked that everyone rise and explained to them the concept of making *Kiddush* and all that it represented. Upon the completion of his thoughts he raised the cup to begin. Just then there was a knock on the door.

One of the guests walked over to the door and to the amazement of all, thirty more guests stood by the entrance of the apartment.

"Okay. Don't worry, there is plenty of room. We'll just pick up the tables and chairs and move outside to the front lawn." Rabbi Machlis was not fazed in the least. Did it matter if there were seventy guests or a hundred? Slowly the tables and chairs were moved outside and set up again. And finally, when most people might have normally ended their *seudah,* the Machlises began theirs.

Just getting everyone to wash and find their proper seats was an ordeal in and of itself. However, their charm and sincerity enabled the Machlises to work the magic that drew these people to them in the first place. Many of the guests conversed with each other and periodically Rabbi Machlis himself would share a Torah thought with his company. The chicken soup was delectably spiced and each bowl contained a delicious matzah ball.

Shabbos songs and Torah thoughts flavored the meal, and eventually the hour grew late. Dessert was served and as a calm quiet filled the Maalot Dafna night, the Machlis meal was about to end. All the guests knew that they had experienced something unique. But before they left, the time had come for *bentching* — Grace After Meals.

Rabbi Machlis stood up and the crowd immediately quieted down. "We now have a dilemma. On the one hand, the custom in the Machlis household is to *bentch* out loud after the meal. However, because we are eating outside, if we *bentch* aloud we will wake up all our neighbors, and that is stealing one's sleep, which is clearly a transgression. So tonight I propose that we sing the *bentching* together. I will sing it out loud by myself and you will all join in together with me. But instead of singing along with your mouths you will sing along with your hearts."

And so they did, feeling in their hearts that it was a true honor to be in the presence of this wonderful family that made every guest feel special and wanted. As Rabbi Machlis sang aloud, his guests sang along from their hearts and souls. The song poured forth as they thanked Hashem for this unique opportunity. And we can be sure that high above, the heavenly angels joined in to sing together with them.

The Blind Cripple

THE NORMALLY FESTIVE AURA THAT ACCOMPANIES THE holiday of Simchas Torah was replaced by the fear and trepidation felt by all in view of the impending war. General Erwin Rommel and his Afrika Korps were marching across North Africa, meeting little resistance. A horrible feeling of uncertainty loomed large over all of Palestine. No one knew what to expect. The rumors about Hitler's diabolical plan had been confirmed – to the complete and utter horror of all. Jews by the millions were being murdered. How was one to handle the whirlwind of emotions?

The Shomer Emunim shul located in the heart of the back alleyways of the Meah Shearim neighborhood was generally regarded as a special place to be on Simchas Torah. But not this year. Maariv had just concluded, *Atah Haraisa* had been recited and the Sifrei Torah had been distributed – but the feeling in shul was more like Tishah B'Av than Simchas Torah. The singing and dancing began but the dancers were listless and the singing was without heart. After five minutes the Rav of the shul, Rav Aaron Roth, banged on the *bimah* and ordered the dancing to stop. This was highly unusual, considering that normally *Hakafos* lasted the better part of four hours. The dancing stopped and the crowd grew silent. All eyes were focused on the Rav and after a moment he looked up and began to speak.

"My dear friends, there was once a king who decided to send out letters throughout the land. It was his birthday and he wanted the best dancers in the land to come and dance for him. From far and wide they came to celebrate. The finest musicians and the most creative choreographers all joined to rejoice on the king's special day. The musicians came early and set up their instruments, while the dancers brought beautiful, ornately designed outfits. After weeks of preparation the grand event finally got underway.

"It was a glorious sight to behold. The music was befitting a royal palace, while the dancing was coordinated to synchronize precisely with the ebb and flow of the melody. The invited guests stared in awe as the evening proceeded beautifully.

"In the middle of all the bravura the king noticed out of the corner of his eye an old crippled man enter the grand ballroom. He was attempting to make his way to the back of the room but constantly kept bumping into tables and chairs. Observing his every move the king realized that this cripple had another disability. He was blind.

"A few moments later the disabled man made his way to a seat in the back. The king was intrigued by this poor fellow and watched him closely. Suddenly a smile formed on the king's lips. He watched as the man hobbled around on his crutches and tried his best to 'dance.' In the meantime, one of the professional dancers approached the king and waited expectantly by the side of the king's throne. Acknowledging the man's presence, the king granted him permission to speak.

"The nervous subject began, 'Your royal highness,' he stammered, 'I have been watching his majesty for the last hour or so and I don't understand. The best dancers in the country are performing the finest choreographed dance steps and your royal highness is not even looking! Instead you've been watching that old cripple in the corner.'

"The king smiled and explained. 'All of those who have assembled to perform for me are truly talented and their performance is without question something to behold. But I ask you, are they enjoying what they're doing? Most certainly! Are they dancing solely for me or is it not also for themselves? But the blind crippled man in the corner is dancing *only for me*. Look at his face! Look at the pain he's in! But he continues to dance and hobble around only to please me — and that is what makes his dancing so dear to me.' "

"*Morai VeRabosai*," Rav Aaron concluded, "In other years when we danced and rejoiced on Simchas Torah, besides fulfilling the Will of the Almighty we also enjoyed ourselves. However, this year, with Hitler on our doorstep and the plight of the Jewish people on the forefront of our minds, we have the unique opportunity to dance solely because our Father in Heaven asked us to. *Nu, lomir tantzen* — Let's dance!"

Resilience and Resolve

The following incident was told by Reb Shlomo Brevda, who heard it from Rebbetzin Greineman, the Steipler Rebbetzin's sister. It is a tribute to the Steipler Gaon's determination and tenacity regarding the sanctity of Shabbos.

RAV YAAKOV YISRAEL KANIEVSKY, WHO LATER IN LIFE was simply known as the Steipler Gaon, was about to become engaged to the Chazon Ish's sister. But before he determined to make her his *kallah*, he felt that it was important that he share with her an incident that taken place while he was in Siberia.

The forced labor in the Russian army in Siberia was back-breaking. Aside from the bitter cold and blinding snow, the actual labor required pure brute force. The Steipler had been inducted into the army against his will, yet regardless of the terrible conditions and the impossible work, he knew in his heart that only one task mattered — serving the Master of the world. He would do whatever was needed to accomplish that task.

One of the first obstacles he had to overcome was the army system itself — the ordinances dictated that everyone must work seven days a week. To the Steipler that was absolutely unacceptable. He approached the officer in charge, a brutal anti-Semitic ogre, and requested that he be granted a furlough every Saturday. The official paused for a moment and then belted out an evil cynical laugh.

Immediately he answered that he would grant the request on one condition: the Steipler first had to prove himself to be a valiant warrior. He quickly ordered his men to form two rows and arm themselves with truncheons. The young Steipler watched the soldiers move into formation and heard the words of the evil officer, "Kanievsky, here is the deal. If you are able to make it through these lines and survive the blows from my officers, then you may rest on your Sabbath. However, if you don't — " His voice trailed off, and he belted out a hearty, evil laugh. Clearly he was enjoying his little game.

The Steipler did not flinch. Instead he quietly whispered a heartfelt prayer to the A-mighty to help him survive this difficult test. He knew that he could give up and the game would be over. But if he admitted defeat, then his attempt to be released from working on Shabbos would be over. The guards motioned to their commanding officer that they were ready; the officer and his comrades then stood back to watch the fun.

The Steipler approached the path and again murmured one last plea. He held his hand over his head and ran between the awaiting guards. With all their might they began to pummel him and beat him incessantly. The pain was unbearable, but the Steipler persisted and trudged forward. Blood trickled into his eyes but he continued to move forward. Step by step he inched ahead until finally he reached the end of the treacherous path. He collapsed at the finish line. As he lay there a smile formed on his lips. He had won. He was in incredible pain — but he had won! The Shabbos was still holy and he would be able to observe it. The commanding officer grudgingly informed him that he would not have to work on Saturday. Nobody helped him off the ground but it did not matter because he had survived.

The Steipler finished recounting his tale to his *kallah*. He explained to her that this was his level of *mesiras nefesh*. "The blows had hurt but I was happy to have had the privilege to suffer for the sake of the Shabbos." He then asked her if she was prepared to join him in his continuous sacrifice for Torah. She replied that she was, and they became *choson* and *kallah*.

Sleep Well

YOUNG YOSEF DOV HOCHTUCH PEERED OUT FROM HIS cramped sleeping quarters and then walked over to the area where the middle-aged man stood. Shlomo Mussbacher, 42 years old, had been an accountant, with a lovely wife and children, when suddenly everything in his world turned upside down. He was dragged out of his home by the Nazis, his wife and children screaming for someone to help him, but their German neighbors turned away. They were indifferent to the horror taking place around them — they acted as if their neighbors, their friends, were not being brutally beaten and dragged off before their eyes. They somehow were able to pretend that it was not their business. All the men from Shlomo's village were taken away. With no time to say good-bye, Shlomo quickly grabbed what was most dear to him, his *tefillin*, and was dragged away.

And now, in Blechhammer, it was impossible to relate the horror of this life to the sweetness of what had been his, just days before. The cold. The cries. The only way to survive was to become robotic — to lock into a routine where day and night no longer mattered, where indifference was the only way. But Shlomo was able to set aside one part of his day, early in the morning when everyone else was still sleeping, for something special. With the first rays of the sun, Shlomo would steal away a few precious moments to put on his *tefillin*. The other inmates knew, but told no one about it. But this morning the newcomer from Denmark, Yosef Dov Hochtuch had seen this peculiar behavior. He remembered that his father on occasion had donned these black boxes on his arm and head but he himself had never done so, not even at his Bar Mitzvah.

Yosef quietly introduced himself to Shlomo and inquired about the *tefillin*. His genuine interest touched Shlomo, who offered him a chance to wear them. Although there was a considerable age gap, almost twenty-five years, between the two, they soon became close friends. Shlomo taught Yosef how to put on the *tefillin* and what to say while wearing them. They could not spend too much time davening — at any moment the guards could arrive. In Blechhammer being found with a religious article was punishable by death. In addition to the davening in the morning, Shlomo would say *Shema* with Yosef before they went to sleep at night. And he would conclude by teaching Yosef one *pasuk*, *"Beyadcha afkid ruchi padisa osi Hashem Keil emes* — In Your hands I shall entrust my soul, You have redeemed me, Hashem, G-d of truth." The young man thought the *pasuk* said it all. What could be a more important thought than this declaration of belief? He was so inspired that he promised Shlomo and himself that if he ever made it out alive he would become a fully observant Jew.

Three weeks passed and every day Shlomo and his new friend put on *tefillin* in the morning and recited the verses of faith at night. But one day a midday roll call was announced. Normally roll call was twice a day: at morning and at night. But this midday check meant that some of the inmates would be transferred out. Both Shlomo and Yosef found themselves among those who would be moving on — this time they were going to Buchenwald. Their destination was known, but they feared that almost certainly they would not be together in the same barracks.

Unfortunately their fears were realized. Shlomo was placed on the opposite side of the camp. The conditions in Buchenwald were even more difficult than in Blechhammer. The morning to night backbreaking labor was only for those who were strong of body — those who were weak or did not possess a valuable skill would not live. Those unfortunate souls would either go to the gas chambers, or if they were lucky enough to collapse and die from weakness and starvation, their bodies would be dumped in a pile with others whose bodies could not withstand the rigors, suffering and anguish of Buchenwald. Many succumbed and died.

Shlomo was walking in an unfamiliar part of the camp. Normally he would follow the rest of his workforce and labor together with them, but on this day he had been assigned a task on the other side of camp. Shlomo felt himself lucky to have been chosen for this work — perhaps it would mean an extra morsel of bread; he always took advantage of these opportunities when they arose. As he was walking, he heard an eerie sound.

"Shlooommo." The voice seemed to come from heaven. Shlomo looked around but saw no one.

"Shlooommo." This time he clearly heard it. It was not his imagination. But from where had it come? He looked all around and still saw no one other than some guards in the distance. And then — about twenty meters from where he stood was a pile of sickly looking dead bodies. On the bottom of the pile, almost unrecognizable, was his friend Yosef Dov Hochtuch. Shlomo ran over to his dying friend and tried to pull him out. Clearly he was suffering and could barely speak. His eyes were sunken in and his cheekbones jutted out. He looked like a human skeleton.

"Leave me, Shlomo. I can't move." Shlomo did not want to listen and he attempted to pull out the boy whom he had taken under his wing. Yosef was the only one in the pile of bodies that was still living, but Shlomo was afraid that by pulling too hard he could kill him.

"What can I do to help you?" Shlomo asked. He had not seen his friend in the last two months and desperately wanted to help him.

"Tell me over what you taught me to say before we would go to sleep." Yosef was struggling with every word he spoke. "I forgot it. Please."

Shlomo held his hand and bent down closely to him. He could feel Yosef's slowing breath and knew that he did not have much time to live. He slowly recited the words of *Shema Yisrael* with him. And then the young boy joined with him as he said, *"Beyadcha afkid ruchi ...* In Your hands I shall entrust my soul ..."

Shlomo held tightly on to Yosef's hand. He did not want to let go. But as the sound of the barking dogs grew louder he knew he had to say good-bye. Shlomo wasn't sure of much anymore, but of one thing he was certain: his young friend's precious soul was entrusted in safe, protective, loving hands.

Forever.

Hashem yinkom damo — May Hashem avenge his blood!

A Ticket to Gan Eden

ENRY BORENSTEIN KNOCKED LIGHTLY ON RABBI Nelkin's office door and waited to be admitted into the rabbi's private room. The door opened and Henry was cheerfully greeted by his good friend. "What can I do for you this morning, Henry?"

Henry was a no-nonsense type of guy. Well advanced in age, he had been a member of his shul for close to fifty years and although the rabbi was young enough to be his son he respected him and had come to seek out his advice this morning.

"Rabbi, I'm here to tell you that I'm going to die."

"We're all going to die sooner or later," Rabbi Nelkin joked, in an attempt to lighten up the conversation.

"I mean it, Rabbi. I'm not fooling around." Henry's serious tone indicated that this was as serious a discussion as any.

"Have you been to a doctor lately? What makes you think that you're going to die, Henry? You look perfectly fine to me." Rabbi Nelkin tried the best he could to calm Henry's nerves, as he seemed to be on edge.

"What can I say? I just know that it won't be long now. And I have a request. I don't want to buried in *tachrichim*."

The request surprised Rabbi Nelkin. A proper Jewish burial was something even the nonreligious took quite seriously. What could Henry's reason possibly be?

"Instead, I want you to bury me in the prisoner clothing I wore in the concentration camps. I'm afraid that after I pass away I'll come before the A-mighty and He will ask me how come I didn't keep Shabbos and *tefillin* and kosher for over three years of my life. I will be able to respond, 'G-d, look at what I'm wearing. I went through the horrors of Auschwitz and I still raised an observant family.'"

Rabbi Nelkin stared at Henry in disbelief. The request was one that was highly unusual but he assured Henry that when the time came he would address the matter, figuring that he had plenty of time until Henry passed on. However, that wasn't the case. Three weeks later Henry died suddenly. He had gone to sleep one night and never woke up.

Immediately Henry's sons began to make the necessary arrangements for the funeral. The *chevrah kadisha* was called and preparations for the *taharah* began. They asked the family for Henry's *tachrichim, tallis* and *kitel*. His children gave over everything but mentioned to those who would be doing the *taharah* that they should wait until the family met with Rabbi Nelkin.

"Rabbi, we are aware of our father's unusual request regarding his burial shrouds; however, we ask you not to bury him in those garments."

In all Rabbi Nelkin's years in the Rabbinate this issue was definitely one of his most unique ones. He thought for a moment and then responded to Henry's sons. "Why should we not bury him in his prisoner's uniform? That was his final request from me. I told him that I would consider it, but I really have not delved into the halachic side of the matter, although I can't imagine why you would be opposed to it."

Moshe, Henry's eldest son, stepped forward and spoke on behalf of his brothers. "My dear Rabbi, allow me to explain the family's hesitation. Each year we gather together as a family for the Pesach Seder. Thank G-d, there were already four generations of my father's descendants. You might wonder why we would go through the trouble of all being together when it would be more manageable for us to have our own separate Seders.

"The answer is that every year after all the children would ask the *Mah Nishtanah,* my father would get up from the table. With all his grandchildren's eyes watching his every move he would walk deliberately to the closet, take out a hanger, remove the plastic from it and then hang it from the chandelier. As the children stared at their grandfather's prisoner uniform, my father would announce in a loud clear voice, '*Kinderlach, Avadim hayeenu leHitler beGermania.* Children, your grandfather was a slave to Hitler *ym"sh* in Germany. He tortured and killed millions of our brothers. And some thought that we would never escape the nightmare. But *Vayotze'einu Hashem*

Elokeinu misham, Hashem took us out of there and He allowed us to rebuild our lives. It is to Him that I owe my thanks for all of you.'

"Rabbi, it is that cry of faith that left an indelible impression on each of us and we don't want to relinquish this family heirloom."

Rabbi Nelkin held onto Moshe as he cried for his father and his children's grandfather.

With a new understanding of the importance of these hallowed garments, the chevrah kadisha buried Henry in the traditional burial shrouds and placed the precious uniform inside the aron as well.

Ayy Ayy

"AYY — AYY — AYY — AYY," SHLOIME MOANED silently. Shloime Greenwald, an elderly well-respected member of the Orthodox West Hempstead community, operated a thriving and flourishing corporation. Moreover, there was not a committee in town where Shloime was not involved. Treasurer of Bikur Cholim and Chairman of the Board for Yeshivas Bais Yehudah were both full-time jobs, yet Shloime skillfully juggled them together with his other full-time job — father and husband of the Greenwald's industrious household. And all things considered, Shloime lived a wonderful, perfect, life.

Only one thing was not so wonderful — Shloime's constant, disturbing "*krechtz.*" This low, sorrowful whimper was barely audible to most, but loud and clear to his family, who wondered about it but never dared ask from whence it arose.

Yanky, the youngest of the Greenwald clan, had recently become engaged and was extremely troubled by his father's embarrassing sigh, and worried about how his fiancée and her family would react to it. He gathered his courage and pleaded with his father to bring this *krechtz* to a halt.

Shloime, a kindhearted and caring father, desperately wanted to satisfy his newly engaged son. He understood that his Yanky was extremely concerned and wanted to impress his new *kallah* and her family. The last thing Yanky wanted was for his "strange" father to tarnish the "L'Chaim" with his peculiar moaning.

It was three short days before the *vort* when Shloime pulled his busy son aside and asked him, " Yanky, tell me, why do you think that I cry out like that?"

Now beginning to feel uncomfortable, Yanky shifted uneasily as he searched for the appropriate response to his father's question.

"Well — um — I always assumed it was because of something that happened in the war, though you never really told me, Ta." Yanky already felt foolish for his misguided request, as he stumbled through his reply.

"The truth is that an explanation has been long overdue." Shloime paused deliberately as if transporting himself back to a different time, and a much different place.

Shloime sat down on the living room sofa alongside his youngest son and journeyed back through time to a place he had hoped never to revisit.

"It happened so suddenly. When the Nazis *ym"sh* stormed into our peaceful little town, we had just enough time to gather a few bits and pieces before we were herded into the suffocating cattle cars. Two endless days passed — no sleep, no food, no water. Suddenly growling dogs and barking humans greeted us. Commotion ensued and before I ever had a chance to say good-bye to my family, we had been separated. Forever."

Shloime paused to regain his composure and collect his thoughts. He pulled his son Yanky closer to him, tenderly holding his hand, and continued, "There I was, still a young boy, not yet 13 years of age and over a chaotic period of two harrowing days I had lost everything. My parents, brothers, sisters — everything."

Yanky sat transfixed — his father had never told this story before and Yanky knew that this was a pivotal moment in his own life. He watched his father with great love and the deepest intensity.

"Weeks had gone by," his father continued, "and as the initial shock wore off, depression began setting in. Despondent and all alone, I felt like giving up until — I saw them. There they stood before me, like angels sent from Heaven, my close friends from back home, my *landsmen,* Pinchos and Dovid.

"We hugged each other tightly not wanting to let go, as each shared his family's horrifying fate. As the last one had completed his traumatic tale of woe, we knew that we had to stay together, though by now we had certainly learned that we weren't the ones in charge. We needed a plan.

"Desperate for some form of inspiration and short on time, Pinchos suggested a clever idea, 'Even though we physically cannot always be together, what if every time we saw each other we reviewed one piece of Gemara that we had previously learned in yeshivah?' We were thrilled and without delay, right there and then, we implemented the plan with the first Mishnah of *Eilu Metzios.*"

Yanky sat incredulous – to think that his father had suffered so much – it was beyond comprehension.

Shloime, oblivious to his son's observation, pulled out his handkerchief, wiped his brow and continued. "The plan worked to perfection the first few times we tried it but then one day the most brutal of all the SS men, Ivan, noticed that we appeared to be scheming as we each mumbled something every time we were together. He pulled us aside and began to shout at us. Unaware of the crime we had committed we tried to explain that we had done nothing wrong. This sent him into a maniacal frenzy, as he took out his metal truncheon and pummeled us ferociously.

"There we lay on the ground beaten and bloody, physically broken but with the pulse of our spirit still beating strong. Pinchos suggested we revise the plan. Instead of gathering together to review Gemara, we could murmur a chapter of *Tehillim* whenever we made eye contact. Satisfied with our revision, with new resolve we instituted 'Plan B' with our first chapter of *Tehillim*, '*Shir Lamaalos.*'

"But Ivan was looking for us. With close surveillance of our every move he spotted each of us speaking softly to ourselves, and like a dog chomping at the bit he jumped at the opportunity to yet again inflict pain and punishment. That time, Ivan left us lying on the floor more dead than alive. Our plan had all but failed. We needed an even more clever scheme to deceive Ivan. But how?

"After some deliberation, Pinchos, the shrewdest of our small group, proposed a brilliant plan. 'What if we developed a code where the Germans would assume we were crying out in pain, while simultaneously that very same cry would give us the *chizuk* we so desperately needed?'

"Dovid and I gave each other puzzling looks as we speculated about Pinchos' most recent plan.

" 'That's right,' continued Pinchos, his tone reflecting his ever-growing excitement and optimism. 'Ayy — Ayy — Ayy — Ayy.'

" 'It's the *roshei teivos* (an acronym) for the six *yesodos* (principles) that a Yid must always embrace.' Pinchos continued, strength mounting in his voice. *'Alef — Ahavas Hashem* (Love of G-d); *Yud — Yiras Hashem* (Fear of G-d); *Yud — Yichud Hashem* (G-d's Oneness); *Aleph — Ahavas Yisrael* (Love of a fellow Jew); *Yud — Yekadeish Shemo Berabim* (Public sanctification of G-d's Name); and *Yud – Yesh Eloka Mimaal* (Cognizance of G-d Above).'

"Pinchos, with the fearless facade of a warrior facing battle, looked at the two of us and in a soft whimper began to cry softly, 'Ayy, Ayy, Ayy, Ayy.' And together Dovid and I proudly joined in with our cry of *emunah*, 'Ayy, Ayy, Ayy, Ayy.'"

Shloime, exhausted and emotionally spent, removed his handkerchief once again to wipe the tears glistening in his eyes, then turned to his son and explained that which needed no explanation. "My dear son, the cry of 'Ayy, Ayy' is not a cry of pain; rather, it is our secret battle cry of *emunah* that I have never forgotten and it is because of this that I continue to cry out."

Yanky sheepishly attempted to apologize for his foolish request. His deep feelings and pure intense love for his father were evident on his young face. And, in response, Shloime pulled his son close and sighed, "Ayy, Ayy, Ayy, Ayy."

Always Together

ORDINARILY, ONE IMAGINES A *TZADDIK* NOT ONLY AS A pious individual, but also as someone who devotes his life to Hashem's commandments without a thought for material comforts, even living in utter destitution, totally impoverished. However, Reb Yisroel Rizhiner, the scion of the Rizhiner dynasty, believed that a *tzaddik*, and in particular a Chassidic Rebbe, was required to live his life otherwise.

Instead of living on bread and water, dressing in rags and existing in a hovel, Reb Yisroel felt that he should comport himself as a holy representative of the King of kings, the *Ribbono Shel Olam*, and should therefore live as royalty.

From his stately home, a beautiful palace filled with the finest furnishings, to his elegant clothing, made of rich, exquisite fabrics, nothing seemed to be lacking. Most striking of all the eye-catching extravagance were R' Yisroel's elaborately designed, custom-made boots – both ornate and flamboyant with engraved imprints etched into the soft leather. All of this for one reason — to show the royal essence of the *Ribbono Shel Olam* through his holy servant, Reb Yisroel.

However, Reb Yisroel took meticulous care in gaining no personal pleasure from his surroundings. External impressions aside, R' Yisroel reasoned, "If indeed this display is solely for the A-mighty, then who am I to benefit from it?" As an example of this, his famous boots, as lavish as they looked on the outside, held a secret which bespoke R' Yisroel's true *neshamah* – they had no sole! In essence, Reb Yisroel was walking around barefoot, since he wished to deny himself any pleasure from the display he took upon himself to pay honor to his Creator. Neither his garments nor his surroundings were of any significance. Uncompromising *Kevod Malchuso* (Honor of His Kingdom). This was R' Yisroel.

In the still of a cold dark winter night in the year 1847, as R' Yisroel sat inside his secure home hovering over a *sefer*, all seemed placid in the quiet town of Rizhin when suddenly a deafening pounding shattered the silence of the night.

"Open up at once!!" barked the burly Russian policemen who had arrived at the Rebbe's door searching for him. Banging furiously, they forcefully demanded that the Rebbe surrender at once.

The Rebbe's *gabbai* bravely protected the Rebbe, and asked the police what they wanted with Reb Yisroel. "The Rabbi must come with us at once!!" they responded. They went on to accuse the Rebbe of circulating false propaganda and being disloyal to the Czar. Reb Yisroel and the *gabbai* knew that denial would earn them nothing but more severe treatment; in this time, in this place, the truth was not the concern of the Russian police. There would be no negotiation.

Ignoring the *gabbai's* persistent pleas, the muscular guards seized the blameless Rebbe, carelessly dumped him in the back of their dingy wagon, brought him to the prison and wildly hurled him into a dreary, dark prison cell no more than six feet by eight feet in measure.

The crushed Chassidim despondently attempted to arrange for their beloved Rebbe's hasty release but it was to no avail. Several prolonged, anxious weeks passed but their heartfelt attempts to free their precious Rebbe left them with more frustration than fruition. Their helpless leader lingered in that dismal, awful cell.

At last, after two agonizing months, the shaken Chassidim were finally able to procure sufficient funds to bribe the greedy officials for the privilege of visiting their dear Rebbe.

They could never have prepared themselves for what they saw. As the door to the prison cell slowly opened and the timid Chassidim tentatively paused by the foreboding doorway, they peered inside and watched in utter horror as the rats and vermin that had surrounded their pure Rebbe now scurried about. The Rebbe of Rizhin, a prince of a human being, had been diminished to rags and indigence as he sat crumpled and weeping on the cold hard floor.

The Rebbe, who had learned to fear any time the door to his cell opened, tentatively turned toward the door with his tear-filled eyes. He peered upwards and beheld in front of him his devoted Chassidim. Aghast at what they had witnessed and appalled at their

Rebbe's wretched conditions, they could not control themselves and burst out in tears.

Their concerned Rebbe curiously looked at them and asked "Why are you crying, my dear children? Why do you seem so pained?"

His shattered Chassidim rhetorically responded, "Dear Rebbe, you wonder why we are so pained? We are anguished by the reality that someone of such stature and greatness, someone of such *chashivus,* someone so undeserving is forced to exist under such hideous circumstances. It's horrifying! Rebbe, you yourself are crying."

The Rebbe pondered for a moment, wiped away his tears and then lovingly replied, "My dear Chassidim, you do not grasp the true reason for my tears. It is not for my own discomfort and pain that I cry, rather it is for an altogether different reason.

"Dovid HaMelech declares, '*Gam ki eileich begei tzalmaves lo ira ra ki Atah imadi —* Although I walk in the shadow of death, I need not fear evil for Hashem is with me.' My dear Chassidim, Dovid HaMelech is conveying to us that no matter where we journey to, regardless of how low we might have fallen, the *Heiliga Shechinah* constantly accompanies us."

He gazed intently at his devoted Chassidim, then at the appalling conditions of his cell, and, with pain and anguish in his voice, continued, "Why is it *ra? Ki Atah imadi —* Because You, Hashem, are with me. This means that, sadly, right here amidst the darkness and gloom of this cell, the A-mighty resides with me. And that is the cause of my intense pain. Why must *He* suffer? Why does *He* need to be desecrated and defiled just because of *me*?"

Now, merely beginning to comprehend their Rebbe's unfathomable sensitivity for his Creator, the humbled Chassidim sat down on the cold hard floor beside their broken Rebbe and wept together with him.

Alive and Well

I T WAS 1984. YINGHI BRAUN, WHO WORKED FOR EL AL for many years, starting off as a baggage handler and then working his way up the corporate ladder to the position of vice president, enjoyed his job. Yinghi was a quiet unassuming man, and although he was well liked by his peers, he kept mostly to himself. He had come to the shores of Eretz Yisrael shortly after the war, some forty years ago. His fellow workers were conscious of the fact that he was a war survivor although he rarely spoke of it. In fact, he *never* spoke of his past. His co-workers learned quickly that Yinghi was terribly uncomfortable talking about his war experiences, and did not bring up the subject with him.

In Israel, preparations began for the fortieth anniversary of the liberation of Auschwitz. Journalists worldwide scurried about, searching for stories of interest. The media hunted for personal accounts from those who had survived the war. The fact that they were opening wounds that had been sealed long ago did not concern them. A story, no matter what the cost, was a story.

One of Yinghi's co-workers insensitively suggested to him that perhaps, as a prominent member of Israeli society and an important corporate executive, he should volunteer for an interview. Yinghi shrugged off the proposal and hoped that the idea would be put to rest. None of his other colleagues dared suggest it again, and Yinghi was grateful — his memories had been buried long ago and perhaps that's were they were best kept.

The matter had been put to rest and months passed without incident. Those who had overheard the insensitive suggestion had admonished the associate who had recommended the interview. All of Yinghi's acquaintances now knew to never again mention the subject.

Yinghi regularly received a newsletter for war survivors, and in the current issue, the headline shocked him: "Dr. Mengele alive and well in South America." Yinghi studied the newsletter carefully, reading and rereading every word of the article. His blood boiled as he pictured in his mind the sadistic doctor's cold, cruel demeanor. Vivid memories raced through Yinghi's mind; his face contorted, reflecting his inner torment — reliving nightmarish experiences that he wished would remain buried and feeling that familiar sense of utter rage that demanded revenge. His very soul was struggling with this news.

Later that day, in his office, the telephone rang. It was a woman from New Zealand who worked for the German weekly news magazine, *Der Spiegel*. She explained that she had been looking for a personal account from a Holocaust survivor and had been given his name. In light of the recent rumors that Dr. Mengele was alive, would he be interested in doing the interview?

Yinghi thought long and hard. The thought that Dr. Mengele roamed free made him feel physically ill. After thinking over and over about the interview, he finally relented, utterly surprising himself. "Most certainly," he stated emphatically. They agreed to meet at Yinghi's home the next day.

Yinghi slept uneasily that night. Twisting and turning, memories that had been locked up for forty years were creeping ever so slowly back to the forefront of his mind. He envisioned long lines of confused families being directed to life or death with the uncaring movement of a man's index finger as if he had been selecting paint colors. He remembered how he and his twin sister volunteered when the call went out for twins to step forward. Screaming, he woke up in the middle of the night shaking and sweating. Perhaps this was all a mistake. Why go through it? Let the past die!

The remainder of the night and during early morning Yinghi thought of canceling the interview. But somehow he just could not cancel. At 10 o'clock the doorbell rang and Lisa Dubois introduced herself as the reporter from *Der Spiegel*. Yinghi invited her in, set out two cups of coffee and they sat down and spoke.

At first, his words came out as if pulled by an invisible chain — slowly, with great effort. Then, as he went on and watched the interviewer's sympathetic face, he realized he was speaking more freely. He recalled for her the sickening experiments performed on him and his sister, pausing briefly to regain his composure. His emotions twisted into a whirlwind of pain, grief and anger. Lisa listened, awed by the description of what had happened to this man and what he had endured.

Two hours later, Yinghi finished his narrative, exhausted and emotionally spent. Then, Lisa asked him one final question. "What would you do if you met up with Dr. Mengele today? What would you say to him? What would you do to him?"

He thought for a moment, having reviewed the scenario over in his mind countless times prior to this question. He knew what he would say, because he had been saying it his entire life. "Dr. Mengele, I want you to know one thing. After all your hatred and malice, in spite of all your efforts, we have won and you have lost. I have two children — young, healthy boys. Every day they go to school and study G-d's Torah — and that is our badge of conquest, our symbol of triumph. I appropriately named them *Ud*, 'a spark,' and *Amichai*, 'my nation is still alive.' " Yinghi's eyes blazed with fire and spirit as if he had actually just spoken with the infamous doctor who had altered the lives of millions.

Lisa had stopped writing long ago. She had heard what she came for, now understanding that the legacy of the Jewish nation will indeed last forever.

The Time Machine

Yael had been scanning the Sunday morning *Jerusalem Post* classified section searching for an intriguing summer job, and one specific ad caught her eye:

"Looking for Hebrew teachers to educate recent Ethiopian immigrants."

She was vaguely familiar with the fascinating account of Operation Moses, the dramatic operation that had airlifted 25,000 Falashan Jews out of Ethiopia. It had caused quite a sensation in both the religious and political Israeli circles. Overwhelmed by the sheer numbers of these immigrants, the Israeli government had established absorption centers for the sole purpose of acclimating these new citizens to an unfamiliar culture.

Yael possessed an outstanding command of the language and enjoyed teaching as well. Satisfied with her choice of job opportunities, she was thrilled to be accepted for the post. Uncertain about what to expect, she began to prepare diligently, making the most of her creative abilities.

The opening day of the semester fell on a Tuesday. Yael arrived early and braced herself for the out of the ordinary. Her students' ethnic colored clothing spoke volumes about where they had come from. Men, women and children of all ages attended the *ulpan* to become acquainted with the language of their new home. Following the initial commotion of finding their seats and discussing their surroundings, the crowd settled down to listen to their first lesson of *Ivrit*.

"This is the letter *aleph*," announced Yael, grabbing the attentive group's interest. She held up a white poster-board displaying the shape of the letter accompanied by pictures of *aleph* words.

"*Abba, Imma, aviron* … " Yael continued to flip through board after colorful board, rich both in color and content. Judging from the expressions on most of their faces, Yael seemed satisfied that her students were understanding the lesson, and prepared to move on to the next letter.

"This is the letter *beis,*" Yael confidently declared as she held up the *beis* collection of pictures, "as in *bayit,* house." She spoke clearly, articulating each and every letter while presenting a handsome drawing of a typical house. Her students nodded as she moved onto the next sketch.

"Or as in *Beit HaMikdash.*" Yael raised the diagram high in the air to ensure even those in the rear of the room a clear view of the beautiful illustration depicting the Second *Beis HaMikdash.* Inexplicably, some looked puzzled while others stared blankly at their instructor.

Where did I go wrong? wondered Yael, as she persisted. "Does everyone understand?"

Just then a young boy, no older than 8 or 9 years, raised his hand and impatiently inquired, "Have you ever seen it?"

Confused about the question, Yael shrugged and responded, "Of course not."

A few moments later as Yael presented the letter *dalet*, the youngster again lifted his hand and interrupted, "Well, why haven't you seen it?"

At this point Yael was becoming slightly irritated and she annoyingly responded, "Because it isn't here anymore." Yael had accepted this unusual job because she assumed it would be challenging; however, she hadn't expected any chutzpah. And this child's smart-aleck responses were bordering on impudence. However, the child quieted down and she continued. An hour later, slightly frazzled from the give and take, she began to review the lessons before ending the class when the child blurted out again, "What happened to it?"

Exasperated, Yael cynically responded in a matter-of-fact tone, "Nearly 2,000 years ago the Romans destroyed it. Does that satisfy your curiosity, young man?"

She watched closely as the expression on his face was transformed from that of curiosity to one of terror. She immediately regretted her snappy retort. She wished she had not responded so curtly, but it was too late now.

"Liar! You're a liar!" the vulnerable child shouted as he swiftly dashed out of the room.

She was shocked. *Impatient? Maybe. Intolerant? Perhaps. But a liar? What I told him was completely and entirely true. The Beis HaMikdash had indeed been destroyed by the Romans 2,000 years ago,* she reflected, her heart filled with remorse.

With feelings of confusion and anxiety, and convinced that she had been quite unsuccessful, Yael ended the class, gathered her belongings and got ready to leave. As she pushed open the door she was startled to be confronted by the offended lad and his entire family — father, mother, sisters, brothers, aunts, uncles, cousins and grandparents — all clad in ancient tribal dress.

Shocked and surprised at this uncomfortable encounter, Yael regretted the day she applied for this thankless job. But she kept her professionalism and asked politely, "Hello, how can I help you?"

"Why did you lie to our grandson?" asked the apparent patriarch of the family in a stern and commanding voice.

"I didn't lie to him, though I'm sorry he became so upset with what I told him. All I related was that the Romans destroyed the

Second *Beit HaMikdash*, 2,000 years ago," Yael firmly avowed in her defense.

"Why do you lie again?" the stately grandfather accused.

"I'm not lying!" exclaimed Yael. "It was destroyed! I promise!" As the heartrending words left her mouth and she observed the grief-stricken reaction of the family, tears began to stream down her cheeks as well.

In a shocking moment of realization — pain, fear and horror all at once overcame this long-lost family. Amazingly, in their millennia of bitter exile, they had never been informed of the destruction of the *Beis HaMikdash*.

Yael's eyes opened wide and she drew in her breath. She suddenly understood that she was *zocheh* to witness the true anguish a Jew feels over this singular, most terrible loss in Jewish history.

Broken beyond words, the orphaned family ripped their garments, sat on the ground and cried bitterly.

Chazal tell us that every year the Beis HaMikdash is not rebuilt, it is as if it has been destroyed. Sadly, for this broken family, never have the words of Chazal rung truer.

Tefillah /
Prayer

A Bubby's Tears

WHEN THE STATE OF ISRAEL WAS FIRST FORMED, Prime Minister David Ben-Gurion appointed his cabinet. Among those selected was Zalman Oran, a non-religious Jew, who was to serve as Minister of Education. His convictions, though secular in nature, were sincere. He served his post with dedication and commitment and took his job quite seriously.

Zalman Oran's wife, also secular like her husband, nonetheless lit Shabbos candles every week, a custom passed down from her mother. Every Friday night she would cover her eyes and pray that her children should grow up to be as great as the greatest Jew she knew — David Ben-Gurion! This was her heartfelt prayer, week after week.

Early on, in the formation of the statutes of the State of Israel, Ben-Gurion met with the venerated sage, Rav Avrohom Yeshayah Karelitz, the Chazon Ish. They discussed many important issues during that momentous meeting, and Ben-Gurion came away from the encounter incredibly impressed and somewhat awed by the Chazon Ish's saintliness and sensitivity.

A few days after that meeting, Ben-Gurion met with Zalman Oran and other members of his cabinet to discuss certain policies and he began by describing the Chazon Ish and how amazed he was by his angelic presence. That night Oran went home and related the entire episode to his wife.

The next week when she lit the Shabbos candles, Mrs. Oran's prayer for her children was modified. Instead of wishing that her children grow up to be like Ben-Gurion, she now prayed that they become like the Chazon Ish, a man she knew nothing about other than the fact that Ben-Gurion was unusually impressed with him and held him in great esteem.

This incident was related by Rabbi Boruch Heyman, a Rav in Yerushalayim, and a Torah scholar who is involved with myriad Torah organizations — and the grandson of Mrs. Zalman Oran.

When they began to search for a new chief rabbi of Yerushalayim, the name of Rav Chaim Yaakov Levin was brought up. His father, Rav Aryeh Levin, was a much revered *talmid chacham* and beloved *tzaddik* and Rav Chaim Yaakov seemed to be a logical choice and a viable candidate. However, when he was approached, he asked if he could be privy to the names of the other nominees. One of the names mentioned was that of Rav Betzalel Zolti (who was eventually chosen for the position). Upon hearing this name, Rav Levin immediately withdrew from consideration.

At the time the committee did not understand why Rav Levin had withdrawn his name. It was only many years later that he revealed his reason by relating the following story: My father, Rav Aryeh Levin, was once walking late at night in the dark quiet streets of Yerushalayim when he noticed a woman sitting outside her tiny home, bent over, stitching a pair of pants in front of a dim kerosene lamp.

The hour was late and the light was so dim that my father could barely see in front of him. "Excuse me," he asked, "but why do you sit out here so late at night stitching up these pants?"

She looked up from her work and noticed that the Rav was standing right near her. She quickly sat up and began to explain. "You see, I must work extra hard because I need the money to pay for my child to have a good *melamed*. I am a widow and have very little money and this is the only way we can afford it." As she spoke, tears ran down her cheeks and one could hear the pain in her voice.

Rav Chaim Yaakov Levin concluded, "Do you know who that woman was? It was the mother of Rav Betzalel Zolti. Her grueling work paid for the *chinuch* of her orphaned son. Who can measure the strength hidden in the painful cries of an *almanah*? The tears she shed watered the field of Torah that her little *yasom* planted. And the harvest they produced together enabled Rav Zolti to become the Rav of Yerushalayim."

The Most Valuable Thing in the World

IS NAME WAS SIBERIAK. A SHORT STOCKY MAN WITH a weathered look, he spoke in front of a group of survivors who were like himself. They did not have much left of their own lives. Hitler, Stalin and years of loneliness had taken an immense toll, but the group gathered together occasionally to share their emotions. And now it was his turn:

I always thought that the most important thing in the world was money. After all, what could be more valuable than gold? That is, until I came to Siberia. Together with other prisoners, I was given the task of mining gold. We would work long hard days, sometimes up to 18 hours with little or no rest. Our sleeping quarters were horribly cramped and our food rations were minimal. But when I saw where we would be working, I was immediately overcome with a feeling of joy. Our group was going to be working in the gold mine. And although the work was difficult I managed to bring along a small pouch in which I was able to smuggle out a few golden nuggets each day.

One night as I was counting my bag of golden nuggets one of the inmates noticed what I was doing and burst out laughing. He called over some of his friends and enjoyed a hearty laugh. They mocked me and ridiculed my little pouch. "Don't you think we all could smuggle out golden nuggets? You fool, what value does a golden nugget have here in the cold abyss of Siberia?" It was at that moment that I realized that gold is not the most valuable thing in the world. At least not here in Siberia. What good could it bring me?

The hunger pangs gnawed at my insides as I dreamt of a thick juicy slab of meat, something I had not tasted in years. *That's it!* I thought to myself. *The most valuable thing in the world is not gold but good food to alleviate my hunger pangs. There could be nothing that is more valuable than that.*

And so the daily grind of finding food continued. It was comical in a sad way that those glistening golden nuggets were no more valuable to me now than the dirt into which they were wedged. They were worth nothing to me. All I could think of was the gnawing hunger. Every moment of every day my thoughts were focused on food — until one of the passing guards walked by while he was smoking a cigarette. The smell of the cigarette wafted through the cold Siberian air and the aroma filled the surrounding area.

All of a sudden my hunger pangs dissipated and the craving for a cigarette became my focal point. Nothing else mattered. Food was something that lasted for a short while but a cigarette provided much more than that. There was something that was more meaningful about it. The calm feeling and relaxation it provided were significantly deeper than the food or gold that I had previously desired.

But a cigarette was something that was more difficult to come by. Although tobacco was readily available and fairly easy to obtain, the paper in which it needed to be wrapped was scarce. Even the guards had a tough time getting hold of the elusive paper. I now realized that the most important thing in the world was not gold or food or even tobacco: it was paper.

For days I would look forward to the next opportunity to smoke and the feeling from those few moments would provide me with enough satisfaction for the next few days. And so it developed into a routine. But one day I came across a peasant from a neighboring village. The older man approached me and asked if I knew how to read. He explained that I appeared to be slightly more educated than the rest of the prisoners and he had a favor to ask of me. His son, an officer in the Soviet Union's army, was stationed hundreds of kilometers away and would periodically send a letter to inform his father of how he was managing.

"Recently another letter arrived and I need someone to read it for me. If you help me I will give you the envelope to use for wrapping the tobacco."

I could hardly believe my good fortune. I figured that I could probably roll at least two or maybe even three cigarettes with the envelope he had. I assisted him with his letter and thanked him for his "gift." And then I took the letter back to the barracks where I slept. I removed a small pouch of tobacco and placed the envelope on the floor. But just as I was about to empty the pouch into the envelope something caught my eye. I had to look closer to make sure that I was not dreaming. Lo and behold! In front of my eyes an envelope was made out of paper that had Hebrew lettering on it.

I carefully read it and saw that the writing was words from davening. I had not prayed in many years but I was familiar and fluent in my reading. I picked up the paper and carefully folded it into my pocket.

There was a man whom we called the "Rebbele." It's not that he was so learned but he was someone who kept track of when the Yamim Tovim were and so he was the closest thing we had to a rebbe. When I showed him my newfound treasure, he could not believe it. Here we were, thousands of miles from the closest sem-blance of Yiddishkeit and G-d had sent us, a page of a *siddur*. We figured that if He had not forgotten about us, then we should not forget Him. So we began a *minyan*. It was certainly not conven-tional in any sense. We only had this one page of a *siddur*.

At each *tefillah* the *shaliach tzibbur* would read from the enve-lope. Whether it was a Shacharis, Minchah, Maariv or Shabbos and Yom Tov davening, the *shaliach tzibbur* would stand up and read from the envelope. The formerly depressed inmates found strength and solace through this *tefillah* gathering that I had helped organize.

Watching the transformation of these poor wretched souls tak-ing place was nothing short of a miracle. The prisoners now walked around and conducted their daily lives with a sense of purpose. Their lives had meaning and for that they were forever grateful. And then one day it hit me. I had discovered the most valuable thing in the world. It was not gold nor was it food. It wasn't a ciga-rette or the paper it was rolled in. It was "Prayer." The ability for one to connect with his Creator for but a few moments a day was something invaluable.

But perhaps what was most incredible about the envelope was the prayers that it contained. To receive an envelope that was made from some recycled *siddur* page was in itself a mira-cle, but the prayers it contained were the timeliest and most potent messages we could have ever hoped for. The page began with the declaration from *Az Yashir:* "*Hashem yimloch le'olam va'ed* — G-d will rule foreve!" And the small lettering on the page continued until the heartfelt plea found in middle of *Ahavah Rabbah,* "*Avinu, Av HaRachaman, HaMeracheim, racheim aleinu* — Our Father, our Compassionate Father, Who is merciful, have mercy on us!"

A Mother's Prayers

*T*HE STATE OF ISRAEL WAS AT WAR WITH LEBANON IN 1982 and a group of five soldiers bravely attempted to flush out an Arab ambush deep in the heart of the Bekaa Valley. The fighting was furious and, tragically, after a valiant battle, all five soldiers were killed by Lebanese troops.

The devastating news reached the city of Cleveland where Moshe and Yehudis Spero lived. Yehudis' brother, Daniel Haas, a sergeant in the Israeli army, was one of those who had been killed, and at the time Yehudis was pregnant with her fourth child. When her son was born she named him Daniel in memory of her slain brother, and prayed at the time that no further Jewish blood would ever need to be shed. But *hashgachah* would dictate otherwise.

Moshe and Yehudis moved to Eretz Yisrael a few years later and their son Daniel became a sniper in the elite Tank Scout Unit. He has served on missions guarding the Jewish settlements in the *shtachim* (West Bank and Gaza). He and his commanding officer are generally at the front of the group while the soldiers at the rear are instructed to scout the rooftops for possible terrorist attacks. One Friday night they were assigned the task of patrolling the area and keeping guard. With the recent hostility in the vicinity, it was a dangerous assignment.

Yehudis had recently suffered from some lower-back pain. She had gone to specialists but the discomfort had persisted. Friday night she twisted and turned in bed but could not fall asleep. Though she was tired, the pain in her back would not allow her to sleep. Finally, at 3:30 in the morning, she got up and went downstairs to recite a few chapters of *Tehillim*. She had always found comfort in the words of David HaMelech.

She sat down on the couch, began to daven and was overcome with emotion. Her thoughts drifted to her children — somehow she had a very strong feeling that they were in peril. After davening for a while she started to feel drowsy and with the pain in her back subsiding she went back to sleep. The rest of Shabbos passed uneventfully and comfortably.

Immediately after Shabbos the phone rang. Moshe answered. It was Daniel.

"*Abba*, I have to speak with you." Normally Daniel asked to speak to his mother first but he seemed to have something urgent to share with his father. He whispered quietly "*Abba*, I almost died Friday night."

"Is everything all right? What happened?" Moshe's heart was beating wildly and he dreaded to hear what was coming next.

"Well, I was on *shemirah* together with the rest of my unit when the quiet of the night was broken with a distinctive 'klink' at my feet. I looked down and saw that a grenade lay unexploded next to my feet. A second later another one fell and this time it was sparking. Although it was too late to do anything, we screamed and ran for cover. We waited for an explosion but nothing happened. We continued to wait for a while and then carefully walked back toward the grenades and defused them."

Realizing that most often these stories are told after soldiers have been killed, and not by those who have survived, Moshe whispered a silent prayer of thanks to the A-mighty and informed his son that he should recite *Bircas HaGomel*. Almost as an afterthought Moshe asked Daniel when this incident had taken place. Daniel paused for a moment and answered, "It was 3:30 in the morning, why do you ask?"

Recognizing the *hashgachah* and power of a mother's *tefillos,* Moshe told Daniel about how his mother had said *Tehillim* in the middle of the night. Yehudis, regaining her composure, picked up the phone and Daniel managed to mutter the words, "Thank you, *Imma,* for saving my life."

Tehillim and Tumults

THERE'S NOTHING LIKE IT. IT'S TRULY A "TUMULT." Without any prearrangements or plans, over 2,000 *bochurim* and *yungerleit* gather together in Lakewood's Beth Medrash Govoha on the first day of the *z'man* to decide who will learn with whom. No words can describe the feeling, the rush and the commotion. There is a sense of urgency in the air, for it is imperative that each young man find a good *chavrusa*. A good *chavrusa* is vital to having a good *z'man* of learning; hence, the success of your entire *z'man* hinges on that one day.

A constant tension fills the air. It is almost like a *shidduch*. Each student needs to find a *chavrusa* with whom he will be compatible — and compatibility means something different to each young man. Some want to serve in a mentor capacity, some look for a *chavrusa* who is on a higher level — someone to learn from. Everyone has his own theories about what is best. It is therefore a difficult and tense day. And so, often, a *chavrusa* partnership was formed only to end after a few weeks, with each individual then searching for a new partner.

One *yungerman*, Yosef Goldstein, who had been learning in the yeshivah for a number of years, was somewhat of an enigma. Yosef hadn't endured what others had — entering into a *chavrusa*, finding it doesn't work, looking for another, and on and on until the right match is found. Yosef was very fortunate. He always seemed to find *chavrusos* with the best *bochurim* and *yungerleit*. He enjoyed learning with those on a higher level because he himself was not too advanced in his learning, but it was still a wonder why Yosef, not one of the yeshiva's "stars," found the best *chavrusos* with whom to learn.

One day, Shimshi Braun decided to follow Yosef around on the morning of the *chavrusa* tumult. Shimshi had found great *chavrusos* for himself, but wondered if he could be doing something differently, and wanted to learn Yosef's secret. He watched from a distance for an hour or so and observed Yosef approaching a few fellows who were his age but clearly much better than he was in learning. He looked for something unusual but didn't find it. He wondered if perhaps Yosef would send someone else over to speak on his behalf but again noticed nothing of the sort. Finally, Yosef walked downstairs and slipped into a phone booth. Passing by, Shimshi could not help but overhear the conversation.

"Hello, Ma?"

"Yes, hello, Yosef."

"Ma, you can stop saying *Tehillim*. The *chavrusa* I wanted to learn with agreed to learn with me."

Shimshi smiled and understood that the power of a *Yiddishe mama's* "*Tehillim un treren*" (Psalms and tears) can never be underestimated.

The Mysterious Letter

Reb Shabsi Yudelevitch zt"l related this amazing true incident. It delivers a poignant message about the sincerity of tefillah and what one can achieve through it.

EIGHT-YEAR-OLD JUAN DIEGO PEERED OUT OF THE WINDOW of the small Peruvian village's orphanage where he lived and saw a beautiful scene. A family of four, impeccably dressed, were strolling down the road. Mother, father, son and daughter walked together as a family, something Juan had never experienced. Orphaned as a young boy, Juan had never known his parents nor his siblings. The only life he had known was the one he had now. The empty cold rooms felt more like a hospital than a home for children. Toys were minimal and in poor condition. The food, though nutritious, was bland. Sometimes Juan thought that the missing ingredient was the T.L.C. he longed for.

The harsh voice of the guardian ordering the children to complete their chores snapped Juan out of his reverie. He caught one last glimpse of his dream family and ran to finish his household tasks. Today he had been assigned to wash the kitchen floor and he hoped it wouldn't take too long.

An hour and a half later Juan returned to his room, completely exhausted. He staggered through the door, collapsed onto his bed and fell into a deep sleep. In his dream he imagined himself living in a posh palace surrounded by servants and, more importantly, by family — a mother with warm eyes and a gentle smile and a father who playfully wrestled with his children. Juan envisioned himself as part of this family.

"Come on, children, it's time to get up!" The shouting jolted Juan back to reality. The familiar pain in his heart had been growing and deepening over the past months, and he made a promise to himself to do whatever he could to actualize his dream.

The postal worker looked at the peculiar letter and placed it on the table to get a better look at it. He had never seen anything like it before. The letter was addressed to "G-d." No return address and no name. The simple solution would have been to open the letter; however, the time-honored custom in Peru was never to open someone else's letter. Some pointed to superstitions, others to tribal curses that had been placed on the one who violates the custom. Regardless, now he was in a quandary as to what do with the letter.

Having brought the mysterious letter to each of their respective supervisors, the postmen had no idea what the next step should be. The unusual envelope had caused quite a stir in the media and it caught the attention of several government officials. After weeks of being shuttled from office to office in the Peruvian government, the letter landed on the desk of the prime minister himself.

Prime Minister Espinoza brought the envelope into his private chamber, grasped his elegant silver letter-opener and gently sliced open the small crumpled envelope. Out fell a note written in large lettering. He put on his reading glasses and began to read:

> *Dear G-d,*
> *My name is Juan Diego but I'm sure You know that because You know everything. I'm 9 years old and live in an orphanage. I miss my mother and father and really want a family very badly. Please help me. You're the only one Who can.*
>
> *Your son,*
> *Juan*

The prime minister wiped away the tears from his eyes. Those who really knew him realized he was a compassionate man. He emerged from his office and immediately met with his advisers in order to decide what to do.

He discussed the matter with his wife as well, and they decided to meet Juan. An intense investigation began and every orphanage in Peru was searched. Finally the authorities located the young orphan and brought him by limousine to the presidential palace. His charming personality won the hearts of the Espinozas and to the amazement of all, they took a bold and wonderful step — they adopted him. Juan's dreams had become a reality.

Reb Shabsi, in his deep, raspy voice, concluded this incredible story with a powerful thought. It says in the *pasuk*, "*Karov Hashem lechol korav* — Hashem is close to all those who call Him," but He endears Himself especially to "*lechol asher yikra'uhu* — all those who call out to Him," Reb Shabsi repeated, then looked up and smiled, "*be'emes* — sincerely!"

> *If you call out to Hashem sincerely, like a hopeless child who desperately needs His help, then He will endear Himself to you and answer your cries!*

A First Time for Everything

The following story is especially dear to me as I was personally involved in this unusually beautiful series of events. It is not a miraculous episode, though it sends us a powerful message in a subtle manner.

THE NIGHT HAD GONE WELL. SHAVUOS NIGHT CAN BE quite difficult and arrangements sometimes complicated, with so many boys learning. But the learning in Yeshivas Chofetz Chaim Talmudical Academy of Baltimore this particular year was filled with energy. Excluding several coffee breaks, the *bochurim* had exhausted themselves for the last six hours by toiling in learning. Unfortunately, after the night-long intense learning, sometimes the Shavuos morning davening does not hold the energy that it should. Some are trying to fend off the urge to sleep, and others simply submit and catch a quick catnap. This time, the davening concluded uneventfully and the crowd dispersed to their homes and beds for a well-deserved morning of sleep.

I myself was happy to crawl into bed after a beautiful night of learning with the students. My wife tried as hard as she could to keep the house quiet, but I ended up waking a bit early from my sleep, and was a bit groggy as she told me that we would be entertaining company for the *seudah*: two T.A. boys would be joining us for the meal.

At 12:30 the young men arrived and sat down politely on the couch as we waited for the preparations for the meal to be completed. I sat down next to the boys and we spoke about the previous night of learning, the excitement still palpable. Nathaniel Persky, a sweet recent newcomer to the yeshivah, graciously offered to help in the kitchen although the meal was now ready to begin.

The delicious dairy feast of sweet-and-sour salmon and gourmet lasagna was complemented with home-made butter croissants, rare dairy treats for a Yom Tov meal. The sweet sounds of

Torah and song infused the *seudah* as the enjoyable meal began winding down. *Mayim acharonim* was passed around the table and I motioned to Nathaniel to lead us in the *bentching*. Looking at me, he hesitated, and responded by regretfully declining the honor, explaining that he was uncomfortable leading the *bentching* as he had never done it before. I told him that I would help him along and encouraged him to give it a try.

Nathaniel smiled, shrugged his shoulders, and agreed to give it a go. "You know, it's ironic that I'm doing this for the first time because today was also the first time that I've ever said all the words in davening."

Could it really be? I knew that due to his weak background Nathaniel had trouble reading. But to never have *davened* all the words before? I was surprised and admired his determination. Nathaniel announced, *"R-a-b-o-s-a-i N-e-v-a-r-e-i-c-h,"* slowly pronouncing every letter, stumbling over some, mispronouncing others.

Those present replied with the appropriate response of *"Yehi shem Hashem mevorach ..."* Word by word, Nathaniel plodded through the entire *Bircas HaMazon*. It took him much longer than the rest of us, his *kavanah* evident to all. When he finally finished, he looked up triumphantly, kissed his *bentcher* and thanked my wife for the delicious meal.

I could hardly wait to tell the other rebbeim in yeshivah about Nat's accomplishment. Before Minchah I approached Rabbi Shraga Hershkovitz, the *mashgiach*, to share the story with him as I knew he would be particularly proud of Nat.

After relating the entire episode I asked Rabbi Hershkovitz if he had observed Nat's davening this morning. He responded that he had not only had the privilege of watching him during davening but afterward as well. I was slightly confused. What could have happened after davening that would be noteworthy? I knew that the rest of us had hurried off to sleep, and I wondered aloud what Nat had been busy with.

"Would you believe that although the *tzibbur* had concluded the davening at 7 o'clock, Nat remained here afterward for over an hour, diligently fighting to pronounce every single word of davening?!" Rabbi Hershkovitz declared emphatically. I was amazed.

Merely saying all the words was quite an accomplishment on a Shavuos morning when most people are focused on their sleep. But to utter them with such concentration when one can barely read was astounding and very inspiring. I could not help but think back to my own davening that morning and was overcome with feelings of shame and humility.

"If you think that is amazing, I have to tell you something. Nat asked me a *she'eilah* after davening," Reb Shraga continued. "He asked me, 'Rebbi, do I need to recite a *Shehecheyanu*?' So I asked him why he thought that he had to. He looked at me with such a shy expression, but so full of pride. 'Rebbi,' he said, 'today I davened the whole davening for the first time.' " Reb Shraga looked at me with tears in his eyes, but a huge smile on his face.

Babies and Bubble Gum

THE TAXI PULLED UP QUIETLY AND ONE BY ONE, STOP BY stop, the women piled into the vehicle. They were only the first group to arrive. There would be more. Twenty-one women in all. They came as their children and the rest of Yerushalayim slept. Some came with kerchiefs covering their hair, some in snoods. Others had put on *sheitels*, as they were going to visit the hallowed ground where so many before had come to pray, the Western Wall, the Kosel Maaravi. They came from Ramot, Mattersdorf, Har Nof and Bayit Vegan. Some were already in their mid- to late-40's while others were in their late 20's. But they all came for one purpose: to answer Amen at the Kosel Maaravi.

Standing in line at the local supermarket, Ruchi Goldfarb felt very uncomfortable. As the other mothers, both in front and in back of her, explained to their children why they couldn't have the chocolate and bubble gum that they wanted, she was piling the same types of items on the counter.

"So I guess someone in your family is having a big birthday party." The woman did not know Ruchi Goldfarb and she clearly did not intend to hurt her, yet the words stung because not only was it not her child's birthday, she didn't even have her own child. Many nights she had soaked her pillow with heartfelt tears begging the A-mighty for a child. But she had been married for seventeen long years and remained childless.

Last Shabbos, her husband Boruch had come home earlier than usual from yeshivah and had found her crying on the couch. She had tried her best to conceal her emotions and pain, but today she had been "caught." She apologized for losing control and Boruch, feeling terrible for her, suggested that they go again for a *berachah*. He set off to visit Reb Ahron Karliner, the Stoliner Rebbe.

Boruch waited patiently to see the Rebbe, and after a few moments he was escorted in. The Rebbe greeted him warmly, and listened to Boruch's recounting of the entire ordeal: the visits to specialists and the frustration and pain they felt as a couple. A compassionate man, Reb Ahron enumerated the *zechus* of an "Amen" and "*Amen yehei shmei rabba.*" He then suggested an unusual proposal. If one "*yehei shmei rabba*" can destroy an evil decree, then just imagine what many of them can do. Boruch looked at the Rebbe with a puzzled expression. He did not understand what the Rebbe was driving at.

The Rebbe took Boruch's hands into his own and told him that there is nothing more precious to the A-mighty than the sounds of Amen from little children. He then told him to prepare little packages of candy and any child who would answer Amen loudly would be given one after davening.

And so Ruchi stood in line together with all the other mothers waiting to buy her candy. After all, what was the cost of a few candies compared to the value of an extra Amen? Ruchi took the bag home and emptied the contents on the table. The jellybeans and peppermint candies mixed with licorice and chocolate rumballs. With tears in her eyes she picked up two or three of each type of candy and filled the little paper bags. It took her almost an hour to make all thirty bags.

That Erev Shabbos, Boruch, who had spoken to the Rav beforehand, walked into shul with a huge bag of candy and a few extra pieces just in case. Little notes had been distributed to the children in the neighborhood informing them of the exciting new development in shul. Many children came early to ensure that they would be included in the prize for answering Amen loudly.

The *chazzan* began to say the first *Kaddish* and the congregation erupted in an *Amen yehei shmei rabba* ... The adults seemed to have been inspired by the children's excitement. The rest of *Kabbalas Shabbos* took on a life of its own. The singing of *Lechah Dodi* was even more beautiful than usual. And at the end of Maariv the eager children all lined up to receive their rewards. Boruch put his hand into his bag and pulled out package after package filled with candy. He left the shul that Friday night beaming and described the entire scene to his wife who was hopefully optimistic though somewhat skeptical. Could a few children's Amens really make a difference?

One year later the Stoliner Rebbe was invited to be the *sandek* by the Goldfarb boy's *bris*. After the *bris* someone asked Boruch which particular *zechus* he felt had brought about this miracle of a child. When Boruch answered that he thought it was the Amen, it was suggested that he lend the *zechus* to someone else. And so the chain began.

From one childless family to the next, the sacred custom of bubble gum and candies was passed around. And as each of these women wished to express her thanks in some lasting way, they created a special group which goes to the Kosel before dawn, before their precious children arise to start their day, to answer Amen to each other's *berachos*. The group has now reached twenty-one.

The glorious rays of the sun begin to rise above those ancient stones. It is almost time for these mothers to go home, as their children will soon wake up and will need to be cared for. The last one of this small group of women finishes reciting the last *berachah* of *Birchos HaShachar* and the rest of the group all answer in unison: Amen.

Torah

Hunger Pains

The Ponovezher Rav would often point out that in bentching the words, "al Torascha shelimadtanu" (for the Torah which You taught us), are placed before the phrase, "ve'al chaim chen vachesed shechonantanu"(and for the life, grace and kindness which You granted us), because without Torah what "life" is there?

WHEN THE ENTIRE NOVARDIK YESHIVAH WAS PLACED behind prison bars by the Communist government the intent was to prevent them from learning Torah and serving G-d. Religion was frowned upon, especially the intense observance found among the young men in the Novardik Yeshivah.

The prison guards attempted to weaken the resolve of the students by depriving them of basic physical needs. They were served only enough food to barely stay alive and they were constantly damp and cold due to the stone walls and floors of the prison cells. They had neither coats nor blankets and the temperature was usually well below freezing. But what pained them more than anything else was that they were robbed of their most prized possessions: their Gemaras.

The boys' families were allowed to bring food packages, and one of the young men came up with a clever plan. At the time of their arrest, the yeshivah students had been learning *Maseches Makkos*, one of the shorter tractates. The entire *mesechta* was only twenty-two pages long. The "prisoners" sent word to their families that they needed packages of cheese: twenty–two packages to be exact, each wrapped in another page of Gemara. In this way they would able to smuggle in the entire *mesechta* and share the Gemara. The unwary guards never suspected a thing and before long the young men from Novardik had their entire *mesechta*.

> *The question arose as to how they were allowed to disgrace the pages of Gemara by using them as wrapping paper for cheese if the halachah clearly states that the honor of Torah is even more important than Torah itself. Rav Eliezer Rabinovitch, the Rav of Minsk, answered that not learning Torah for these boys was a matter of life and death and for matters of life and death it is permissible.*

> *Perhaps the following story will help us to understand why these bochurim learned with such self-sacrifice and resolve. It was their Roshei Yeshivah who were role models and provided the inspiration.*

Reb Chaim Efraim Zaitchik, the Novardik Rosh Yeshivah, had been exiled to a Soviet labor camp in Siberia for the "atrocity" of learning and teaching Torah. The food rations were sparse and the hunger pains which gnawed at the men were a constant reality. The water which they drank was brought from a spring located three kilometers away in a thick forest. Carrying the water was a thankless job as the pails were heavy and the path treacherous. But one day Reb Chaim volunteered for the position of water-carrier. Why? Because he had heard that there was a village at the other end of the forest where there might be another Jew.

He made his way through the forest and after a few hours reached the spring, put down his pails and trekked to find the village. Seeing a clearing in the distance he made his way to the small town. Searching door to door, Reb Chaim was thrilled to finally find a little hut that had a *mezuzah* on the doorway. He knocked softly and the door was opened a small crack by a poor middle-aged woman who obviously did not have much extra food in her home. Nevertheless, she slipped an extra slice of bread through the small crack and sent Reb Chaim away.

But Reb Chaim persisted. "It is not food that I want. Please just give me a *sefer* to learn from." The woman called her husband to the door and he greeted Reb Chaim. "I'm sorry but I'm not a very learned man. I own only one *sefer* and I'm not about to part with it."

Reb Chaim pleaded with him, "Please just give me a page of the *sefer*. I'll take any page, even the opening page. I beg you. I'm starving for learning. Don't send me away with nothing!" The sincerity in Reb Chaim's pleas moved the poor villager and finally he brought the *sefer*.

"I'll tell you the truth. The *sefer* is a Gemara, with two *mesechtos* in one, *Nedarim* and *Nazir*. I'll give you one." Reb Chaim tore the volume in two and gave Reb Chaim *Maseches Nedarim*. He hid it under his clothing and thanked the man profusely for his priceless gift.

Returning back to camp with the buckets of water, Reb Chaim's body was sore and his bones ached. But the smile on his face would not go away because as he held onto his Gemara he knew that he had acquired something much more valuable than anything else in the world.

> *"Lo raav lalechem velo tzama lamayim ki im lishmoa es divrei Hashem! We did not hunger for bread nor thirst for water — but only to hear the Word of G-d."*

The Holy Sweater

Kavod HaTorah is easily defined. It means the honor one bestows upon the Torah and those who learn it. And most often one imagines this as a public display by those who wish to show their honor openly. However, there are times when the subtlety of the moment helps convey that message in a more significant manner. It is not always the hoopla and attention that best characterize kavod HaTorah.

RAV FORSHLAGER IS NOT A WELL-KNOWN FIGURE IN THE Torah world, though he should be. A brilliant *Poilishe gaon* whose *sefarim* exude unusual knowledge in every facet of Torah, his genius in learning was matched only by his relentless and indefatigable *hasmadah*. When Rav Ruderman *zt"l* first came to Baltimore, the city where he would establish Yeshivas Ner Yisroel, he stayed in Rav Forshlager's home. However, after a few weeks he moved into another residence. When asked why, he explained that the schedule of learning which his host had kept was so extreme that it had worn him down and he was no longer able to continue in such a fashion. Rav Forshlager would sleep sometimes less than three hours, waking as early as 3 o'clock in the morning to learn. Rav Ruderman would wake up then as well to learn with him but found it too difficult to maintain the schedule. Such was Rav Forshlager's level of *hasmadah*.

Once Ner Yisroel was established, Rav Ruderman would send students on Friday afternoon to "talk in learning" with the *Poilishe gaon*. On one occasion Moshe Lefkovitz and a friend were chosen to go. When they walked into the old, sparsely furnished apartment they immediately took note of the obvious poverty in which this Torah scholar lived. Whatever furniture there was in the house was chipped and broken. The paint was peeling and the floor covering was faded and worn. But perhaps what was most notable was the sweater that this man wore. The fabric was discolored and worn out, filled with holes. It was amazing that the sweater stayed together. Never had they seen anything like it before. But they did notice that the entire apartment was geared toward one purpose — the learning of Torah. Rav Forshlager welcomed his young guests and sat them down by the dining-room table which was piled high with *sefarim,* some open and piled on top of each other, while others were piled in a way which indicated they had been recently used.

Before they began to learn he excused himself, left the room and then a moment later he returned. Curiously he had changed his sweater into one that was slightly less torn and discolored, but still by no means luxurious. Though Moshe noticed the change he dared not mention it. But Rav Forshlager himself brought up the subject.

"I would like to explain to you young gentlemen why I just changed my sweater. You see, I own two sweaters — one for the weekdays and one for Shabbos. Before you walked in I had been wearing the weekday one. But when I saw that I would be speaking to two fine young Torah scholars like yourselves I felt it was important and the proper *kavod HaTorah* to change into the nicer sweater."

Rav Moshe Lefkovitz, now a great-grandfather many times over, looks back on the incident and relays the message that Rav Forshlager imparted to him and his friend that Friday afternoon. When one learns Torah, he becomes important. Whether he is an aged scholar with Shas and poskim in the palm of his hand or a young yeshivah boy beginning his journey into the world of Torah, the honor of Torah and those who learn it must be guarded and kept forever.

Shortcuts and Shtieging

NESTLED AWAY FROM THE REST OF THE WORLD IS the Meah Shearim section of Yerushalayim. If one weaves his way through its alleyways he will discover that right near the Meah Shearim *shtieblach* lives one of the greatest Torah giants of our generation, Rav Elyashiv. He is a man to whom the entire Torah world looks for advice and guidance on personal, communal and worldly issues. Whatever the topic, he guides countless people who turn to him in times of need.

His sons-in-law are well-known Torah giants and personalities as well, and have also assumed leadership roles in guiding those who come to them for advice. One of them is Rav Chaim Kanievsky, and another, Rav Yitzchok Zilberstein, is the Rav and *posek* of Ramat Elchanan, a growing community in Eretz Yisrael.

Last year, one of Rav Chaim's grandchildren had a baby boy, the first great-grandchild for Reb Chaim and the first great-great-grandchild for Reb Elyashiv. Immediately after the child was born, the parents who live in Bnei Brak, called up their great-grandfather Reb Elyashiv to wish him a "mazal tov" and inform him about the *bris* which would be G-d willing in one week.

Reb Elyashiv was overjoyed at the news of becoming a great-great-grandfather but when he was asked to be *sandek* at the *bris* he politely refused. The surprised great-grandchildren seemed bewildered, but they assumed that Rav Elyashiv probably did not want to commit to something that was a week away.

Another week passed and it was the night before the *bris*. Once again the great-grandchildren called their grandfather to ask him if he would accept the honor of being *sandek* at their child's *bris*. But this time the offer had an added incentive. Someone had notified the young couple that being a *sandek* at one's great-great-grandchild's *bris* carried with it an added benefit — that one can automatically secure for himself a direct ticket to *Olam Haba*.

Rav Elyashiv thanked them for their kind offer but again he refused. Without pursuing the issue any further they wished him a mazal tov and said good-bye.

With a smile on his face, Rav Elyashiv explained, "I'm an old man and I don't have the strength I used to. For me to have traveled to Bnei Brak and back would have tired me out for the day and I would not have learned so well. I've been learning Torah my entire life to get to *Olam Haba* and I'm not interested in taking any shortcuts."

Just a Piece of Paper

*I*T'S JUST A PIECE OF PAPER. A SMALL SCRAP OF PAPER THAT was found after the war and made its way into a museum as a relic of a nation's history. But the story behind this piece of paper is perhaps the key to survival of the Jewish people.

It was found in a bunker in the Warsaw ghetto. The message that the paper carries with it reveals why it was saved against such horrific odds. A group of people had been hiding in a bunker of the ghetto for weeks. The food supply was scarce. The only thing they had in abundance was fear. The knowledge that at any moment they could be discovered and immediately shot was a fact they lived with at all times. And yet they persevered.

The greatest proof of that perseverance is the scrap of paper found in the bunker. It is not an ethical will nor is it a letter to be delivered in the event of their death. But perhaps that is what was so special about it.

The paper contained the sentence: *Ashrei yoshvei veisecha od yehallelucha selah*. Underneath that phrase were the letters *aleph, shin, reish* and *yud*, together with the *nekudos* that accompanied them. This scrap of paper was a lesson in *aleph-beis*. Hiding in a cold, wet bunker, fearing for his life every second of the day, a father wrote these words in order to teach his child the *aleph-beis*. Life, learning and Torah went on even in these impossible conditions. With the sounds of machine-gun fire in the background drowning out the voices of the anonymous father and son, the torch of *mesorah* was being passed from one generation to the next. We do not know who they were nor do we know from where they came. We don't know if they lived or were killed with millions of others just like them. But one thing we do know — that they touched eternity. Amidst the fires and inferno that surrounded them, this father and child escaped to a world where they became invincible, where nothing could touch them or hurt them — a world of Torah that will exist forever.

The Strongest Rock in the World

AFTER THE WAR IN 1967, TENSIONS RAN HIGH IN ERETZ Yisrael. Many had lost children in battle and were furious over the fact that only their sons had to risk their lives while the young men in yeshivah continued learning in the security and safety of their study halls. At times, when the yeshivah boys boarded buses they would be subjected to jeering and shouting from passengers who were bitter about the situation.

The issue came to a head and the Israeli cabinet decided to address it with a debate. Many feared that although Prime Minister David Ben-Gurion had initially established the rule that yeshivah boys need not serve in the army, that edict had run its course and change was inevitable. Heated discussions escalated both in and out of the Israeli political world. It became the water-cooler conversation of the moment.

The *gedolim* issued statements regarding an increase in *tefillah* (prayer) to help prevent the law from changing. Perhaps what was most nerve racking was the overwhelming desire among those who wielded power in the government to once and for all force the young men in yeshivah to serve.

However, the famous general Moshe Dayan took up the cause for the yeshivah boys and his considerable political influence carried the day. The proposal for change was rejected and the situation remained status quo. The irony of Moshe Dayan defending the right's position was in itself a small miracle, and the Roshei Yeshivah and *gedolim* wanted to personally express their thanks and appreciation to General Dayan.

Rav Hutner, Rosh Yeshivah of Yeshivas Rabbeinu Chaim Berlin, arranged to meet with Dayan and express the gratitude of the Torah world. In conversation with the famous general, Rav Hutner could not help but wonder what had caused him to back the cause of the yeshivah *bochurim*. Dayan was a left-wing secular Israeli and here he was defending everything that seemed to be diametrically opposed to his way of thinking.

Dayan received the Rosh Yeshivah warmly and smiled when he was asked the obvious question. He explained, "I grew up in a home where breakfast and lunch were served on Yom Kippur as though it were a regular day. Yet one day in high school our class was assigned a project: to recite a poem by Bialik. I chose the poem entitled *Hamatmid*. It speaks of the power of a child who learns Torah. '*Mi atah shamir umi atah chalamish laamod lifnei naar haosek baTorah* — Who are you, emery stone, and who are you, flint stone, to stand in front of a child who learns Torah?' "

Dayan turned to Rav Hutner and smiled. "If Torah is the rock that has allowed the Jewish people to persevere over the last 2,000 years, then who am I to shatter it?!"

Rav Hutner was amazed that even a nonbelieving poet and a secular leftist general had understood what the power of Torah can achieve. How much more so must we guard our responsibility of learning the Torah with which we have been entrusted.

Accusations and Incriminations

REB YITZCHOK SHMUEL ELIYAHU FINKLER, THE REBBE OF Radoshitz, led the people of his hometown Pietrokov in continuing their observance of Torah and mitzvos in the face of the Nazi persecution which engulfed their lives. Many people from miles around came to the Rebbe for advice and direction in this period of darkness. Some risked their lives to meet with the Rebbe one last time to discuss what they should do with their families and how they should respond to the ongoing threats of attack.

Even after the Jews of all the surrounding areas were crammed into the ghettos many Jews flocked to the Radoshitzer for comfort and hope. The Rebbe would always soothe the spirits of those who came to him and reassure them with encouragement, strength and words of inspiration. Somehow they would all leave feeling better although on the surface nothing seemed to have changed. But the Rebbe's perspective always made things seem a bit brighter.

Even after the Rebbe had been deported to Scarszysko, a forced-labor camp, he continued to infuse those who were in contact with him with an undying sense of hope that things would soon be better. His uncanny ability to lead the people who surrounded him is what made him so unique. Many of the inmates who had recently been transferred there wondered if the change was for the better. And even if it was not, the Rebbe would always be able to assuage their fears.

As was common practice in all of the concentration camps, as soon as people arrived they were stripped of all their belongings, and especially their religious articles: *tallis, tefillin* and any *sefarim* they had brought. Not a volume of Talmud was to be found until the day the Rebbe arrived. He had smuggled in with him a half-torn Gemara *Bechoros*. They could not believe it but there it was. Many had thought they would never see a Gemara again for the rest of their lives. Every day, after 14 hours of backbreaking labor, the men would gather around him and he would give them a *shiur*.

The Rebbe's amazing expertise in Gemara allowed him to enlarge upon the *sugya* being studied and to quote verbatim other passages from *Shas*. The inmates, worn and weary from an exhausting day and lack of nourishment, would look forward to the *shiur* every day with excitement and enthusiasm. They knew that if they were ever caught with the Gemara they could be killed instantly. But that did not deter them from risking their lives to learn the sacred words of Torah from their revered Rebbe. The Rebbe had ignited a spark of life in these near-dead souls as he taught Torah to them in the midst of the horror and torture.

One day as the Rebbe sat down to give the *shiur*, the door burst open and the kapo stood before them with the commandant. As the Rebbe looked up he stared at the commandant. "*Der Yid lernt aleh mol Torah!* — The Jew learns Torah all the time!" the kapo screamed in an accusatory manner, but at the very same time the Rebbe realized that he had discovered the reason and purpose for our nation's existence.

The commandant asked the Rebbe if the accusations were true. The Rebbe proudly responded that they were. Every day they gathered together to learn. There was no denying the truth.

"Then we will never defeat you!" And just like that the man who was responsible for the deaths of so many turned and walked out. They all looked at each other and silently thanked Hashem for the miracle that had just occurred. And as if nothing had happened, the Rebbe continued the *shiur* where he had left off.

Happy Birthday

THE ROSH YESHIVAH MENTIONED IT ONLY IN PASSING BUT some of the young men in yeshivah decided to act upon it. Rav Meir Shapiro, the founder of the *Daf Yomi* program and the Rosh Yeshivah of Yeshivas Chachmei Lublin, had remarked recently that his birthday was approaching. He had been born on the seventh day of Adar. As the young men gathered around their rebbi, they asked what he would like for his birthday.

Rav Meir thought for a moment as the *bochurim* wondered how he would respond. After all, this was not a common question that one posed to a Rosh Yeshivah. Rav Meir finally answered as he looked at the young man who had asked the question, Chaim Levovitch. He replied that he wanted *Shas*.

Chaim was startled that the Rosh Yeshivah had responded at all. But his response was puzzling. The yeshivah had numerous sets of *Shas*. The Yeshivas Chachmei Lublin was somewhat unique in its magnificence and stately appearance. It had everything a yeshivah needed, including a beautiful *beis medrash* fully stocked with every available *sefer*.

Rav Meir noticed the puzzlement on the faces of his students, turned toward Chaim and smiled. "I want the young men in yeshivah to finish *Shas* for me by my birthday."

All of a sudden, this was no longer a little joke between the Rosh Yeshivah and a few young men. They quickly calculated that there were over 3,000 *blatt* in *Shas* and a little over 300 young men in yeshivah. Each boy would need to learn close to ten *blatt*, a reachable goal but a difficult one to achieve.

A small group was appointed to administer the distribution of pages to the young men. And that evening, by sunset on the sixth day of Adar, the learning began. An intensity stormed through the *beis medrash* unlike any that had been experienced before. They had set a goal for themselves and were determined to achieve it.

The fire of learning spread throughout the *beis medrash* and the large majority of the young men in yeshivah stayed up even later than usual to accomplish the awesome task they had undertaken. Anyone with a difficulty in the material he was learning would ask one of the other boys or one of the rebbeim who had volunteered to join the project. The special learning program continued throughout the night and stopped only temporarily for a recess of davening and a quick meal.

The frenzied pace and thunderous sounds of learning permeated the *beis medrash*. And as the afternoon progressed not an empty seat or a wasted moment could be found. The sight and intensity of the learning was a spectacle to behold. *Lo pasak girsa mipumayhu!* The words of Torah flowed ceaselessly from their mouths!

And then as the sun began to set, Chaim knocked on the door of the Rosh Yeshivah's office and asked him to come into the *beis medrash*. They had a present to give him. Chaim escorted their beloved rebbi into the *beis medrash* and as the Rosh Yeshivah walked through the door he smiled.

A loud bang on the *bimah* brought an immediate halt to the tumultuous din of voices raised in learning; and the group that had arranged the project acknowledged that their colleagues had finished their assignments. "*Rabbosai*, in honor of our rebbi we have successfully completed the entire *Shas* in twenty-four hours. We would like to honor the Rosh Yeshivah with the *hadran*." Rav Meir beamed proudly and, with tears in his eyes, thanked his disciples for the most wonderful birthday present he could have ever received. He then recited, "*Hadran alach Talmud Bavli*...We will return to you once again, Babylonian Talmud ..."

The Very Last One

IN 1941, RAV ELYA MEIR BLOCH AND RAV MUTTEL KATZ, Roshei Yeshivah of Telshe, came to America from war-torn Europe. Together they intended to rebuild the great yeshivah of Telshe, which had been entirely wiped out by the accursed Germans. Both of the Telshe Roshei Yeshivah had been unable to save their families and had lost everything. They came to the city of Cleveland, a city with one of the strongest Reform populations in all of America, and declared that they would rebuild the *Yeshivah HaGedolah VeHaKedoshah DeTelshe*. Very few believed they could.

At that time Rav Mordechai Gifter was a rabbi in Waterbury, Connecticut and was invited by the Telshe Roshei Yeshivah, who happened to be his uncles, to join them in Cleveland to help re-establish the yeshivah. Rav Gifter, a dynamic brilliant *talmid chacham,* was American born and an oustanding orator. He accept-ed the invitation and moved to Cleveland where he became a *maggid shiur* in the yeshivah.

On one of those early days Rav Elya Meir invited Rav Gifter to join him as he purchased a volume of *Ketzos HaChoshen* at a Hebrew bookstore on New York's Lower East Side. They introduced themselves to the elderly storeowner and asked him if he might have a *Ketzos HaChoshen* in stock. He walked to the back of the store and began searching through the stacks of books in storage. There were plenty of "Jewish books," though almost nothing that quite resembled a *sefer*. A few *siddurim* were piled on one of the shelves and assorted Judaica sprinkled throughout. A set of candle-sticks and a plain-looking *challah* cover were lying on top of a few *talleisim*. Otherwise the store was almost bare.

Finally, after searching on one of the bottom shelves, the owner pulled out a large black volume covered in dust. It had been hidden under a pile of *Chumashim* and had probably not seen the light of day since it had first entered the store. The man removed it and wiped off the dust so it would look somewhat respectable, and then handed it over to the Rosh Yeshivah.

But before he relinquished his grasp on the *sefer* he looked Rav Elya Meir in the eye and spoke. "I will sell you this *sefer* on two conditions. Number one, I understand that you lost your entire family in the war and that you intend to rebuild what was lost in Europe. Please listen to me. Don't try it! There is only so much heartache that a man can take. You'll never succeed."

Reb Elya Meir nodded, not agreeing but waiting to hear what the second condition would be. The bookstore owner thought for a moment and continued. "Second, let's be honest, America is not the type of country where Torah will flourish. What we had in Europe is now gone and what Hitler destroyed cannot be rebuilt. So treat this relic as a valuable piece of history because this *sefer* that I'm selling you might quite possibly be the last *Ketzos* that is ever sold in America."

The words stung and pierced through Reb Elya Meir like a dagger. Perhaps a man who had not suffered as he had might have been discouraged, but not one who pledged his entire existence to rebuilding what the fires of the Holocaust had destroyed. He stared at the man and defiantly responded, "My dear friend, the answer to the first question will resolve the second. I appreciate your concern but soon you will see that you are wrong. The Torah that was lost will be rebuilt and the *kedushah* restored. And when that happens you will see that more *Ketzos HaChoshens* will be sold at that time than were sold from the time that the *Ketzos* wrote it until now!"

Reb Elya Meir purchased the sefer and kept true to his word. The Telshe Yeshivah and the many institutions that have blossomed forth from it are a testimony to that fact. The "Etz Chaim," Tree of Life, that was planted by those great men who rebuilt the glory of Torah in America now has many branches. And these branches have given rise to more learning of Gemara, Rashi, Tosafos and — Ketzos!

The Delayed Breakfast

FTER THE PASSING OF HIS WIFE, THE *GADOL HADOR*, Maran Rav Laizer Shach, would be escorted home every day after davening by a young man who would prepare breakfast. The honor was given to a rotation of students who jumped at the opportunity to serve a *talmid chacham* of Rav Shach's stature. The actual work was minimal. The Rosh Yeshivah was not a big eater. Generally he ate an egg with some vegetables and a piece of bread. The job of serving breakfast to the Rosh Yeshivah entailed escorting Rav Shach on his short walk home and then preparing his breakfast while he sat and learned by his table.

Shimon Blackman woke up early that morning. He had never been privileged to spend time with the Rosh Yeshivah before and was thrilled when he was approached to serve his Rosh Yeshivah breakfast. Immediately following davening Shimon walked up to Rav Shach's *shtender* and introduced himself. Since the Rosh Yeshivah had become older he was not familiar with every new boy in the yeshivah. Although Shimon was nervous about the venture he was pleasantly surprised to find that making conversation was very easy. He had to constantly remind himself that he was speaking to the *gadol hador,* as Rav Shach asked him about his family and where he had learned prior to his arrival in Ponovezh.

He held the Rosh Yeshivah's frail hand as they walked slowly out of the yeshivah building and into Rav Shach's apartment. He took his rebbi's coat and hung it up in the closet as Rav Shach sat down and opened a *sefer*. Shimon had been told by the one who had appointed him that normally the Rosh Yeshivah ate one scrambled egg. Shimon excused himself to prepare the small breakfast. It was 8 a.m.

Five minutes later Shimon appeared with a plate of scrambled eggs, a piece of toast and some sliced vegetables. He walked into the dining room where Rav Shach was sitting and placed the plate of food on the table. The Rosh Yeshivah looked up from his *sefer* and asked Shimon what time it was. It was 8:05. Rav Shach told him to take the food back. Surprised, Shimon did as he was told but he was confused. He had been instructed to prepare this exact breakfast and had followed the directions to the tee. Why had the Rosh Yeshivah told him to take it back?

He waited inside the kitchen and five minutes later again reappeared with the food that he had attempted to keep warm. The Rosh Yeshivah asked him once again what time it was and Shimon answered that five minutes had elapsed since he had last tried to serve the breakfast. For a second time Rav Shach apologized but requested that the food be taken away from him. By now Shimon was really bewildered.

This unusual scene repeated itself once more and finally, at 8:20, Shimon appeared for the fourth time and placed the reheated food in front of the Rosh Yeshivah. Rav Shach thanked Shimon for his patience and excused himself to wash. After returning to the table he noticed that Shimon, although too respectful to question outright, waited for an explanation about the delays.

"Let me explain to you what happened. Every morning at 8 a.m. there are one million children in this country who go to schools that teach *kefirah*. Their curriculum is based on blasphemy and is entirely anti-Torah. One million Jewish children! I tried to eat but thinking about that tragedy made it too difficult. And so I kept asking you to return in five minutes. I'm sorry that I troubled you, but how can one eat when he's thinking about so many lost *neshamos*? I know that I have to eat but sometimes it takes me 15 to 20 minutes in the morning to gather up the strength to do so."

Seeing the sensitivity the Rosh Yeshivah had displayed, and the genuine pain he had felt for Jews whom he had never met, gave Shimon a clearer understanding of what it means to be a *nosei be'ol chaveiro* — one who carries the burden of his fellow Jew.

My One and Only Mitzvah

*R*AV BINYAMIN DISKIN WAS A WELL-KNOWN *GADOL* WHO lived in the town of Brisk. A genius in learning, he was known for his punctuality and meticulousness in mitzvah observance.

During the entire year he was careful about which foods he ate, where he walked and to whom he spoke. And this was all the more so prior to the *Yamim Noraim*. The Days of Awe filled the air with trepidation over the uncertainty as to what the new year would bring; the *tefillos* in Brisk took on a new meaning. One was able to sense the apprehension in each and every member of the community and to feel it in Reb Binyamin's *davening* as well. His sincerity and heartfelt tears were matched only by the awe in which he stood in front of his Maker.

One year as the shul filled for *Kol Nidrei* the Rav's seat remained empty. Murmuring began among those who had already assembled: normally, Reb Binyamin was early for this important event. The sun started setting and more and more people filled the room. The entire shul was practically full but still there was no sign of Reb Binyamin. Some questioned if he was feeling well, though that would not have prevented him from coming to daven on *Kol Nidrei* night.

Another 15 minutes went by and by now everyone was whispering, "Where is Reb Binyamin? What could he possibly be occupied with that is more important than davening on Yom Kippur?" At the same time the bizarre situation could not prevent others from wondering if indeed something terrible had happened to their beloved Rav.

Search teams were sent out to cover the town and look for the Rav. They carefully traced the roads and examined every possible alleyway he might have passed through but each possibility they explored produced no results. They finally made their way back to his home and knocked on the door, fearful of what they might find. At first they heard nothing and braced themselves for the worst. But then as they were about to forcefully enter his home, they heard voices inside.

Again they knocked, but this time with a little more force. "Rebbi, are you okay? Is everything all right?"

Suddenly the door opened and before them stood Rav Binyamin attired in his white *kitel*. He looked at them and looked back at the wooden table in his house. At the table sat his son Yehoshua Leib with two large volumes of Talmud opened in front of him. Rav Binyamin had apparently just been learning with his son.

The members of the congregation excused themselves for intruding but mentioned that they were concerned since the hour was late and the Rav had not yet come to shul. Rav Binyamin looked at the dark sky outside. It was long past sunset, the time when *Kol Nidrei* is normally recited. He then looked back at the *baalebatim* and explained. "You know that tonight is Yom Kippur. It is the day when our mitzvos and *aveiros* are weighed. And I began thinking about how I could spend the last moments before this awesome day. There are not many mitzvos that I perform properly but there is one that I know I fulfill correctly, and that is the mitzvah of *veshinantam levanecha* — learning Torah with my son."

The stunned men realized that in fact everything was fine in the Diskin home. The silence lasted for a long moment.

"*Rabbosai*, I beg you. I need all the *zechusim* I can get. Please don't take away the one mitzvah that I do correctly."

Slowly the once anxious *baalebatim* walked back toward the door through which they had entered. What they had witnessed was truly incredible. To Rav Binyamin the one thing that mattered most was learning Torah with his son and he would allow nothing to interrupt him. True, the *kehillah* was waiting, but he was simply unable to pull himself away from what mattered most. A moment passed and a reluctant father closed his Gemara and walked to shul with his beloved son, Yehoshua Leib, who would one day be the Rav of Yerushalayim.

The Happiest Man Alive

HE WAS THE HAPPIEST MAN IN THE WORLD. NO, HE DID not own a large house nor did he possess fancy cars. In fact his home was small, old and dilapidated. His clothing was ragged. His shoes had been stitched up countless times. His jacket was faded and worn. But perhaps most distinctive was this *tzaddik's* hat. It carried pinches in every place it shouldn't have. Washed out and discolored, it was one of a kind. The small brim could not manage to produce even a tiny shadow over his forehead, yet on walked Reb Betzalel Goldstein or, as he was better known, Reb Betzalel Milchiger – the milkman of Shaarei Chesed, Yerushalayim, and the happiest man in the world. Why was he so happy? Because to him material luxury meant nothing. A delicacy was a *shtikel Torah,* a *kasha* or *terutz*, a *rayah* or *upshlug*. These were the treats for which Reb Betzalel longed. All he possessed was Hashem's holy Torah. That was all he had and that was all he needed.

The city where your standard grocer was a *Shas mentch*, the shoemakers *mekubalim* and the water-carriers *lamed vovniks* had a milkman like Reb Betzalel. This was the heavenly city of Yerushalayim.

Legend has it that once a wealthy man passed by Reb Betzalel. The man noticed that Reb Betzalel's hat smelled awful and went to buy him a new one. Reb Betzalel reluctantly accepted the gift and promptly proceeded to make a visit to Hersh Meir the fisherman and dipped the hat in a barrel of pickled-herring brine. When the donor of the hat saw him again, he sniffed the air and looked puzzled. Reb Betzalel then offered the following explanation, "Generally, when I deliver the milk the man of the home is not there. I don't want to see the wife if she's not dressed properly so I make sure that my hat doesn't have the most pleasant aroma. This way when I come to the door the wife keeps her distance and I just leave the milk by the door."

His personal tragedies were kept to himself. Few if any knew of his tragic life. Some had mentioned that he had lost a family in the war. Reb Chaim Shmulevitz, the Mirrer Rosh Yeshivah, with whom he had learned as a *bochur,* met him after the war, took one look, covered his eyes and wept. Perhaps it was the impression that Reb Betzalel gave of being an impoverished beggar, but more likely Reb Chaim cried that a man so deserving of honor was given none because so few were aware of his greatness. Some had said that he was orphaned as a young child. Reb Betzalel's difficulties were to remain his secret forever. He carried them around with him together with his milk cans, more as a badge of pride than the burden they were.

Little else was known about the mysterious figure who seemed to just emerge from the Shaarei Chesed pathways. It was no wonder, as his house was difficult to locate. Nestled deep within the obscure alleyways of Shaarei Chesed was a tiny room containing his *sefarim,* a bed that was rarely used, and a table with a damaged stool that struggled to stand on its own. It was here that the happiest man in the world lived.

And the small community understood when their milk was not delivered. When the children had to wait for their milk, the mothers explained to them that Reb Betzalel Milchiger, the "*illuy* from Bialystok," was lost. Not on a street but in a *Rashba.* He had no doubt met up with Reb Shimon Atik, the other milkman in the community, and they were discussing a "*shvere Tosafos.*" Such was the life of Reb Betzalel Milchiger – the happiest man alive.

During Israel's War of Independence, each evening in the *miklat* of the Gra's shul Reb Binyamin Zev Cheshin would deliver a *shiur* on *Sefer Daniel,* revealing some of the secrets of the Torah. The sounds of exploding bombs a few blocks away were drowned out by the constant hum of Torah learning between Reb Betzalel and his *chavrusa,* Reb Mordechai Shteinovitch. Their excitement and total disregard of the danger surrounding them had a calming effect on the crowd that had gathered there. Such was the type of gift that this poor man gave to all around him.

On all nights, his neighbors fell asleep to the sweet sounds of his learning. It lasted until the wee hours of the morning when Reb Mendel Brunner, who awoke early to say the entire *Tehillim* before davening at *netz,* would hear him at 3:30 in the morning. On the morning of the 28th of Nissan, when Reb Mendel walked to the Gra's shul, a stillness filled the air. The song of Reb Betzalel's learning was missing. Sensing that something was wrong Reb Mendel went to the door of Reb Betzalel's room, knocked a few times and then let himself in. He was shocked to find Reb Betzalel's lifeless body.

The crowd gathered. The grocers, shoemakers and water-carriers of Yerushalayim all came. Mothers brought their children and all cried bitterly and wondered who would now protect the streets of Yerushalayim. And at the end of the long sad day as they escorted him on his final journey, they all said their final good-bye to their milkman, Reb Betzalel Milchiger – the happiest man in all of Yerushalayim. The next morning the mothers cried as they poured the milk for their children, milk that had sometimes come late, or not at all, because the Milchiger was immersed in Torah. Today, the milk had arrived on time.

In the Shadow of the Kremlin

PRIOR TO THE COLLAPSE OF THE IRON CURTAIN, LIVING IN the Soviet Union required survival skills. You knew whom to talk to and whom to ignore; whom you could trust and whom you couldn't. Everyone you met was suspected of being a K.G.B. agent. No one was above suspicion. Agents and spies masqueraded as friendly neighbors.

At this time, the international Jewish community took steps to reach out to their brethren in the USSR. Special *shelichim* visited to bring religious materials and any other assistance they could provide. However, the government imposed strict security measures to prevent the spread of political and religious propaganda, and as a result airport and customs officials confiscated many of the religious materials. *Shelichim* had to be wary of every move they made.

Rabbi Tzvi Bronstein, a renowned *mohel,* had visited Russia nine times before. Each time there he had secretly performed many *brisim,* in addition to smuggling in countless religious items for Jews who needed them. One time, the day after he arrived, Rabbi Levin, the rabbi of the Moscow synagogue, approached him immediately after Shacharis and whispered in his ear that a Jew by the name of Reb Yitzchok Isaac Krauslitzkiev was waiting for him in the hospital. He explained to Rabbi Bronstein that it was urgent that he go there immediately. Reb Tzvi, sensing the necessity, rushed out the door and headed in the direction of the hospital.

Reb Tzvi was familiar with Reb Yitzchok Krauslitzkiev. Although he had met the Torah giant on only a number of previous occasions, his scholarly reputation was well known. He had learned by the great Mirrer Rosh Yeshivah, Reb Eliyahu Baruch Kamai, and he had authored the last-published Hebrew manuscript in Russia — an explanation on the *Rambam.* Since Reb Yitzchok had spent the last forty to fifty years as a "librarian," word had leaked out that he had written a monumental work on *Talmud Yerushalmi,* The Jerusalem Talmud. Reb Yitzchok had served in the Rabbinate of Poltova through the early 1930's but the political environment had forced him and many other rabbanim to abandon their posts. Summoned by Reb Yitzchok, Reb Tzvi viewed it as an honor and privilege to help the *"Gaon* of Poltova."

Entering the hospital, he asked to be directed to Reb Yitzchok's room, explaining that he was a nephew of the 80-year-old patient. Reb Yitzchok shared a room with three other patients who had visitors at the time. Reb Tzvi approached the bed and saw that his older friend was quite weak. His glassy eyes barely opened and his white parched lips moved slowly. Recognizing Reb Tzvi, a small smile formed and he pulled him closer.

"Listen to me carefully." RebYitzchok's words were barely audible yet the urgency in them was evident. "We don't have much time."

Reb Yitzchok's breathing was heavy as he struggled to get out the words. "As you know, many years ago I wrote an explanation on the *Rambam.* The second volume was never published. Place your hand near my forehead as if you are taking my temperature.

Underneath my pillow I have smuggled in a notebook of my *chiddushim*. Instead of placing your hand on my forehead reach behind my head and under my pillow and take the notebook and hide it in your jacket pocket. But be careful that you don't draw any unnecessary attention to yourself. If the authorities are the least bit suspicious they will send you off to a gulag in Siberia."

Reb Tzvi did as he was told and surreptitiously concealed the precious notebook inside his jacket. Reb Yitzchok again summoned the strength to speak, though his voice was barely audible. "Promise me that you will print my writings — and I promise you that you will be greatly rewarded."

"But Rebbi, I don't even know if I'll ever make it out of here safely. How can I promise you that I'll publish your *sefer*?"

"Then at least promise me, if you get out of here, you'll do as I ask."

Reb Tzvi nodded and humbly accepted the awesome responsibility. Reb Yitzchok gasped for air and was visibly struggling for each breath. "One last thing. For the past forty years I have lived in the shadow of the Kremlin and worked as a librarian. I had two rooms. In one room I slept and in the other I wrote. They always thought that I was doing some other work in there but really I was writing a *peirush* on *Yerushalmi*. I knew that at any moment I could be caught and sent off to Siberia. But I felt I had to do it.

"Now, my daughter in Leningrad has the thousands of pages of notes that I wrote. They are safely hidden but I ask you to visit her and publish those as well. Please. I beg you."

Reb Tzvi was entirely overwhelmed by the task he had undertaken, but given no choice he agreed to try to publish the cherished manuscript.

"One last question." Reb Tzvi did not want to trouble this *tzaddik* but he had to know one last thing. "Tell me, why would a disciple of Reb Eliyahu Baruch Kamai and a student of the Lithuanian method of learning spend the last thirty to forty years of his life writing and learning *Talmud Yerushalmi* when the vast majority occupies themselves with *Talmud Bavli*?"

At first Reb Yitzchok's eyes stared off in the distance but then he cleared his throat and bit by bit began to formulate his answer.

"For many years," Reb Yitzchok eyes took on an other-worldly glow and his face seemed to radiate with joy, "I dreamed of reaching the shores of Eretz Yisrael. I tried every method I knew but it was all to no avail. It was obviously not so simple for a Russian Jew to achieve this elusive goal. So instead I resolved to reach Eretz Yisrael the only other way I could — by swimming in the seas of its Torah, the *Talmud Yerushalmi,* where I would learn the *mitzvos hateluyos baAretz* (commandments concerning the Land of Israel). When I started, it was a *Shemittah* year so I began to learn and write *chiddushim* on *Maseches Sheviis.* And by immersing myself in those hallowed waters I finally found myself attached to and inseparable from that beloved land. Once I was there I could never bring myself to leave. And this is why I spent my later years learning and writing about the Torah of *Talmud Yerushalmi.*" Exhausted, he closed his eyes and said good-bye. Reb Tzvi, inspired as never before, wiped away the tears that streamed down Reb Yitzchok's cheeks, bent forward and kissed him on his forehead.

The next morning a small sad *levayah* moved through the cold streets of Moscow. Few knew this great man but Reb Tzvi Bronstein did and as he quietly whispered words of *nechamah* he hoped for the day when the bones of this great man would rise to finally tread on the sacred ground for which he had longed.

*Reb Tzvi fulfilled his promise and published the second
volume of Reb Yitzchok's work on the Rambam. The sefer
"Toldos Yitzchok" on Talmud Yerushalmi was released as
well, and it is in that precious sefer's introduction that
this amazing incident was recorded.*

For Now and Forever

I T WAS JUST AFTER THE END OF WORLD WAR II. HE WALKED in with a dazed look on his face. The explosive sounds of Torah in the Ponovezh beis medrash had surprised him. Searching up and down the rows he looked for a familiar face, though he did not expect to find one. Finally he approached a prestigious-looking individual with a long grayish beard streaked with white and asked him for help.

"Who are you looking for?" the kind man asked, his eyes brimming with warmth.

The bewildered boy, rail thin with jutting cheekbones and eyes set back deep in their sockets, mentioned that he was searching for Rabbi Kahaneman, the Ponovezher Rav.

"I'm Rabbi Kahaneman. How can I help you?" The young man seemed genuinely lost.

"My name is Shloime Reichberger and I would like to come to your yeshivah and learn here. I wasn't sure if I should come here or go to learn in Kfar Chassidim so I figured I would try to come here first and see what happens." The boy spoke clearly yet his thoughts seemed to be focused elsewhere.

The Rav asked him where he had come from and what had brought him here. The young man's response shook the Rav to the core.

"I come from Auschwitz." Shloime spoke as if there had been nothing before and nothing after that dreaded place. The words resounded in the Rav's heart with a deep and utter horror.

Rav Kahaneman now stared at the young man who stood in front of him. He no longer viewed him as a child but instead as an adult. He should have known from his skeletal build that he had come from a concentration camp.

"Do you have any family that survived the war?" Shloime's silence was telling. He obviously had no one. *He* was all that remained. The Rosh Yeshivah's heart cried for this lonely boy.

"Shloime, where did you learn before the war?" Shloime responded that he had studied in a yeshivah in Hungary, but that was four and a half years ago.

"Do you remember which *mesechta* you learned at that time?" The Rav watched with respect and admiration as Shloime closed his eyes and allowed himself, for the first time in many years, to travel back in time and remember the warmth of the yeshivah where he had learned. He heard the sounds of learning and recalled the fire of Torah that had infused the *bochurim* who were now no longer among the living.

"Yes. I remember that we were learning *Maseches Chullin* before we were sent away." Shloime tried to picture the room where his rebbi had given *shiur*. He imagined the rebbi sitting in the front of the room swaying back and forth in front of the *shtender* explaining the *sugya* they had been learning. He envisioned himself asking a question on the *Tosafos* which had just been explained. These images had been all but buried in the deep recesses of his soul and Shloime was proud and a bit shocked that he was able to unearth these memories.

"Can you tell me anything that you remember from the last *sugya* you learned?" This was quite different than the standard entrance examination to gain admittance to the yeshivah. The Rav was hoping that this young man had retained something, anything, from before he went through the Gehinnom of Auschwitz.

Shloime thought long and hard. The furrows of his forehead wrinkled as he struggled to recall a piece of Torah he had learned. Finally he looked up and proudly declared. "The last piece of Gemara we learned was *daf mem ches amud beis* (page 48b) in *Maseches Chullin*. I remember a *machlokes Rashi* and *Tosafos*." Shloime proceeded to tell over what he remembered. Each word he spoke served as a testament to his determination to prevent the flames of Torah from being extinguished.

Rav Kahaneman watched as Shloime spoke, the boy's emaciated face beaming with joy. As he concluded, the Rosh Yeshivah grabbed him and held him tightly. "Shloime! Shloime!"

He placed his arm around the boy's shoulders and ran out the doors of the Ponovezher *beis medrash*. Holding onto the boy's hand, he ran through the streets of Bnei Brak toward the humble home of the *gadol hador*, Rav Avrohom Yeshayah Karelitz, the Chazon Ish. When they arrived at the home the Rav burst through the door and shouted, "Rebbi, *Netzach Yisrael Lo Yeshaker! Klal Yisrael* and the Torah will survive forever! This boy lost everything in the war. He has no mother! He has no father! No sisters or brothers! There is only one thing he has left. Torah! This *bochur* held onto a *machlokes Rashi* and *Tosafos* through the Gehinnom of Auschwitz."

The Rav brought Shloime close to the Chazon Ish and the three of them shed bittersweet tears over all those who had died — and for Hashem's Torah that had survived.

Shomer Yisrael, shemor she'eiris Yisrael ...

For the Sake of a Gadol

*I*T WAS A THURSDAY NIGHT, THE SECOND DAY OF KISLEV, A cold dark December day in 1961 and the void was felt throughout the Jewish world. The venerated Torah giant, HaRav Aharon Kotler *zt"l*, had passed away. That day, Rabbi Amos Bunim, son of Rabbi Irving Bunim, received a call from a few students of Beth Medrash Govoha. They wished to escort the *aron* to Eretz Yisrael and wanted to know if he could help them obtain ten tickets. He told them that he would do what he could and thus began a whirlwind of activity.

El Al was the first airline he called. He explained the situation but his request was met with an abrupt negative response. The only other choice at the time was TWA. Early Friday morning, Amos called them and pleaded for their help. He was transferred from one person to the next and, as the day wore on, his frustration mounted. Left with no choice, since Shabbos was starting so early and time was running out, he hung up the phone in disappointment. All his efforts had seemingly been for naught.

An anxious Shabbos came and went. *Motza'ei Shabbos*, Reb Yaakov Kamenetsky called Amos and told him that he had heard he was trying to arrange tickets for the students to escort Reb Aharon's *aron* to Eretz Yisrael. He relayed that Reb Aharon had refused to fly with El Al during his lifetime because they flew on Shabbos. And thus, without Reb Yaakov knowing that El Al had already refused to cooperate, he mentioned that Reb Aharon's *aron* should not be brought on El Al as it would not befit his honor.

After another series of run-arounds on the telephone, Amos was finally connected to the president of TWA, Thomas Cunningham. Mr. Cunningham was understanding and considerate but explained that his hands were tied. He informed Amos that only one man would be able to help them, Jay Wilson Reed, who was head of TWA's federal aviation division, and when necessary dealt with issues between customers, the F.A.A., and the U.S. State Department. He, and only he, would have the power to override any company policy in case of unusual circumstances. Cunningham told him to call Reed at 8 o'clock Sunday morning.

In the meantime El Al called back. They had received word that *The New York Times* would be writing a piece on the funeral of this great sage and did not want the negative publicity over their refusal to be of assistance. However, Reb Yaakov's earlier phone call had already ensured that El Al was no longer in the picture. Bunim told them that they had lost out on their opportunity and were no longer a viable option. Instead, he notified them, they would be going with TWA. He hoped he was right.

Sunday morning, 8 a.m., finally arrived. Amos picked up the phone and dialed the number of Jay Wilson Reed. He explained to him that a very special individual, a great Torah sage revered by the entire generation, had passed away and his students wanted to honor him one last time by escorting him on his final journey to Israel. Reed listened and sympathized — he was impressed by the dedication and devotion — but explained that the State Department was closed on Sundays. All final decisions would have to be postponed until the next day. Instead, he directed Bunim to inform TWA of their conversation. They would issue him the tickets free of charge and the matter would be resolved between the two of them the next day. He gave his personal phone number in case any problem would arise. Satisfied, Bunim did as he was told and although he would now have to forgo his ticket as one of the ten in order to resolve the matter on Monday, nevertheless he felt proud that he had helped in the Rosh Yeshivah's *kavod acharon*.

In addition, Reed arranged for hangar number 80 to be entirely cleared out so that eulogies could take place there, and he agreed to have only the rabbi's students handle and carry the casket. Ten police cars escorted the crowd to the plane and when they arrived to load the *aron,* an area of the baggage compartment was roped off to ensure that no other cargo be placed on top of the *aron.* Reed ended with one final thought, "Amos, we feel very honored as an airline to have the merit of carrying the remains of this great person on our airplane."

The next day Reed called back and relayed the conversation he had had with the State Department. They expressed hesitation concerning the precedent it would set if they allowed the ten free tickets. Tuesday, Reed rallied several senators to speak on his behalf. However, they were refused as well. The State Department would not budge from its position. Finally an exhausted Reed told Amos that he would be unavailable the next day but they would speak on Thursday.

Amos asked his new friend why he would not be able to contact him on Wednesday as this had been a matter that had occupied most of their time over the past five days.

Reed paused and spoke quietly, "My son is suffering from cancer and is undergoing a very critical operation. The doctor has given me permission to stand by his side during the operation. They don't know if they can remove the growth but we have to try."

Amos comforted Reed and assured him that he would pray along with the students of the yeshivah on behalf of his ill son. He wished him a speedy recovery and promised to have him in his prayers. Reed was moved by Amos' sincerity and thanked him for his wishes.

Thursday morning Amos called Mr. Reed to see how his son's operation had gone and to finally resolve the entire plane ticket matter. Reed answered the phone and began to speak in a reverent tone. "Rabbi, I want you to know that during the operation something happened, something that left the doctors bewildered. The spreading of the cancer had reversed itself. I saw the way they looked at each other. None of them had ever witnessed anything like this. We still have a long way to go but it looks as though my son will G-d willing make a complete recovery."

"Amos," he continued, "make no mistake about it. The two are connected. I know that the only reason my son's life was spared was because of the last respects we showed to this great man. Clearly G-d was repaying me for the efforts we showed." Reed cried as he spoke, having witnessed the Hand of Hashem in a very powerful manner.

Amos was awed by the *kavod HaTorah* he was hearing from this man. After all, he was a gentile. The feelings he had shown and his recognition of the Divine Providence were unlike anything he had witnessed before.

Reed regained his composure, "Amos, if we don't receive permission from the State Department, would you have an objection if we would instead give you a check for charity written out to Beth Medrash Govoha for the entire amount of the checks? They in turn can reimburse you for the tickets." After Amos agreed, Reed informed him that a messenger would deliver a check from Mr. Cunningham, the president of TWA, within an hour.

One hour later, Amos, check in hand, marveled at the *hashgachah* that had led to this incredible honor for the sake of Torah and thanked Hashem for allowing him to be a part of it.

Chesed / Kindness

Angelic Inmates

RABBI ARYEH LEVINE *ZT"L* WAS WELL KNOWN, BOTH IN his homeland Eretz Yisrael and worldwide, for the unbridled love which he displayed to every single Jew. No act of kindness was beneath his dignity; no *chesed* too small. In his eyes a Jew was a Jew, and deserved to be treated like someone special. The tales of his kindness are legend. One such episode occurred, oddly enough, in a prison.

Reb Aryeh had a custom to daven on Shabbos with a group of prisoners. Arriving early Shabbos morning he would spend the next few hours davening with the inmates and sharing with them words of inspiration and Torah. To these disheartened criminals Reb Aryeh's visit was the highlight of the week. Their lives were generally void of spirituality and relatively empty of all meaning. When Reb Aryeh spent time with them, it gave some measure of meaning to their lives. It made them feel special that a rabbi would make such a sacrifice and spend Shabbos with them; it was truly the best day of their week.

On this particular Shabbos Reb Aryeh, as usual, trekked to the prison to daven with his unique group. In the middle of Shacharis a messenger burst into the room where they had been davening. "Rabbi — you must come — immediately!" the man shouted, urgency in his voice. "It's your daughter. Something terrible has happened." The bearer of the unfortunate news could hardly catch his breath as he had obviously run as quickly as possible to relay the information.

Reb Aryeh apologetically excused himself and hurried home.

He walked through the door and was instantly directed to Shaarei Tzedek Hospital where his daughter had been admitted.

Reb Aryeh's wife greeted him at the entrance of the hospital. She detailed the chain of shocking events that transpired that Shabbos morning. She had been preparing the Shabbos meal in the kitchen when she noticed her daughter lying motionless in the adjacent room. Her head was burning hot and she was completely unresponsive. She retold the frightening episode in its entirety, clutching her *Tehillim* and tissues in her still trembling hands. Reb Aryeh calmed her as they were led to their daughter's room.

The child was lying there in a near-comatose state, and the doctors were at a complete loss as to what had happened to her. Around the clock *Tehillim* vigils were organized as word spread throughout Yerushalayim. Heartfelt prayers stormed the gates of Heaven but none seemed to alter her frail condition. Reb Aryeh himself altered his schedule so that he could spend maximum time at his sick daughter's bedside.

A stressful week passed and there was no apparent change in the young girl's condition. Shabbos came and Reb Aryeh decided that although he had not left the hospital for any other reason, he had to be at the prison *minyan*. How could he not? The prisoners waited an entire week for his visit. Leaving instructions as to where he could be found, he set out for the prison.

As soon as he arrived a buzz filtered through the quarters, "Reb Aryeh is here!" They couldn't believe he had come. They were painfully aware of his daughter's sad predicament and were shocked that he had come. Gathering around their Rav they inquired about the little girl's welfare. Reb Aryeh informed them that there had been no apparent improvement over the last week and that the doctors were concerned. *"Hashem yaazor,"* he declared, the inmates witnessing the sincerity and faith in his voice.

The crowd settled down and Shacharis progressed uneventfully. After Shacharis the *chazzan* placed the Torah down on the makeshift *bimah* and prepared to read from the Torah. Uzi, one of the prisoners, had the first *aliyah*. At the conclusion of his *aliyah*, the *gabbai* began reciting the *Mi she'beirach*, pausing to hear the amount which Uzi wished to donate.

Uzi looked around the room. His gaze settled on Reb Aryeh and he wondered if he could somehow use this moment to help alleviate his teacher's suffering. And then it hit him.

"I would like to offer one day of my life to the daughter of the Rav." Reb Aryeh, startled, turned toward the *bimah* to ensure that he had heard *correctly*. "Uzi — but —" Reb Aryeh did not know how to respond. He could not believe what he had just heard. Ignoring his rebbi's protests, Uzi motioned to the *gabbai* to proceed with the remainder of the *Mi she'beirach*.

The next *oleh* took his cue from Uzi and the unusually touching scene repeated itself. The *Levi, shelishi,* and *revi'i* as well presented first weeks and then months from their respective lives to Reb Aryeh's ill daughter. Reb Aryeh was completely overwhelmed by the outpouring of love and sacrifice that these men had exhibited.

Finally, *Maftir* was announced and Dov Tamari, a middle-aged fellow with a tough exterior, strode forward to recite the blessings on the Torah. The portion was read and the group turned around to pay close attention to Dov's *Mi she'beirach*. Most expected him to follow suit and donate another week. Some, however, were skeptical and whispered their reservations to one another.

But Dov shocked everyone with his proclamation. "What is our meaningless life in this prison worth when it is weighed against the pain of Reb Aryeh and his sick daughter? I wish to give over the rest of my life to Reb Aryeh's little girl." Not a week or a month. Not even a year. *The rest of his life!*

Reb Aryeh looked around at these men. Some had made mistakes during their lives, perhaps squandering opportunities given to them. But not today. Today these men achieved more than one could ever imagine. For a short time they did not seem like prisoners, rather they resembled angels. Or maybe, they were simply reciprocating to a special man by giving back a little bit of what they had received.

Reb Aryeh returned to the hospital that day and was greeted by the astonishing news that his daughter had opened her eyes. No one was able to explain the young girl's sudden "miraculous" improvement. No one, that is, except for Reb Aryeh.

Looking for Direction

REB CHAIM OZER GRODZENSKI, ONE OF THE TORAH giants of the previous generation, would customarily walk home with throngs of disciples at his side, thirsting for more of their teacher's great wisdom and insight. Though they had just listened to his intricately woven *shiur* — Reb Chaim's lectures were renowned for both their depth and their wide-ranging scope — the students eagerly hoping for more.

The bitter Vilna cold spared none from its fury. Swirling arctic winds lowered the single-digit temperatures to well below zero. Anyone caught outside in such weather was certain to suffer from the frigid conditions. But Reb Chaim Ozer's dedicated students stood the test of the blustery wind and accompanied their rebbi home each and every day. Nothing seemed to stand in their way, even when he warned them to go inside and stay warm and not to risk becoming ill.

One particularly frigid day, in the course of answering a student's question on the lesson, a young man approached Reb Chaim Ozer and waited to ask him a question. Not recognizing the fellow, the Rosh Yeshivah glanced up and stopped in middle of his thought.

"Yes, young man, how can I help you?" Reb Chaim Ozer, flanked on each side by ten *talmidim*, looked quite intimidating.

The young man, no older than 15, answered, "C—could the R—rosh Yesh—ivah p—please t—tell m—m—me how t—to g—g—get to th—th—this str—street?" It had seemed like an eternity until the question was finally completed. Clearly the boy had a stuttering problem and standing in the presence of this Torah giant had only exacerbated the condition.

"Most certainly," the Rosh Yeshivah replied. And although he was only a block or so from his home, he turned around and began to walk in the opposite direction. Most of the *talmidim* had never even heard of the street the young man had mentioned.

The throng of people moved through the streets of Vilna. Ten minutes had passed and the students looked at each other, wondering where exactly they were heading. In the meantime, Reb Chaim Ozer walked leisurely, holding onto the boy's hand as he engaged him in conversation. Another 10 minutes passed and by now most of the boys had no idea where they were walking.

Finally, after wandering 25 minutes out of their way, through alleyways and obscure streets, Reb Chaim Ozer pointed to the street the boy had requested. "Th—Th—Thank you," he finally stammered and ran off in the direction he had been shown.

The *talmidim,* many of them shivering from the gusty winds that had frozen their fingers and toes, stared blankly ahead, their faced numb from the cold. They were about to begin the harsh trek back to the yeshivah that would take them another 25 minutes. Not only that, but their rebbi, on whose shoulders rested many of the problems of Jewish people from around the world, had "wasted" almost an hour of his time. And for what? Couldn't he have simply told the directions to the young fellow? At the very worst, the boy would have had to ask again if he had lost his way.

The Rosh Yeshivah looked into the eyes of his students and remained silent for a moment. "Do you know who that was?"

They began to wonder if perhaps he was the son of a great Torah scholar or related to one of the supporters of the yeshivah, although none of the boys recognized him.

"That boy had a stuttering problem. He has difficulty speaking and was clearly embarrassed from the question he had asked. Had I just directed him to the obscurely located street across town he would have been forced to ask again for directions and that would have caused him further embarrassment. So as not to bring about further humiliation and discomfort to another Jew I deemed it necessary to take us out of our way and show him precisely where the street was."

The young men then understood that their rebbi had given them one of their most important lessons — how far one must go not to cause shame to another Jew.

The Everlasting Friendship

IT HAD BEEN AWHILE SINCE REFAEL AARON ELAZARY HAD been back in his yeshivah, Yeshivah Beth Moshe in Scranton. His illness had caused him to miss much of the past two years of learning. As a student, he was known for his high level of energy and emotion, which permeated the *beis medrash*. His warm energetic personality had endeared him to his friends and rebbeim alike. There was a special excitement in the air when his friends heard that Refael Aaron would be returning for the unique *Yamim Noraim* davening that the yeshivah was known for.

When Refael Aaron walked through the door, those who had not seen him in a while were shocked. He had lost significant weight and was only a shadow of his former self. Though he was not feeling all that well, and those around him could detect his utter weakness, he seemed very excited to be with his rebbeim and friends for the most meaningful days of the year.

Armo Kuessous, who was a good friend of Refael Aaron, was very thankful that he would be able to daven next to his friend. Just watching him in the middle of davening provided more of an awakening than any *mussar sefer* he could have learned. He thought about the suffering and pain that his friend's family had endured over the past few years and could not help but daven that Refael Aaron had experienced the last of his troubles.

The davening was beautiful that year. The *baalei tefillah* as usual were exceptional, and the young men, especially those who sat near Refael Aaron, seemed to be able to focus on the words and their meaning even more than usual. Both before and after davening, those who were around Refael wished him a healthy year as well as the traditional wish, *kesivah vechasimah tovah* — may you be inscribed and sealed in the book of life for good.

Late that afternoon, Refael peeked over Armo's shoulder and noticed that Armo was studying from a halachah *sefer*. Refael mentioned to him that a new *sefer* entitled *Yalkut Yosef* had recently come out, a compilation of Sephardic laws and customs on the *Yamim Noraim*. Rafael told Armo that he would bring it back for him when he returned to the yeshivah for Yom Kippur.

Tragically, Refael Aaron never returned to Scranton for Yom Kippur — but the *sefer* did. After Rosh Hashanah, Refael Aaron's condition deteriorated. He had been in remission but now his fever began to rise and by the end of the week he was in critical condition. Unfortunately he died on the eighth day of Tishrei.

The entire yeshivah came to Brooklyn for his funeral. The *maspidim* spoke of Refael Aaron's unusual *chein*. Everyone seemed to have liked him. He was an outstanding student in learning and was well liked by all his friends.

As Armo was preparing to leave the funeral and head back to Scranton a friend came over to him holding a *sefer*. "Rabbi Betzalel Elazary, Refael's father, asked that I give this to you. He said that Refael Aaron wanted you to have it."

Armo stood there frozen. He realized that he was witnessing true greatness. A man whose child had just died had the presence of mind and sensitivity to carry out an act of kindness for another young man! And a young man whose life was ebbing away felt the importance of performing a favor for a friend no matter how insignificant it might have seemed at the time. Armo accepted the *sefer*. He wanted to say thank-you to his friend who was no longer here. He clutched the *sefer* tightly and thought of Refael Aaron.

It is now almost fifteen years later, and as Yom Kippur approaches so too does Refael Aaron's *yahrtzeit*. Armo thinks back to the day when a selfless father carried out a favor for his dying son. And, as always, Armo will learn a few halachos from the *sefer Yalkut Yosef*, in memory of his good friend, Refael Aaron Elazary.

What a Wedding

As the Grossman children, grandchildren and great-grandchildren surrounded their beloved Bubby and Zaidy at their sixtieth wedding anniversary celebration, one of the grandchildren marveled that this wonderful couple had been fortunate enough to be together for so many years, and have such beautiful nachas. Upon hearing this, the elderly couple smiled at each other and Reb Dovid began to recount their incredible tale of hashgachah pratis.

The preparations for the wedding had taken months and everything had been arranged just so. In the city of Yerushalayim, the weddings were quite simple but that did not diminish the way the *choson* and *kallah* felt about their most special day. For Moshe Schwartzman, the *choson*, and his *kallah*, Baila Goldberg, it was going to be one of their most memorable days.

Shidduchim had not gone easy for Baila. She had been dating for several years and nothing seemed to be appropriate. Quite often she would think that she was going to get married to a certain young man and then for one reason or another one of them would decide that it was not a match. But the years of frustration made it all the more satisfying when she finally became a *kallah*.

The excitement in the Goldberg home was palpable. The approaching wedding brought with it many responsibilities and tasks to be accomplished, but finally the months of waiting came to an end. The big day had arrived. Baila arrived at the Bnos Yerushalayim wedding hall very early and soon afterwards the *choson* arrived. He appeared to be nervous but sat down at the *kabbalas panim* and tried to calm himself. Many of the guests arrived and were enjoying the festivities. However, as the *chuppah* was about to begin, it became apparent that the *choson* was nowhere to be found.

His parents began to explain nervously — feeling responsible for this terrible turn of events, but not knowing what to do — that he had come to them terribly distraught, saying he did not want to go through with the wedding. They had tried to convince him not to leave but all their efforts were in vain, as were the efforts of his friends. Moshe's mind was made up and he refused to reconsider. He just did not want to marry this girl. For the meantime, the impending disaster was kept quiet, but it would only be a matter of time before the *kallah* would hear the devastating news. Everyone there tried to think of a way to break the news to the *kallah* but no one seemed to have a good idea of how to go about it.

Rav Yosef Chaim Sonnenfeld, the Rav of Yerushalayim, was at the wedding and was immediately informed of the crisis. The Rav inconspicuously slipped outside to where the *choson's* friends had gathered and were already discussing what had happened.

"Who wants a guarantee for a long life and *nachas* from all your children and grandchildren?" All the boys looked up and were surprised to see the venerated Rav standing next to them. "Anyone who is willing to marry this girl and prevent her from the shame she will incur from this embarrassing incident will be guaranteed a wonderful long life with endless amounts of *nachas*."

One by one the young men, although impressed and tempted by the offer, declined. But one boy was willing. Quickly his parents were asked and with their consent he spent a few moments with Baila. Her initial shock caused her to hesitate but she finally consented. And so they got married.

It is sixty years later and their children, grandchildren and great-grandchildren smile and are forever grateful that their Zaidy's unusual display of chesed allowed for their Bubby and Zaidy to meet, get married and spend a long and happy life together.

Stammering and Stumbling

As HE LOOKED AROUND THE ROOM, THE ALTER OF Slobodka, Reb Nosson Tzvi Finkel, mentioned to his student that he would like to daven for the *amud*. His student, who had spent many years at the Alter's side, was surprised by the unusual request. He did not recall such a request from the Alter ever before, but he was nevertheless not about to question his beloved teacher.

The *gabbai* immediately acquiesced and approached the Alter with a *tallis*. He told the great man what an honor he felt it was to have him davening in their shul. The Alter took the *tallis* and walked up to the *amud*. The *gabbai* banged on the *bimah* and in a loud voice announced, "*Ashrei yoshvei veisecha*," initiating the Minchah davening. The Alter led the rest of the *tefillah*, but after he ended *Ashrei* something unusual happened. To everyone's shock, he began to stumble over the words of *Kaddish*, reading them as if he were a young child who was unfamiliar with the words.

What was even more unusual about the entire episode was the fact that this continued throughout the repetition of the *Shemoneh Esrei* and up until the last *Kaddish*. The congregation seemed very surprised though many of them had never heard the Alter speak before. They dared not snicker or show a lack of approval over his seeming inability to lead the congregation in davening. Instead they did their best to show no reaction whatsoever. After the Alter finished the last words of *Aleinu*, a *Kaddish Yasom* was recited from the back of the room. It wasn't loud or clear and it certainly wasn't fluent. The simple, clearly unlearned man struggled mightily to recite the difficult Aramaic words that he was not accustomed to reading. Line by line he plodded through and as he finally neared the end of *Kaddish*, he took three steps backward and recited the words, "*Oseh shalom bimromav...*," getting stuck on the word *bimromav*. The congregation waited patiently and finally responded with a loud Amen at the conclusion of the *Kaddish*.

As he walked out with his rebbi, a knowing smile formed on the face of the student to whom the Alter had first put forth his request to daven for the *amud*. He realized what had happened. The Alter noticed his smirk and confirmed what his disciple already suspected.

On the way into the shul the Alter had seen this simple man and heard him practicing the words of *Kaddish* in the back of the room. He listened carefully and heard the numerous mistakes the man had made. He feared that the man, who had obvious difficulty reading the words, would attempt to daven for the *amud*, as he was obligated to, and that the congregation would be horrified that this man, who could not even read properly, was performing so poorly in front of the venerated sage. So as to save this villager from incurring the shame of a frustrated congregation, the Alter decided to lead the congregation himself.

His student understood the incredible sensitivity that his rebbi had for a fellow Jew. Nevertheless, one question remained. Why was it necessary for him to purposely mispronounce the words of davening that he was so obviously familiar with?

The Alter smiled at his student and explained that he was still afraid that the man would read *Kaddish* at the end. He knew that the man could not read the familiar Hebrew words, let alone the difficult Aramaic words of *Kaddish*, and did not want him to be ashamed in his attempt. Therefore he himself pretended to have difficulty with the words of davening. In this way the simple man would not feel awkward with his own halted reading. Disregarding the fact that he may have embarrassed himself in front of the congregation, the Alter was concerned only with making this simple Jew feel comfortable.

All the King's Horses ...

AS THE GREAT NAPOLEON BEGAN HIS MISSION TO conquer Russia, he heard tales about the famed Reb Chaim Volozhiner, who was reputed to be a man of G-d. Reb Chaim, he was told, might be able to offer insight and sage advice concerning the upcoming battles with the Russian army. Napoleon's army approached Volozhin and he commanded the Torah sage to come before him. Reb Chaim, who shied away from predicting the future, explained to the great general that he was not a fortune-teller, but a simple Jew who tries his best to serve his Creator.

Napoleon was not deterred, and he insisted on hearing what Reb Chaim had to say about the upcoming battle, all the while promising that no harm would befall him, regardless of what he said.

Reb Chaim finally agreed to speak. "I'll explain it to you through a parable. There was once a wealthy duke who traveled from town to town to see what his subjects were doing. His carriage was drawn by four of the finest horses that could be found. A tall strong stallion hailed from Saudi Arabia, its dark mane in stunning contrast to the light brown of its body. The second came from Egypt, a thoroughbred with unusual speed and agility. The third was the finest stallion in all of France and the fourth, the strongest of the bunch, had recently arrived from Holland. They were an awesome group in both size and appearance, finely groomed and well fed.

"One stormy day the windswept rain pummeled the carriage as the duke's wagon was passing from one town to the next. The wagon stayed on the road and the trip was relatively uneventful until the horses slipped on the wet muddy path and the wagon fell into a ditch on the side of the road. The wagon driver snapped his whip onto the back of one of the horses but it did not seem to help. The horses each responded to the whiplashes by pulling, but alas did not pull as a team, in unison. The duke became frustrated and angry. Just then a small dilapidated wagon pulled up on the road where the duke's wagon was stuck. The peasant driver immediately surveyed the situation and offered to help. Snickering, the duke did not wish to insult the poor man and accepted his offer. But when the man unhooked the duke's regal horses and harnessed his own two horses, the duke began to protest.

"The duke's protests were stilled as he watched the peasant snap his whip once onto the back of one horse. Immediately the two horses pulled as one, dragging the carriage back onto the road. The duke thanked the man profusely but admitted his surprise. 'I don't understand. How could your two horses accomplish what my four strong thoroughbreds were unable to?'

"The simple man smiled and answered, 'Your four horses are truly quite impressive. However they come from four separate countries and in essence have nothing to do with each other. Whipping one will have no impact on the others. But my two horses are a mother and her child. They care deeply for each other and the moment I whip one of them the other responds immediately to help the one that has been hit.' "

Reb Chaim turned to the ruler of France and applied the parable. "Your army is indeed impressive. They are skilled and talented in all areas of battle. However since they come from all over the world, some from Spain and others from France and yet more from other countries, when one battalion is hit, the others are not inspired or motivated to try harder. But the Russians are one family. They are fighting for the same cause and the same country. They are in fact brothers and care deeply for one another. If one is hurting the others will rally and do what they have to, to save him. And that's why I think that they will defeat even your great army."

A few months later history would prove that Reb Chaim's prediction was correct.

Two Are Better Than One

THE COLD HARSH WINTERS OF RADIN, HOME OF THE Chofetz Chaim, produced heavy snowfalls and freezing cold temperatures. The bitter winds would force most people to remain inside their poorly heated homes for weeks on end, except for an occasional trip to the market to purchase some essentials.

One time a wealthy man came to visit the Chofetz Chaim during one of these wintry weeks. After spending some time with the great sage, he decided to leave behind a gift — an expensive pair of fur-lined gloves — for the Chofetz Chaim.

At first the Chofetz Chaim shied away from accepting the present, but seeing that the man very much wanted to give him the gloves, he agreed and kept them. A few days later, the Chofetz Chaim had to travel to a neighboring town for an important meeting. A few of his disciples escorted him onto the train and after purchasing their tickets the small group was shown to their compartment.

The compartment was small and had just enough room for the group. Although the trip was to last for an hour and a half, the Chofetz Chaim remained in his coat, though he removed his gloves and put them into his pockets. Thirty minutes into the journey the cabin began to get stuffy and one of the students opened the window to get some fresh air. The Chofetz Chaim was shifting from one seat to another and in the commotion his coat brushed against the open window causing one of his fur-lined gloves to fall out of his pocket and out the window. Immediately a *talmid* notified his rebbi of what had happened and to the amazement of his students, the Chofetz Chaim threw the other glove out the window as well.

Seeing the confused look on his students' faces he explained, "Someone is going to be walking along the train tracks one day and will see this beautiful glove, but since he will only find one, he will not be able to benefit from it. So I thought to myself, what good will one glove be to me? I might as well allow the one who finds the glove to find a pair of them."

While most of us tend to think first of ourselves, the Chofetz Chaim had trained himself to innately think of others and reacted to an unfortunate situation by thinking of how he could turn it into an opportunity to help a fellow Jew.

Measure for Measure

*T*HE MOMENT HE ARRIVED HE KNEW THAT HE WOULD NOW be faced with horrors which he had never seen before. Mauthausen, one of the most barbaric death camps, located in the Austrian Alps, was the new home for Yechiel Annisfeld. The sullen gray skies and the awful stench of death permeated the air. As soon as the Jews were rushed off the trains, the growling and barking of the wild German shepherds terrified them and they obeyed the orders to form two rows. Once in line, they waited for their fates to be decided — life or death. Yechiel was one of the fortunate ones.

That first day the temperature hovered around 30 degrees below zero. Just for their amusement the Nazis *ym"sh* decided to force the tired, weak inmates to stand barefoot in the camp's square for many hours. The pain of the biting winds slicing into their barely clothed bodies was absolutely unbearable and many succumbed. But Yechiel stood defiantly, and after a few hours the SS officers beat him. The bottoms of his feet had become frozen to the ground and the skin was ripped off them. His open wounds caused an immediate infection to set in, his fever rose quickly and intense pain wracked every inch of his body. All of this on his first day in Mauthausen!

Yechiel staggered toward his barracks and found his way to the slab which served as his bed. Six others joined him in this minuscule excuse for a bed. The frozen concrete they lie upon was perhaps even colder than it was outside the barracks, and the only way they could defy death was to lie with their bodies pressed against one another. The body warmth would warm them and allow for a few moments of much needed rest until the next morning.

In the middle of the night Yechiel turned to the man sleeping next to him, Yiddel Moses, and begged him to show him the way to the infirmary. His fever had risen to the point where Yechiel felt delirious. But Yiddel refused to allow him to go. "If you go you're going to die and I refuse to allow you to die."

Yechiel pleaded with him but nothing could persuade Yiddel. He seemed to have an intuition that although one was allowed to periodically make use of the infirmary, tonight was not a good night to use that privilege.

Approximately an hour later, at about 1 o'clock in the morning, shrill screaming, the likes of which they had never heard before, woke them and the rest of the barracks. The screaming was like that of a wounded animal. It was a haunting, chilling yell that came from the camp's square. The inmates in the infirmary, sick and debilitated, were taken there, stripped of their clothes and left to freeze to death. The tortured screams are something that anyone who heard would ever forget. Yechiel thanked Yiddel again and again, sensing that something deep inside connected the two of them, as if they were soul mates.

The wagon pulled up to a small hostel where a number of orphans had taken shelter in the few days since Auschwitz was liberated. Hirsch Meilich Kunreich, together with a few friends, had managed to find a few scraps to eat. Their bodies were weak and their spirits entirely broken. They had lost everything — mothers, fathers, sisters, brothers, homes, possessions, communities. And many had even lost their faith. They were broken in body and spirit. But their innate desire to survive amid all the death allowed them hope that someday something would give them purpose and reason to go on.

A kind-looking gentile man got down from the wagon and knocked on the door. Warily the orphans opened the door, came out and looked inside the wagon where a dead skeletal body lay. The gentile asked them to give this man a proper Jewish burial. He had been found collapsed on the ground right outside the gates of Auschwitz and, in a barely audible voice, had begged to receive a Jewish burial. He asked to be buried in Brigel, the home of the *"Aryei DeVei Ela'i."* The gentile man could not refuse the poor man's dying request.

Hirsch Meilich, one of the orphans, lifted the man out of the wagon and was startled to find that he had the faintest pulse. Perhaps he had a breath or two of life still left inside of him. Hirsch Meilich took him inside the hostel and laid him down in the corner on a small mattress. Not knowing what else to do, or to whom he could look for help, Hirsch Meilich, on instinct, gently squeezed bits of lemon and sugar inside the man's parched mouth, thinking that perhaps this would give him some sustenance. Miraculously, after a day or two the man regained consciousness.

Although he was alive and breathing, the man simply had no strength with which to eat any more — he even balked at the lemon and sugar. He could not chew or swallow. But Hirsch Meilich would not give up. "I can't allow you not to eat because then you will die. And I won't allow that to happen." The man sensed that Hirsch

Meilich was in need of encouragement and *chizuk* as well and before long a deal was struck between the two. The weak sick man agreed to eat on one condition — only if Hirsch Meilich would make a *berachah* for him on the food which he ate. At first Hirsch Meilich balked at the idea. He had forsaken his religious practices as a result of what he had seen over the past few years, and he did not want to begin praying to G-d once again. But he had made a commitment to himself and to this man, and finally he consented to the deal.

Hirsch Meilich would sprinkle sugar on the lemon and then place it near the man's parched lips. Then the two together would make the *berachah* "*shehakol nihiyeh bidvaro.*" And there, in a forsaken little hut a few short miles from the largest death factory in the history of mankind, two lost men gave life back to each other. The sickly man regained his strength and Hirsch Meilich once again found his faith. And they refused to allow each other to die. The man who had been brought there by the gentile was Yiddel Moses, the same Yiddel Moses who had refused to allow Yechiel Annisfeld to go the infirmary that dreadful night in Mauthausen. His pile of lifeless bones was resurrected and Hashem helped him rebuild his life. A few months later he met Chana Felsen, an orphaned girl from Poland. They married in Torneau and a year later were blessed with a little girl, Soroh Gittel.

And Soroh Gittel Moses is my mother.

Heiliga Hakafos (Part 2)

FOR THOSE WHO WERE PRIVILEGED TO WITNESS THEM, Hakafos in the town of Sassov were truly special. The disciples of Reb Moshe Leib Sassover would travel from miles around to witness the Rebbe's dancing. He would close his eyes and the packed *beis medrash* would erupt in song and clapping. The crowd of swaying Chassidim in their *shtriemlach* encircled the solitary figure dancing with great emotion all by himself. The small *beis medrash* sometimes felt as if it were going to collapse from the weight and energy of the massive crowds, but somehow it held strong. The "Sassover," as he was called, spoke beforehand about the symbolism of dancing in a circle. No beginning and no end, just one continuous flow of *Yidden* showing that we are all equally important components of the entity called *Klal Yisrael*.

One year, as the hour of *Hakafos* approached on the eve of Shemini Atzeres, the Chassidim wondered where the Rebbe was. They figured that he was spending a few moments by himself locked in a room so he could prepare himself properly for the work at hand. But as the hour grew late the *gabbai* sent out a group of men to see what could possibly be keeping the Rebbe. They searched every place they could think of but there was no sign of the Rebbe. Growing concern spread and finally they divided up into groups and began to cover the entire small town of Sassov.

In one of the far corners of the village, one of the search groups came upon a dilapidated house and heard some soft singing coming from inside. They peeked through the window and were amazed at what they saw. There was a small child sitting in a wheelchair, and there was the Rebbe, holding hands with him and dancing back and forth. The group outside the window did not want to move — they understood that they were witnessing something unusual and special. But after a few moments they approached the door and knocked softly.

The Rebbe excused himself for a moment and answered the door. He invited the group inside the humble house. Word spread quickly that the Rebbe had been found and with each passing moment more and more Chassidim began to fill the ramshackle house. The Rebbe waited for the house to fill up and finally he spoke.

"I was on my way to Maariv for *Hakafos* but I wanted to spend some time thinking about the *Hakafos*. I walked to the outskirts of our village and as I started to head back to shul I heard a faint crying. I listened and it appeared to be coming from one of the houses nearby. As I reached the home I knocked lightly but no one answered. Finally I let myself in and I saw that a young boy, perhaps 7 or 8 years old, was sitting on a bed."

The Chassidim were hanging on every word that their Rebbe said. By now the house was bursting from wall to wall in every direction.

"I walked over to him and tried to calm him but he had been crying for awhile so it took him some time till his breathing slowed and he was able to speak. A few moments passed and finally he told me that his entire family had dressed up in their finest Yom Tov clothing and as they were about to leave he asked his mother if he could come. She did not intend to hurt him but she told him that it was becoming too hard to shlep him along. He kept on crying throughout his entire narrative so I knew that there had to be more to the story. He then tearfully cried out, 'I just want to be able to dance like everyone else.' Just then I looked down and for the first time noticed that the boy was wearing knee braces. He was crippled.

"I began to cry for this poor child. And since he was so sad I decided to dance with him and cheer him up, and that's why I was delayed."

The Chassidim were silent and waited for instructions as to what they should do next. Assuming that they would now be leaving, they started to empty out of the small house when the Rebbe made a startling announcement. "*Rabbosai,* tonight, instead of dancing in the *beis medrash* we're going to celebrate *Hakafos* right here in this house with my little friend Moishele."

Moishele beamed with pride as the announcement was made. Suddenly the Rebbe began to sing a *niggun*. Soon, like a mounting tidal wave, the Chassidim joined in and circles formed, one inside the other. Before long there was no more room and the dancing overflowed outside, encircling the home on the outskirts of town. And in the middle of it all stood Reb Moshe Leib of Sassov, dancing and holding up a crippled young boy who now cried no longer.

The Wedding Blessing

*R*EB CHAIM SHAPIRO WAS ONE OF A KIND: AUTHOR, *shochet, chazzan,* storyteller, soldier, survivor and Kohen. His book, "Go My Son," is a testament to his incredible journey of survival. His sense of humor and honesty were trademarks of this giant of a man. And now Reb Chaim was no longer.

Avi Shapiro spoke with sincerity and warmth as he stood by the grave at the funeral of his father, Reb Chaim Shapiro, and told this wonderful story.

When Avi became a *choson,* Reb Chaim and his wife chose "Three Star Photographers" to do the photography and videos for the wedding. Their sterling reputation and patience were hallmarks of their business, which made them the top choice. Four weeks prior to the wedding, Freddy Levitz, one of the photographers, called Reb Chaim and asked the usual pre-nuptial questions, so that he could better prepare the photo session. Freddy asked, as he always did, how many children there were in the family.

Reb Chaim told Freddy that he had five children and Avi was his youngest. Freddy jotted down the notes and muttered to himself, "If I could have just one — " Surprised at his own outburst, he quickly grew silent.

Reb Chaim heard the pain in Freddy's voice, and realized the man was at once uncomfortable and yet seeking help and comfort. He decided to say something. He mentioned that he had successfully given *berachos* before to couples who had no children, and suggested that Freddy bring his wife to the wedding, where Reb Chaim could give them a *berachah.* At first Freddy thought it was strange. He had just met this man over the phone and yet the conversation had grown so personal. But then again, the man seemed to be so sincere.

Freddy went home that night and discussed the episode with his wife April. After years of frustration from undergoing treatments that had produced no results, both Freddy and April were touched and hopeful about Reb Chaim's offer. "Why not try it?" He figured. "It surely won't hurt."

In the months between this conversation and the wedding, Freddy was extremely busy with weddings, Bar Mitzvahs and other events. His business was very successful and he worked almost seven days a week. In the rush of his work, he had all but forgotten Reb Chaim's offer. But Reb Chaim had not. Just before his youngest son walked down to the *chuppah*, he turned to Freddy and asked him if he had brought his wife to the wedding. Freddy immediately remembered about the *berachah* but sputtered an apology that he had forgotten to bring his wife to the wedding. Without skipping a beat, Reb Chaim turned to Freddy, placed his hands on Freddy's head and began to cry and *daven* as if he were blessing his own childless son. Freddy was shocked. He barely knew this man and the tears were so real. Reb Chaim then had Freddy call April on the phone and he gave her a heartfelt *beracha* as well. In the meantime, Avi waited to march down the aisle together with his father and mother.

Finally Reb Chaim completed his emotional plea, and the wedding proceeded.

Nine months later Sima Leah Levitz miraculously entered the world. Immediately Freddy called Reb Chaim with the wonderful news, as he had done when he had first discovered that his wife was expecting. Reb Chaim again blessed him that he and his wife should be granted much *nachas* from their little Sima Leah.

Six years later, Reb Chaim experienced chest pains and was told that he would need heart surgery. That day Freddy received a phone call from Reb Chaim's daughter in Los Angeles; she told him that her father had requested a *berachah* from him. Freddy was shocked. He surely was not the "*berachah*-giving" type and asked why Reb Chaim would have wanted a blessing from him.

Reb Chaim's daughter replied that she too had asked her father why he was insistent on a *berachah* from Freddy when there were certainly greater people from whom to receive blessings. Reb Chaim answered that no one in the world feels a greater sense of love and gratitude to him than Freddy and he felt that it is not so important from whom the *berachah* comes but rather the depth of feeling with which it is given. Needless to say Freddy gladly bestowed his *bircas hedyot* and was happy to hear that the operation was successful.

Two years later Reb Chaim ascended to Heaven where he continues to be an advocate for all of the Jewish people.

Avi concluded the story with a beautiful thought. "The reason my father was a great man was not because he gave a *berachah* and it was fulfilled but rather because at his greatest moment of joy my father thought of someone else. *Yehi zichro baruch!* — May his memory be blessed!"

Caught in the Act

EREV YOM KIPPUR IS A DAY WHEN MANY RUSH TO GRAB AT their last chance to do *teshuvah*. Many stories have been told about these last-minute acts of repentance. Observing the manner in which a Torah giant behaves on this day can be inspiring if not surprising. Let's peek into the life of Reb Yisroel Salanter on one Erev Yom Kippur, just a few hours before the beginning of the holiest day of the year.

The disciples had noticed their rebbi sneak off in middle of the day. He appeared to shy away from bringing attention to himself so these young men who were following him kept their distance. Reb Yisroel slipped into an alleyway and looked behind him. His students could hardly wait. No doubt they would be able to observe their teacher in deep meditation, crying in awe before the forthcoming Day of Atonement.

Reb Yisroel came out of the alleyway holding something in his hand. It looked like some sort of utensil although from the distance the students were keeping it was difficult to tell exactly what it was. They had heard of the *minhag* some had to receive *malkus* on Erev Yom Kippur and they imagined watching him dispensing lashes to himself as an atonement. Reb Yisroel walked toward the shul. Clearly that is where he was going to contemplate how he could serve the A-mighty better and reflect on the events of the past year.

Once Reb Yisroel arrived at the shul he again looked around to make sure no one was watching. The students felt somewhat guilty. Here they were secretly spying on their rebbi when he clearly was wary that no one should see what he was doing. But they quickly resolved their dilemma by rationalizing that this too was something they needed to learn. After all, it was Erev Yom Kippur and when else should they observe how their rebbi behaved if not on this auspicious day.

The students peeked out from behind the house where they were hiding and waited until Reb Yisroel entered the shul where the people in the community davened. He checked to see if anyone was in the building and then proceeded to walk upstairs to the women's section. The "spies" who had been following waited for their rebbi to go upstairs and when he did they quietly crept up after him. It was here they figured he would begin his "holy work." They understood that he wanted to serve his Creator in private. They huddled next to each other and carefully observed their rebbi's every move.

But what happened next shocked them. The utensil he held in his hands was not an administering tool for *malkus* but a simple hammer. Watching the scene unfold, the young men could not help but wonder why in the world their rebbi would be using a hammer a mere few hours before the holiest day of the year. They watched as Reb Yisroel ran his hand smoothly over the benches. And whenever he felt a nail sticking out he would take the hammer and nail it in. Over and over the hammer met its mark. After he was satisfied that indeed all the nails had been firmly embedded in their places did he turn to leave. It was then that he first noticed the students who had been watching his every move.

Sensing that his students had expected to find him engaged in a "holy" act, not just banging in nails like a carpenter, Reb Yisroel pulled them close to him and explained the reason for his actions. "Tomorrow many more women will be coming to shul than on a regular Shabbos. Every seat in the women's section will be taken and the women will be dressed in their finest Yom Tov clothing. If they rip their clothing on one of these nails, imagine how much anguish it would cause them. Their entire day would be affected and what a shame that would be — to have their Yom Kippur ruined because of a nail. So I decided to bang in all the loose nails and prevent this from happening."

Reb Yisroel smiled at his dumbfounded disciples and walked home to take care of some unfinished business. After all, it was Erev Yom Kippur, just a few hours before the holiest day of the year.

Caught in the Act (Part 2)

T HE YOUNG MEN FROM GATESHEAD YESHIVAH WOULD frequently go up to the library to research various *shiurim* given by the Roshei Yeshivah. Sometimes when they were there they would lock the door and spend additional time scanning the library for interesting books and pamphlets. Occasionally, although it was against the rules of the yeshivah, they would use this opportunity to take a cigarette break.

Reuven Lowenstein and his friend Yossi Fishbein decided to review the day's *shiur* in the library. They notified their friend Shmuel that in case anybody was looking for them they could be found upstairs. They took their notes from the *shiur* and went upstairs. To ensure that they wouldn't be disturbed, they both agreed it would be a good idea to lock the door. Approximately one-half hour later they heard a knocking at the door.

At first they just ignored it and assumed that whoever was knocking would walk away if he thought that no one was in there.

But the knocking persisted. And so, just for piece of mind, they went to see who it was. Only one person in the whole yeshivah knew that they had gone upstairs and that was their friend Shmuel.

"Is anybody in there?" The voice on the other side of the door continued. "Please open up. It's the Rosh Yeshivah, Leib Gurwicz."

The boys inside knew that it wasn't the Rosh Yeshivah and therefore decided that if the one knocking was interested in playing games then they would play games as well. "Well, we're sorry, Leib Gurwicz, but we're not opening up for you."

"Please boys, open up the door. I need a certain *sefer* in order to prepare *shiur*." The man on the other side was imitating the Rosh Yeshivah to a tee but that was not unusual.

The young men looked at each other and knew exactly what each one was thinking. They were going to drive this fellow crazy. "We're sorry, but the library is not available. It's being cleaned right now." Reuven was proud of the original excuse he had formulated and was happy that the "mystery man" was becoming more frustrated.

"I beg you, please open up!" The young men recognized the tone. It sure did sound like the Rosh Yeshivah's voice. Either someone was doing an incredibly realistic imitation of Rav Gurwicz or these boys were in deeper trouble than they could have ever imagined.

They whispered to each other and frantically thought about what they could do to get themselves out of this mess. They looked at the window and for a moment pondered the idea of slipping out through it, but they quickly decided that it wasn't the smartest thing to do. First of all, it was freezing outside and second, the window led to a ledge, and then what would they do? Left with no alternative they resolved to face the wrath of the Rosh Yeshivah and deal with it like men.

Embarrassed and afraid of what would happen to them
they slowly walked toward the door and opened it. They
could not believe what greeted them.

Indeed it was the Rosh Yeshivah, Rav Leib (Aryeh Zev) Gurwicz. He stood by the entranceway to the library, imposing looking in his long black coat. The boys braced themselves for what was sure to be an embarrassing lecture. But with their heads faced downwards they waited for a few moments and it was quiet.

They looked up and smiled. It was a sight that will forever remain etched in the *bochurim's* memory — he had placed his hands over his eyes so as not to see who it was that had played the trick on him. Now comprehending his intent, the boys dismissed themselves with a quick apology and ran from the room. What could have become a major embarrassment and source of shame for many years to come instead became an opportunity for the Rosh Yeshivah to teach his students an invaluable lesson in *bein adam l'chaveiro* — relationships between man and his fellow man.

The Bidding War

MENDEL WAS A STRONG-MINDED INDIVIDUAL; HE had his particular preferences and wasn't shy about making them known. As a strong activist he had significant influence in his community and expressed his opinion without concern for the consequences. For example, he wanted the *chazzan* to daven in a certain manner, using specific tunes and specific pronunciation of the words. He pressured the Rav speak about the subject matter that he suggested. Veering away from Mendel's agenda was sure to invite his wrath. And Mendel would not be bashful about his disappointment. If you were *lucky*, he would approach you and chide you regarding your performance. Otherwise you would be subject to a cold shoulder until he decided to *forgive* you. No. Mendel was definitely not a relaxed individual. He was demanding in every sense of the word.

In his shul, each Simchas Torah it had become the custom in recent years for Mendel to purchase the honor of receiving the *aliyah* of *Kol HaNe'arim* for his son. Mendel had heard years ago about the *segulah* that the honor carried with it — that the person who was honored with that portion of the Torah reading on Simchas Torah would be blessed with many children. Mendel's son Chaim had been married for six years now and was still childless, and Mendel had watched as his son and daughter-in-law had suffered through doctors' visits and treatments that were difficult, both emotionally and physically.

One Simchas Torah, Sender, the *gabbai*, decided that he would make some extra money for the shul. And as the bidding wars began for the various *kibbudim* he bid on each of them, attempting to up the ante. One by one the prices escalated as Sender offered proposals and counterproposals on the items up for bidding.

The lower-priced items had been sold; *Atah Haraisa* was sold for $250, and now it was time for the serious bidding to begin. Generally *Kol HaNe'arim, Choson Torah* and *Choson Bereishis* went for a few hundred dollars apiece; on a good year even up to $400 or $500. However, this year was to be different.

"I bid $300 for *Kol HaNe'arim,*" Mendel declared, assuming that he would purchase it easily, with perhaps one or two counteroffers.

"Three hundred and fifty," Sender shouted, to Mendel's surprise. Sender was normally not a "player" in the purchasing of *kibbudim* and Mendel wondered why he was beginning now.

"Four hundred."

"Five."

And so the bidding war began. The smirk on Sender's face indicated that he was not as serious as some might have believed about the purchase of the *kibbud.*

The numbers escalated. And so did Mendel's blood pressure. *The nerve of this impudent fool*, Mendel thought to himself. *He knows that I'm buying it for my son and that I'm willing to spend more than anyone.* One did not need to be a genius to figure out what was going on here.

The tension spread in the room as the numbers hit an all-time high.

" One thousand dollars," Mendel announced emphatically, the irritation clearly noticeable in his voice.

"Eleven hundred," Sender coolly responded, pretending to be oblivious to Mendel's anger.

By now the shul had become silent except for the bidding war between Mendel and Sender and the mediation of the one who had been announcing the soaring prices.

"Twelve hundred," Mendel proclaimed. Beads of sweat had developed on Mendel's forehead as he huffed and puffed in seething rage.

And without missing a beat, Sender declared, "One thousand three hundred dollars."

"Take it! Keep it!" Mendel yelled. Simchas Torah's joy had been replaced with a palpable feeling of hatred that filled the entire *beis medrash*. Sender immediately realized that what he had intended as an innocent, well-meaning fundraising ploy for the shul had not been perceived as such by Mendel. And he was now the "proud winner" of an honor he did not want and could not afford. The onlookers in the shul, usually irritated with Mendel's behavior, now sympathized with him. They knew why he wanted the *aliyah*, and felt sorry for him that he did not win the bidding.

The celebration of *Hakafos* proved quieter than usual and uneventful. Many of the members of the congregation had been taken aback by the bidding fiasco that had taken place earlier. The excitement and joy of the Simchas Torah festivities had petered out as Mendel and Sender had avoided each other since Mendel's outburst.

Finally, Shmuel, the peacemaker of the shul, looked up from the *sefer* he had been immersed in. Shmuel was not much of a dancer and usually stayed on the outside of the circles or sat on a chair and shared some Torah thoughts with a sprinkling of jokes for those who would listen. But now an idea popped into his head. He walked over to Sender and sat down next to him in an inconspicuous manner.

"You know, Sender, I have an idea" Shmuel opened the conversation. He knew he was treading on thin ice and proceeded with caution. "I know that you spent an enormous amount of money on *Kol HaNe'arim* — "

"What are you driving at?" Sender interjected. He felt awful about the events that had transpired earlier and wasn't in the mood for Shmuel's jokes.

"I'm not joking with you." Shmuel's serious tone was somewhat unusual and grabbed Sender's attention.

"Just imagine — what if you gave the honor of *Kol HaNe'arim* to Mendel's son. Imagine what type of *shalom* you would bring about. I bet that would cause a commotion in *Shamayim*." The more Shmuel thought about the idea the more he liked it.

And so, as the congregation prepared for the *aliyah* of *Kol HaNe'arim*, Sender whispered something into the *gabbai's* ear. To the amazement of everyone, the *gabbai* called upon Mendel's son for the *aliyah*.

Shocked, Mendel looked at Sender with tears in his eyes and nodded as if to say thank-you. Mendel's son made the *berachos* together with all the children as he, his father and now Sender silently prayed for Hashem to grant this young couple the child they so desperately wanted.

One year later, Mendel bid once again on *Kol HaNe'arim*. But this time — with his brand new little granddaughter in his hands — he purchased the *kibbud* for Sender in appreciation for all he had done. And Shmuel could not help but wonder, "If breaking the barriers of *machlokes* could awaken compassion in Heaven for a childless couple, then just imagine what could happen if we would all put our differences aside."

The Sounds of Silence

THEY CAME FROM ALL OVER: RUSSIA, ROMANIA, POLAND, Czechoslovakia, France, Hungary and even Salonika. They came together as a group and yet as separate individuals. What they had in common was the unique sense of loss that they all shared. And it was to Feldafing that they came to begin rebuilding their lives from scratch.

It was 1945 and the war had ended a few months before. If you wanted to find a relative, Feldafing was a good place to start. And that is where so many of the survivors began reconstructing their lives. Many shuls sprang up in this displaced persons camp and each shul and *shtiebel* had its own *minhagim*. Those in the *Poilishe shtiebel* insisted on their *minhagim* and the Hungarians remained firm on their customs. The same was true for each small group and clique in the camp. The reason these groups were so adamant about preserving their traditions was because that was all that remained, and so they held onto them dearly.

The *Yamim Noraim* were quite emotional that year, culminating with a heartrending *Yizkor* service on Yom Kippur. Each group davened with its own kind and many different *minyanim* were formed. Among other Torah leaders, the Klausenburger Rebbe led one of the larger groups that had gathered. And finally the Yom Tov of Succos was at hand. It was difficult to imagine celebrating in a joyous manner at a time like this. Rosh Hashanah and Yom Kippur had come easier. But to rejoice in happiness seemed impossible when so many had not yet and would never get over what had happened to them over the past six years. Regardless of this, an attempt was made and Succos was celebrated. The usual happiness that had previously been evident at this time of year was lacking. Nevertheless people tried their hardest to adhere to all the mitzvos. A *lulav* and an *esrog* were brought in and hundreds of people shared them. Each person shook them the way he was taught. They were not able to afford the luxury of choosing a specific type of *esrog*, but were happy that it was at least a kosher one.

A certain light-headedness that sometimes accompanies the Simchas Torah davening was missing. And after the congregation davened Maariv the time for *Hakafos* had come. At that moment each group came forward to demand that their style of *Hakafos* be conducted. The German Jews had their manner and the different chassidic groups had their way. Even the Salonikans and other smaller groups spoke up about having their customs observed at this time. The quiet talking among the individuals escalated and before long a full-blown loud argument broke out in the shul. Some peacemakers tried their best to calm the crowd but the tensions ran high. It appeared that this Simchas Torah would just not to be.

Sitting in a corner was a middle-aged man. His name was Shmuel, and he provided a stark contrast to what was transpiring in the shul because he sat so placidly in the corner. Perhaps part of the reason he sat in the corner was because he never spoke. No one ever heard him say a word. Some speculated that he was in shock from the time his family had been killed in front of his very eyes, but no one could be sure. And during the arguing in shul he sat all the while watching and observing what was happening. The hostility grew to the point where some feared that it would come to fisticuffs. It was at that moment that Shmuel stood up.

He walked slowly to the center of the room where the arguments were most intense. One by one those who noticed the usually invisible Shmuel striding to the center of the room immediately quieted down, wondering what he was about to do. He walked through the crowds and by the time he reached the center of the room the crowd was quiet. The tranquility and calm that descended seemed to be at odds with the potential for a thunderous explosion that threatened the sanctity of both the shul and the Yom Tov. But the respect for Shmuel "the silent one" could be felt by all.

All eyes were focused on him and he looked around the room at all the people who waited with bated breath to see what he would do. He opened his mouth and a teardrop formed in his eye. *"S-i-s-u v-e-s-i-m-c-h-u b-e-s-i-m-c-h-a-s T-o-r-a-h."* Four words. And then he moved away. The four words hung in the air. But the message penetrated each and every heart. Those gathered began to think to themselves, "What do we have left? Nothing! *V'ein shiyur rak haTorah hazos* — We have nothing left but the Torah! Let's celebrate what we have left, that which brings us all together."

Slowly and silently the arguing crowds dispersed, and they regrouped peacefully as remnants of a nation that had survived to live for the sake of Torah. No one ever remembers Shmuel saying another word. But those words that he said will never be forgotten.

Sleep, Snow and Siberia

February 17, 2003 produced the worst winter storm in the history of Baltimore. Measurements of two and a half to three feet of snow were calculated, with snowdrifts reaching four feet and even higher! The city was completely frozen, both literally and metaphorically speaking. Tickets of $1,000 were issued to anyone who dared venture out in an automobile, as a state of emergency was declared by Governor Ehrlich. But all this could not prevent Reb Simcha Shafran from venturing out of his home — a mile and a half from the nearest shul — for Minchah and Maariv. When the crowd gathered and some joked with him about the impossible weather conditions, he simply smiled and treated those of us who were privileged to be there to an incredible story of mesiras nefesh of one friend for another.

DURING HIS CHILDHOOD IN SIBERIA, SIMCHA HAD THE unwanted task of guarding the excess summer grain that had been harvested; these stores of grain had to be protected from burglars, and this was always a very difficult job. In Siberia the temperatures at times could dip to 40 degrees below zero. Exposing any part of your body in such frigid weather could result in frostbite or perhaps worse. The watchman was given special boots to wear and a warm fur-lined coat. With snow piled two meters high the only way the watchman could reach his post was by means of a horse-drawn sled which made the two-mile trek from the nearest village.

The weather had reached 50 below and Simcha felt extremely weak. He had felt feverish all day, and now he was aware that his fever was rising. Finally he decided that he had to begin making his way back to the village, otherwise he was going to collapse. He climbed onto the sled and urged the tall strong horse to go forward. Slowly the horse plodded its way through the snow. The heavy winds increased up and the snow swirled in small tornadolike configurations. Simcha held onto the sled with all his strength, but the combination of his weakened condition, the elements and the rugged terrain proved too much for him. He desperately tried to hold on but could not manage to. Having fallen off the sled, he lay face down in the snow and noticed out of the corner of his eye that the horse was moving away.

Simcha turned over and looked up at the sky. He stared at the twinkling stars and began to cry. "Please G-d, don't let me die. If my horse runs away there's no way I can make it back to the village." He poured out his heart in one last desperate plea and looked around. Approximately fifty meters from where he lay helplessly, the horse had suddenly stopped. With great determination he crawled toward the horse and pulled himself back onto the sled. And that was the last thing he remembered.

Somehow the horse managed to find its way back to the village with an unconscious Simcha lying lethargically on the sled. The small village was not equipped with a hospital and so when Simcha woke up in a hospital bed, he had no idea where he was. Unbeknown to him, he had been taken the day after his harrowing incident to a hospital in an adjacent town and therefore did not recognize anyone. Feeling lost and forlorn he began to despair. It was then that Hershel Tushbitzer walked through the door.

His face was red and numb, and his feet — almost frozen — were covered with rags instead of the warm boots normally worn by one who would venture out on a journey in this weather. Hershel had traveled all the way from their village to this hospital, but he seemed genuinely surprised that Simcha's eyes were open. Simcha, though exhausted, was thrilled to see his friend.

Hershel, weary and fatigued from the long journey, sat next to his friend murmuring to himself, "I can't believe it. I just can't believe it."

Simcha was confused. "What do you mean? What can't you believe?"

Bewildered, Hershel recounted the entire incident that had brought him there. A nurse had returned from the hospital and brought with her the terrible news that Simcha had died.

"Well, if she told you that I died then why would you have come here?" Simcha was shocked that they were talking about his life and death. But Hershel's answer taught him a lesson in friendship that he had never learned before.

"When I heard that you died I knew that I had to come and get you. I had to make sure that you were given a proper Jewish burial. And so, even though I didn't have the right boots, I wrapped my feet in layers of rags and managed to walk here. I was shocked, though thrilled, to find you alive. And instead of doing *chesed* with a *niftar,* I got to do *chesed* for a friend who is very much alive."

Simcha could not believe what he was hearing. He thanked the A-mighty for saving his life and Hershel for his unbelievable *mesiras nefesh* for a friend. Reb Simcha remains eternally grateful.

And so do his children, grandchildren and great-grandchildren.

The Torn Tallis

DAVENING IN YESHIVAS MEKOR CHAIM ON THE *YAMIM Noraim* is very special. Those leading the prayers have all the qualifications to serve as outstanding representatives of the congregation. Their melodious voices and heartfelt *kavanah* inspire the crowd to daven with great fervor and devotion. But seven years ago there was an additional element which, had it been known, would have inspired the congregants even more.

Reb Shraga Wollman, the *mashgiach* of the yeshivah, always served as the *baal Mussaf.* He also davened *Kol Nidrei* and *Ne'ilah* on Yom Kippur. His *niggunim* and concentration, as well as his ability to arouse the congregation, is part of what makes the davening in the yeshivah distinctive. And this particular year was no different.

Throughout Mussaf Reb Shraga was his usual sincere self and the congregation responded in kind. However, as Reb Shraga approached the *amud* for *Ne'ilah* something seemed wrong. After a moment some members of the congregation noticed that Reb Shraga's usual *tallis* had been replaced by an old and tattered one; it looked like one of those *talleisim* that hangs near the entrance of the shul for visitors who do not have their own. It seemed strange that he would have simply donned the shul's *tallis*. Didn't he feel more comfortable and inspired wearing his own?

Regardless of which *tallis* Reb Shraga wore, *Ne'ilah* was beautiful and very moving. After *Avinu Malkeinu* the sounds of *Hashem Hu HaElokim* erupted and reverberated throughout the *beis medrash*. The blast of the shofar pierced the air and then the joyous singing of *Leshanah Habaah BiYerushalayim* filled the hearts and souls of the congregants. As the men sang and danced in their white *kitels* and *talleisim*, many wondered if there was a story behind Reb Shraga's *tallis;* it just seemed so odd, so out of place. It was hard for the men not to wonder what was going on.

Finally, after the dancing stopped and Maariv concluded, the crowd gathered downstairs to break their fast on some honey cake, coffee and orange juice. After most had made their way downstairs one good friend of Reb Shraga, Chaim Newmark, approached him and asked him why he had not worn his own *tallis* for *Ne'ilah*. Did this *tallis* belong to a grandfather of his?

Reb Shraga dodged the question and deflected the persistent badgering about the origins of the *tallis*. But Chaim persevered and pleaded with his friend to reveal where the *tallis* had come from. Finally, after giving a *tallis* bag to an elderly woman, Reb Shraga admitted the truth.

He explained that he had walked past Mrs. Rosen moments after *Mussaf* had concluded, when she was on her way home. As he wished her a "Gut Yom Tov" he noticed that she seemed to be down. She acknowledged that she missed her husband a lot as he had passed away earlier this year. She was used to having him around and was sad that he was no longer here. As she spoke tears filled the older woman's eyes.

Reb Shraga thought quickly and asked Mrs. Rosen if he would be able to use her husband's *tallis* for *Ne'ilah*. This way she would know that there was a remembrance of her husband nearby. And so, although the *tallis* might not have looked as nice as Reb Shraga's own, nothing could have been more beautiful than his compassion for an elderly widow.

Tell Him Mo Called

THE YOUNG BOY STARED AT THE GROUND. HE DIDN'T HAVE much to say other than the fact that it was just not fair. Moshe Meir, or Mo as his friends called him, loved his father very much. And now, just like that — he was gone. His mother had told him that their *Tatty* was now up in *Shamayim* together with Hashem and all the big *tzaddikim*. But he still missed him. He hadn't even had a chance to say good-bye.

His rebbi had sat near him during the funeral and had held his hand throughout. He did not remember the *hespedim* at all as he had been crying too hard to actually concentrate on what was being said. His mother was very sad as well. Her husband had been her entire world. He was a Torah scholar, a wonderful father and husband, and a successful businessman. And in one shocking instant all that had changed. One moment he was here — the next gone.

Mo had so many questions to ask, the crux of them being, "Why do bad things happen to good people?" If his father was such a *tzaddik,* then why would Hashem punish him? However since he was too young to verbalize what was going on in his mind, he just kept quiet. Even his good friends from yeshivah could not cheer him up. When they came they were so nervous. Stumbling in their speech, they searched for the proper words of comfort but seemed unable to find them.

He couldn't wait for *shivah* to end. The eerie uncomfortable silences gave rise to an awkward feeling in the room. His uncles had many visitors coming and going and his mother's friends had been very supportive, but he was both lonely and scared.

Finally, on the fifth day of *shivah*, Rav Mattisyahu Salomon entered their home. Mo, who was sitting in the corner of the living room, noticed that an important-looking rabbi had come in but he figured that he was here to spend time with his uncles. They were important people in the community and many Roshei Yeshivah had already stopped by to offer condolences. So Mo was shocked when this man sat down next to him. All of a sudden Mo wanted to be alone again.

"So, young man, what's your name?" Rav Mattisyahu asked him in a beautiful rich British accent. Mo looked up and nervously answered, "My name is Moshe Meir Goldstein."

"Is that what your friends call you?" Rav Mattisyahu was searching for a comfort zone the two of them could share.

"Well, actually my friends call me Mo." Mo was surprised that this nice man had been spending so much time with him, as the crowd in the room seemed to be hanging on his every word.

"How old are you, Mo?" Rav Mattisyahu had noticed that the fragile young boy seemed to be enjoying their conversation and wanted to engage him in further dialogue.

"Seven."

"Really?" The *mashgiach* seemed to be genuinely surprised and smiled as if an idea had popped into his mind. "You know I was also a young boy when my father passed away."

Mo's eyes lit up. Here was somebody who understood what he was going through. The rest of the conversation flowed easily. Mo spoke about his father and how he was going to miss him. Rav Mattisyahu tried to answer all his questions and Mo seemed to respond well to the answers. Those who witnessed the exchange were amazed at how the boy had changed since the *mashgiach* had walked into the room. As Rav Mattisyahu was about leave he proposed a beautiful idea to Mo.

"What would you say about starting a little club with me for *yesomim* who were young when they lost their fathers? And you and I can be the first members of the private club." Mo loved the idea.

"One last thing. The rules of the club are that whenever one of us wants to call the other we are allowed to call him — no matter what the circumstances. And when you call, if my wife or someone else tells you that I'm unavailable, just tell them to relay the following message: 'Tell him Mo called.' I promise to answer immediately."

The *mashgiach* rose from his chair, a giant in understanding human character. Mo glanced up at his new friend and somehow felt a little better. He didn't want him to go now. He wished he could stay a little longer. Rav Mattisyahu stared deeply into the young boy's eyes and comforted him with the appropriate words of solace, reassuring him that there is One Who will never leave him. *"HaMakom yenachem eschem ...* May G-d comfort you ..."

Kaddish on Credit

*I*N A REMOTE HUNGARIAN VILLAGE, MRS. GITTEL HARTSTEIN had an unusually fine custom. Gittel, a fervently religious woman, would scrupulously investigate each time there was a death in the village to see if there was someone to say *Kaddish* for the deceased. If in fact there was no one to say *Kaddish*, she herself would pay the yeshivah to designate someone to do so. In fact, she wouldn't even inform the family that she had arranged it, instead opting to keep it her secret.

Years went by, and Gittel experienced several hardships. Her husband Yeruchem's sudden passing had left her sad and lonely; and her two daughters were having difficulty in their quest for marriage. Rochel Leah, 29, and Sorolah, 26, were both struggling to find their proper mates. It was hard enough to find a young man willing to go out with an older girl, but in this case it was even harder because the Hartsteins had no money to pay for a nice-sized dowry that seemed to be an important criterion in young men's decisions to pursue a *shidduch*.

However, although Gittel's lack of funds prevented her from easing her daughter's sad predicament — and her life was far from idyllic — she would never relax the standards she had set for herself — especially her commitment to those who did not have anyone to say *Kaddish* for them. Gittel would continue to be vigilant in finding someone to honor the memory of the deceased with the recitation of *Kaddish*.

One cold rainy day Gittel followed a funeral procession. Shockingly, it seemed that there were no mourners, for only the members of the *chevrah kadisha* were accompanying the deceased. Immediately she approached one of the members and asked who would be saying *Kaddish* for the deceased. The man sadly responded that he was unaware of anyone who would be able to do so. Gitttel thanked him for the information and turned toward her home.

On her way Gittel took a detour to the local yeshivah and approached the Rosh Yeshivah, Rav Muttel Greenwald, to ask him if someone in the yeshivah could recite *Kaddish* for this poor soul. However, Gittel sadly mentioned that she was short on funds and would therefore like to purchase the *Kaddish* on credit. The Rosh Yeshivah smiled and reassured her that it would not be necessary as the yeshivah would honor her request regardless of her ability to pay. However, Gittel insisted that she would pay as soon as she was able; she knew that she would feel comfortable only when she paid fully for the service being performed.

A few months later, Gittel was walking home alone when she spotted a man standing by her doorway. He appeared to have somewhat of a mystical appearance and he spoke in an angelic tone. "Gittel, have you been struggling lately with your financial commitments?"

Gittel was shocked. How did this stranger know who she was and about her financial struggles?

Persistent in his questioning, he inquired about her daughters' difficulty regarding *shidduchim*. It was all too strange to Gittel. This man knew everything.

Finally he finished his inquiry and gave her the following instructions. "Got to the head of this town's bank and tell him to give you 10,000 *kopeks*. That should be enough for you and your two daughters."

By now Gittel was entirely dumbfounded. "Assuming you have the money in the bank, why should the man at the bank give me the money? How will he know that I'm not making up the entire story myself?"

The old man sent for two *bochurim* to sign as witnesses. A makeshift document was immediately composed and two *bochurim*, one named Yosef Chaim Sonnenfeld and the other Yehudah Greenwald, were brought over from the *beis medrash* to sign the document and validate its authenticity. She thanked the mysterious stranger and entered her home shocked at what had transpired.

Early the next day, Gittel arrived at the bank hopeful yet skeptical. She showed the teller the document she held in her hand, entitling her to the large sum of money. The bank clerk was puzzled by the note and excused himself as he went to locate the bank manager to obtain permission to release the funds.

Immediately the manager, white as a ghost, emerged and asked to meet the woman who had brought the letter. He asked her to describe the old man and she tried to depict him as best she could. After her brief description the manager asked if she would recognize the man if he showed her a picture. He produced a photograph and she confirmed that the man in the picture was indeed the man she had met. And then suddenly he fainted.

After he was revived, the man sat up, sipped a cup of water, and spoke to the small crowd that had gathered. "The man in the picture was my father. Although he was a religious man I did not follow in his ways. And when he passed away I didn't even have the decency to say *Kaddish*. I just didn't care. But there was one woman who did care. She relentlessly assisted those who have no one saying *Kaddish* for them. And this included my father. Last night my father appeared to me in a dream and informed me of the events that would happen today. He asked me to provide the necessary funding to repay this widow and endow her with sufficient money for two dowries for her daughters. And now, realizing my terrible mistake, I intend to repay this woman for her kindness."

The bank manager proved true to his word and granted the woman and her daughters the money that was promised. In a short period of time both of the girls became engaged and their mother continued her wonderful custom. But this time there was no longer a need to buy the *Kaddish* on credit.

Saved by a Favor

SEVERAL YEARS AGO, RAV CHAIM KREISWIRTH *ZT"L* spoke at the "Ezer Mitzion" dinner. There he shared with the crowd his own personal account of how he was saved by a *chesed*.

The year was 1941 and the world was in a state of turmoil and chaos. The Nazis *ym"sh* had begun to unleash their terror on everyone and everything that stood in their path. In Warsaw, some Jews had been forcibly taken away and had not been heard from. Everyone was frightened and worried, but somehow life went on. Amazingly, the flame of Torah continued to burn strong throughout all of Eastern Europe. Yeshivas Ohr Yisroel, a popular yeshivah in Warsaw, had even recently hired Rav Chaim Kreiswirth, a 17-year-old genius, as a *maggid shiur*.

Filled to capacity, the yeshivah was not able to provide every *bochur* with a bed. Some were forced to sleep on the floor while others had to arrange for their own accommodations. But Rav Chaim's status as a faculty member enabled him to receive a bed in the yeshivah's dormitory. One day, the Rosh Yeshivah approached Rav

Chaim and introduced him to a young man who had just arrived in Warsaw. Immediately Rav Chaim noticed something unusual about the young man. He did not look up at the Rosh Yeshivah nor would he even glance at Rav Chaim. At first it appeared that the fellow was simply shy and wanted to avoid eye contact but an exchange of *shalom aleichem* greetings revealed a much more serious issue.

His name was "Yeshayala Mishnah," an appellation bestowed on him due to his outstanding expertise in quoting Mishnayos by heart. Due to a crippling disease he had contracted as a young boy, he was considered legally blind, a disability that pushed him to memorize countless tractates of Mishnah by heart and hence, his distinctive title. Rav Chaim took the newcomer under his wing and accepted the responsibility of finding him a place to live. But that was easier said than done as numerous leads for Yeshayala's lodging arrangements had produced no results. Instead of admitting failure, Rav Chaim took Yeshayala in as his own roommate, choosing to give him the only bed in his own small room while he himself slept on the floor.

Rav Chaim told no one about his sacrifice, and no one would have found out if not for the fact that the *bochur* who entered the room in the morning to wake them for Shacharis noticed Reb Chaim on the floor.

Meanwhile, rumors were circulating around town regarding the fate of those captured by German soldiers. And then, with little prior warning, they came. Storming into the *beis medrash*, the Nazi officers fired off a round of bullets, ripping holes in the ceiling and filling the room with fear. One menacing soldier took charge and marched forward to the *shtender* that stood in the front of the *beis medrash*.

What a *chillul Hashem!* The spot that had until this time been sanctified with the Rosh Yeshivah's Torah-filled *shiurim* was now being desecrated by the craven and merciless enemy. The soldier held in his hands a list of the entire yeshivah body, students and faculty. One by one he calmly called out their names and ordered them to come forward. There they were met by another soldier who escorted them outside and then — a booming sound of a rifle shot splitting the air was followed by an eerie silence. This methodical process continued for the better part of an hour. But the soldiers seemed to be in no hurry, as precision and efficiency were hallmarks of the Nazis' well-oiled killing machine.

Finally Rav Chaim heard his name announced. He walked forward prepared to accept his fate and sacrifice his life as so many others had done. But as the man who was to take his life greeted him, Rav Chaim afforded himself one final plea to his Maker. "*Ribbono Shel Olam,* please allow the *zechus* of my Torah learning to protect me. And if that is not a sufficient merit then allow the *chesed* that I have performed for Yeshayala Mishnah for the last twelve months to speak on my behalf."

As Rav Chaim walked outside he felt the barrel of the soldier's gun sticking into his back. He peered around at his surroundings and saw the pile of dead bodies that lay no more than twenty feet in from of him. The yeshivah's courtyard had been transformed into a killing field and Rav Chaim was next.

The soldier turned toward him, but instead of raising his rifle to shoot he placed his hand on Rav Chaim's shoulder and spoke in a firm but quiet tone. "Listen, you look like a fine fellow. I don't wish to be here any more than you do. I don't want to kill anyone, but if I don't then my superiors will kill me." Rav Chaim could not believe what he was hearing. It seemed more like a dream than reality.

"So this is the plan." The soldier now spoke with urgency in his voice. "I am going to shoot twice into the air to make it appear as though I have killed you. This way they won't suspect anything. But you must run for your life. There are no guarantees that no one else will catch you, and they won't be as compassionate as I am. Now run for your life!"

Two shots cracked in the air. But Rav Chaim did not turn around to look. He ran as quickly as his feet could carry him to the outskirts of the town. And from there he miraculously escaped to safety.

Rav Chaim, the Av Beis Din of Antwerp and Rosh Yeshivah of a number of Torah institutions of higher learning, concluded his gripping tale with a poignant thought. "I have been *zocheh* to be a Rosh Yeshivah for sixty-seven years. Look at what the power of a *chesed* can achieve!"

I Never stopped Hearing Her Cry

S BH, Sephardi Bikur Holim, is one of the largest *chesed* organizations in the world. Ironically it was not founded by a Torah giant, but rather by a layman with a heart of gold. His name was Joseph Beyda — and this is his incredible story.

Susan Farez had her hands full. Living in a cluttered, messy apartment she found it a grueling challenge to manage the two jobs necessary to pay her prohibitive medical bills. Long ago abandoned by her abusive husband, merely coping was becoming increasingly more difficult. Ever since she had been diagnosed with cervical cancer the daily grind had become too demanding. She needed help badly.

Joseph Beyda had left his elegantly appointed corner office in one of his centrally located high-rise Manhattan office buildings earlier that day. The 30-minute commute to his Brooklyn living quarters passed uneventfully. As he walked through the door of his well-designed home, he placed his briefcase neatly in the closet and sat down on the living-room sofa for a well-deserved moment of relaxation.

Thirty seconds later the shrill ring of the telephone cut his rest short. Joseph pulled himself off the couch and answered the phone. The woman on the other end of the line informed Joseph about the plight of one Susan Farez whose dire situation was one that required immediate attention. A look of concern came over Joseph as he promised he would do whatever he could.

Joseph tapped lightly on the shabby-looking apartment door, inadvertently knocking additional peeling paint to the floor. Susan Farez answered the door and opened it just enough to see who could possibly have come to visit her. Joseph negotiated his way into the stuffy run-down apartment and discreetly surveyed the awful surroundings. Susan Farez offered him something to drink but he politely refused.

Moments into their pleasant conversation her 11-year-old son entered the room. Initially he appeared to be somewhat reserved but before long Joseph realized that this young man suffered from autism. As Joseph wondered how the situation could possibly get any worse, a petite 3-year-old girl scampered into the room, crying bitterly.

Why is she crying? wondered Joseph. *Is it because her mother is terminally ill and incapable of providing proper care for her? Could it be due to the fact that all her mother's attention is being directed toward her autistic brother? Or maybe it is for the simple reason that she is just not feeling well.* The possibilities seemed endless.

"Don't worry, honey. Mommy's here," Susan soothingly attempted to console her distraught child, as the hysterical crying intensified. "It'll be okay," Joseph added softly.

I just lied, Joseph pondered, reevaluating the child's sad quandary. *Nothing is going to change. Her father will never return. Her mother is terminally ill and her brother will remain autistic forever.* Joseph had to bite his lip to prevent himself from crying as tears welled up in his eyes. *I just wish there was something I could do.*

Their conversation continued for another half hour though Joseph had difficulty hearing himself over the never-ending cries of Susan's 3-year-old daughter.

Joseph left the Farez's residence with an empty feeling in his heart. The trip home seemed to take twice as long as it did on the way there. He walked into his beautiful home overwhelmed with feelings of guilt. Wherever he turned he heard that little girl's cry. It just wouldn't stop. He poked at his supper, but the cries resonated in his heart and mind.

That evening, Joseph, normally a productive person, tried to rid himself of a cold numbness that had dulled his senses, but he accomplished nothing. Left with no other choice, he decided to retire for the evening.

Joseph went upstairs, showered, went to bed and struggled to fall asleep — but all he heard was that little girl's cry. He twisted and turned throughout the night, all to no avail.

The next morning Joseph "woke up" oddly refreshed. Boasting a proud smile he sauntered down the steps with new vigor. "I've got it," he proclaimed to no one in particular, "we can help Susan and her little girl."

Joseph picked up the phone and called his good friend Jack Dweck. "Jack, we have an important board meeting tonight. I have a matter of utmost importance that I must share with you."

That evening Joseph revealed his historic proposal. "We're going to begin a brand new organization, and we're going to help everyone in need; no expense too great, no task too daunting. Each 'client' will be treated with the respect they deserve." Joseph's address that evening was masterful, conveying to his audience the necessity for establishing such an organization.

And so began SBH, Sephardi Bikur Holim.

Throughout the years many skeptics have attempted to explain to SBH volunteers why this project cannot be achieved or that duty cannot be undertaken. But Joseph, in his inimitable fashion, justifies the need, "because otherwise we will have stopped listening to their cries and that is simply not an option."

Today, SBH is a thriving *chesed* organization with a budget in the tens of millions of dollars a year. Among their many accomplishments is the relocation of over six hundred and fifty Syrian families.

Joseph Beyda tragically passed away at the young age of 57, though he accomplished more in his short lifetime than others have in several lifetimes. Through his crowning jewel — SBH — his legacy lives on.

A Picture Is Worth a Thousand Words

JUNE 12, 1989. SURI AND MOSHE GOLDMAN HAD ONLY recently enjoyed the celebration of their wedding. A beautiful yet modest affair, everything was just right. From the dresses and understated flowers to the band and energetic dancing, it was the dream of a lifetime. The young couple was so happy, basking in the new life they were starting together and savoring every moment and each new experience. As they often talked about and relived the wedding, Suri anticipated the arrival of her wedding photos. She waited daily for the phone call from the photographer. From the time they would meet with Randi, who would be their contact person at the photography studio, it would not take long for the album to be completed. Suri knew exactly how she wanted the album to be layed out.

The phone call finally came. Suri came home and flicked on the answering machine. "I'm calling for Suri Goldman. This is Randi from Three Star. When you have a chance, please call the Three Star office to schedule an appointment."

Excitedly saving the message on her answering machine, Suri quickly called the office to arrange for the earliest possible appointment. Randi gave her a slot between 2 and 3 o'clock the following Sunday afternoon. Before hanging up the phone Suri asked, "By the way, could you just let me know what the balance is on my account?" Suri knew that her parents had exhausted all their funds on the wedding and could ill afford to pay for the "luxury" of a wedding album. "Don't worry," Randi reassured her. "The balance isn't due until you receive the finished product."

The excitement built. Suri and her husband arrived promptly for their 2 o'clock meeting. They were escorted to one of the corners of the Three Star office and sat down as Randi brought in the photos. "Take your time leafing through them," she said. "They really came out beautiful. I hope you enjoy them." Suri's eyes misted over as she looked at page after page of the beautiful prints from her wedding.

Twenty minutes later they thanked Randi and scheduled an appointment to bring in the pictures they had selected for their album. When she called her parents and in-laws, however, Suri's joy quickly turned to apprehension. Both sets of parents, while overjoyed for her that she had received the prints, nevertheless expressed their regret that they would not be able to afford anything more. If that meant forgoing an album for the parents, then so be it. They sincerely apologized but there was simply no money left.

At any rate, Suri prepared her own album, carefully selecting the fifty most important photographs that would create the perfect album. Satisfied with her choices, she met with Randi and showed her exactly how she wanted the album. Randi informed her that she would give her a call when it was ready and wished her well. Before she left she requested the balance on her account. The amount shocked her, but she did not show it. She simply thanked Randi for all her help.

Walking home, Suri began to panic. She wanted this album so very much, but without help from her parents or in-laws, where would they get the $1,500 that remained on balance? She thought of every possible way to make extra money but none seemed likely.

Two months later Suri received a phone call from Three Star; the album was ready. Suri's panic was renewed; she knew that she did not have the money to pay the photographer. She informed them that she needed just a few days to put together the last few hundred dollars and that she would be in as soon as possible. Randi was understanding and notified her that the album would be waiting for her when she was ready.

That evening, Suri sat down with her husband to work through the payment. Sensing her disappointment, he sadly explained to her that their wedding money was already being used and it just seemed foolish to spend $1,500 at this time; it would make more sense to wait until they were a little more financially secure. He felt terrible but what was he to do? Saddened, she tried to hide her disappointment. It clearly wasn't his fault and she didn't want him to feel guilty. "One day we'll get our album," she said. "One day — "

June 6, 2001. Meir and Rusi Silver, a wealthy young couple, was led to the backroom of Three Star Photographers. Randi apologized that there was no better area for them to meet, but good business and the summer rush had caused for an overflow of *chossonim* and *kallos* coming in to pick up their pictures.

Their recent wedding had been everything they had hoped for. A lavish and elegant affair, everything had gone perfectly. From the food to the flowers it was an evening they would never forget.

The young couple would be starting out their married life in Eretz Yisrael. Although their parents were hesitant about allowing their children to live overseas in the age of suicide bombings, nonetheless they were proud that their children were dedicated to a life of Torah and thus supported their decision to live where their son/son-in-law would learn best.

As the young couple sat down in the back room they glanced around at the hundreds of wedding albums adorning the storage-room walls. Curious, they asked Randi why hundreds of albums were stored there when a few sample albums would suffice. She explained that these belonged to customers who had never picked up their final album. "That's odd. Why would someone leave behind a book that would allow them to relive the most special night of their lives?" They could not figure out a reason and with their recent wedding night so clearly etched in their hearts and minds, the mere thought of not being able to ever look back on that night disturbed them greatly.

"Well," Randi responded, "if they don't pay up the balance then we can't give them the album." The policy was not an insensitive one. It was the only way to run such a business. Meir stood up and asked to select an album off the shelf. Randi chose one of the many and handed it to Meir.

Meir stared at the cover. "Moshe and Suri Goldman, June 12, 1989." He flipped through the pages, staring at the beautiful, loving couple, and his heart broke at the thought that they could not have this one lasting memento of their most special day. He wondered what their story was. Why hadn't they paid the balance? He looked at his wife and they tried to imagine how they could help.

Randi flipped through the album as well. She explained that she remembered the young *kallah* who had been unusually excited to receive her pictures. Unfortunately, she could not afford to pay up the balance.

"How much do they owe?" Meir asked. Randi went to check the records and returned a moment later.

"They owe $400," Randi announced. "It says here that she's sent in $100 a year for the past eleven years."

Meir was moved — imagine this young woman steadfastly sending in bits of money as she could afford it, hoping that one day her balance would be paid and she would own this precious item. He promptly removed his checkbook, wrote out a check for $400, and handed it over to Randi. "Could you please tell her to come pick up her album? When she asks who paid for it, tell her it's a belated wedding present." He thanked G-d, Who had given him the opportunity, within his own happiness, to create joy for someone else.

Suri quieted the children and picked up the phone after the second ring. She listened but could not believe what she had heard: Who could have done such a *chesed*? She left a friend to watch her babies and ran over to pick up the album, and with tears in her eyes thanked Randi, and asked, "Who, Randi, who did this for us?" Randi said she was sworn to secrecy, for the donor wished to remain anonymous. Walking out the door, Suri held onto her album, grateful to Hashem for this unexpected gift. She imagined the scene she had envisioned over these past years: her children gazing with wonder at their parents' beautiful wedding album, seeing for themselves the love and happiness that their parents had shared on that day. Now that vision would become a reality. Indeed, some kind soul whose name she would never know had made a very important wish come true.

Ah Freilichen Purim

*I*SRAEL COHEN, OR SRULIK AS HE WAS CALLED, A 17-YEAR-OLD boy living in the Dachau concentration camp, had contracted the dreaded disease of typhus. The nausea, cramps and high fever left him lying listlessly in his barracks. He had mustered every ounce of strength in his skeletal body to finish the workday. His bunkmates, most of them older, had done their best to help him to his "bed" and when he finally reached the hard slab of concrete he collapsed. It was Adar, the joyous month of salvation when Mordechai and Esther helped save the Jewish people from certain destruction. But it couldn't have felt further away. In Dachau every day felt like Tishah B'Av. Never before had the situation seemed so hopeless; but that did not deter the brave inmates from attempting to celebrate the holiday of Purim.

The hunger had been gnawing at them for days and weeks. They craved and dreamed about perhaps finding a tiny morsel of bread. At mealtime, the block elder appeared flanked by his henchmen, the rations were distributed and were consumed in a matter of minutes. A few moments of eating, and they knew that they had to wait a full day until there was more. There was nothing else to do, so Srulik fell asleep hoping that the next eighteen hours would pass quickly until he would receive his next daily ration of the murky liquid they called soup. That night Srulik dreamt of his past life; he dreamt about his family and his visits to the Rebbe of Ger and wondered if he would ever see that world again.

The next morning Srulik was awoken from his dream and once again re-entered his nightmarish life. But he remembered that it was Purim and because of that he felt a little better. Who knew, maybe someone would remember some of the *Megillah* by heart. And just then Itchie Perelman, his good friend, walked in with a *Megillas Esther*. Some way, somehow they had managed to get hold of a *Sefer Shemos* that had a *Megillas Esther* in the back of it. It was a miracle and they were excited to be able to hear the *Megillah* even though it was not being read from a hand-written parchment scroll.

It was soon decided that Srulik, who had read the *Megillah* aloud back home, would do so here as well. They found an old towel lying around and he wrapped it around his head to form a yarmulka. All eighty people in the barracks gathered around and listened attentively as Srulik began to chant in a low, barely audible voice, "*Vayehi bimei Achashveirosh* …" As he read he found that although he was weak his strength seemed to increase; and the spirits of those around him seemed uplifted if only for a moment in time. Everyone drew strength from the timeless story of a wicked man who had tried to destroy the Jews but had failed. At the end of the reading the inmates all cheered and even the block elder who normally was very cruel smiled when he entered to distribute the soup rations. He didn't yell and shout as he normally did. And no one looked jealously at another's portion. For a small moment in time they imagined the future and dreamt of hope and freedom.

Someone had an idea. He took his precious potato and meager ration of bread, walked over to another inmate and held out these two bits of food. The recipient gave him a puzzled look. "*A freilichin Purim*! Take it. It's *mishloach mannos*."

And so these two items made their way around the room. No longer was food important to them. It was the opportunity to perform an act of kindness! Finally, after each one had given this paltry portion to a fellow Jew, the bread and potato were given to Srulik, in appreciation for reading the *Megillah*. Srulik looked up and wished with all his heart, "Please, G-d, *Leshanah Habaah BiYerushalayim* — Next Year in Jerusalem!"

Gevurah / Courage

Sensitivity and Strength

The tests that we face in life are often difficult and push us to the limit of our abilities. We must reach down deep inside ourselves to find the strength to continue and move forward. If we try, then Hashem will help us find the fortitude and courage to endure.

*T*HE IMREI EMES' OLDEST SON, THE BEIS YISROEL, SUCCEEDED his father as the Rebbe of Ger, a post which he served until his passing in 1975. His brother, the Lev Simchah, Reb Simchah Bunim Alter, succeeded him and served as Rebbe until his passing some twenty years later. The Lev Simchah's genius and ability to guide were only outdone by his unusual sensitivity, a trait which he used to give his Chassidim strength to persevere in the most difficult of times.

Reb Simchah was imbued with this trait from the time he was a young man. At the young age of 16 he married. The initial joy of the marriage was tempered by the fact that the couple did not have children for the first ten years of their marriage. Then, when the Lev Simchah was 26 years old, they were blessed with a child — a little girl.

The joy in their home knew no bounds, but tragically that joy was short-lived as complications from the birth endangered both mother and daughter. Both remained in the hospital for a long period of time, their futures uncertain. The doctors expressed doubts and the entire Gerrer community poured out their hearts for the Lev Simchah's wife and daughter. And then one day the little girl passed away, at a moment when her father was at her side. The Lev Simchah pulled himself together and wondered how he could possibly break the terrible news to his dear wife. They had waited ten long painful years for a little baby and now that baby had been taken from them. How would his wife, who herself was still frail from the birth, deal with the tragedy? The doctors were concerned about how her reaction would affect her health.

What the Lev Simchah decided nearly defies human comprehension. He simply did not tell her. Rather, every day when he visited her, he would recount fabricated tales of episodes in their daughter's life. Each day he would spend some time creating stories that could possibly have happened to their daughter. The pain and inner strength necessary to pull off such a plan required every ounce of *gevurah* in the young father and husband. But for nearly six months, as he nursed his wife back from the brink of death, he did just that. Never affording himself a teardrop for the daughter he had lost, he displayed the resilience that only a man of incredible sensitivity and strength could do.

And then, on one sad day, almost six months after they had lost their daughter, he gently revealed the sad news to his wife. It was only then that he finally allowed himself to cry in the presence of his wife. His princely behavior had saved his wife and allowed her the opportunity to recover. It took twelve more years before they were blessed with another child. By then the Lev Simchah had developed into the heir apparent for the Gerrer Chassidim who, in essence, were all his children. And after his brother passed away he guided the flock for over twenty years, caring for each of his nieces and nephews in the only way that he knew — with a Lev Simchah, a heart that, come what may, was ready and prepared to fill others' lives with *simchah*.

The Broken Bus Driver

IT WAS A DAY THAT BEGAN LIKE ANY OTHER. R' ARON Postofsky, Rosh Yeshivah of the *yeshivah ketanah* Bircas Yehudah, had set out early that morning to prepare for school while his devoted wife Chana Leah remained behind busily tending to their seven wonderful lively children.

The usual pre-school preparations — sandwich-making, test signing and knapsack finding — had concluded. Shlomele, the liveliest of the bunch, kissed his mother good-bye and waited patiently with his siblings at the corner for the yeshivah bus to arrive.

Each and every school day the boys from the Ohr HaChaim neighborhood of Bnei Brak would be picked up and dropped off at the relatively quiet Rechov Lapid and Hapisgah intersection. That bright summer morning the bus arrived promptly and the boys were cheerfully greeted by R' Luzer, the bus driver.

When the bus pulled into the yeshivah's parking lot, the boys rapidly exited and raced into the building, darting through the hectic hallways. The day continued predictably for Shlomele and before he knew it, the time had come for him to return home. The boys were loaded into the crowded bus and settled in for their short ride home.

Fifteen minutes later the half-empty bus arrived at the Postofsky boys' stop and Shlomele excitedly jumped off the bus, eager to go home. R' Luzer, weary from his full day's workload, was slowly pulling away when he heard shrieks the likes of which he had never heard before. Luzer immediately stopped the bus, leaped out and looked back in horror.

The details of what transpired were unclear, but it really did not matter. Shlomele was gone. Chaos ensued. The Postofskys, pillars of their community, were shattered. Their little Shlomele was no longer. His shy smile, his delightful laugh. How it tore them apart.

After the heartrending *levayah* comforters filled their saddened home, searching for the proper words of solace that none seemed able to find. How can one comfort parents who have lost their beautiful child?

Simultaneously, skepticism pervaded the splintered Bnei Brak community. Discussions and whispers. Some of them voiced, others hinted to. "How could it have happened? Where was the supervision?" Some cynics spoke candidly about R' Luzer's negligence. But from the Postofskys not a word.

Shivah passed uneventfully as R' Luzer, who had taken the week off, now faced the imposing task of returning to his now unpleasant job. Luzer had heard the murmurs and ignoring them was becoming more and more difficult. Thoughts of leaving the job had registered in his mind. But to what? To where?

Mulling these thoughts over, Luzer's deliberation was unexpectedly interrupted as the doorbell rang. He hadn't been expecting company, considering that he hadn't had any since the tragic accident.

Luzer moved curiously towards the door, and as he opened it, nearly fainted. Standing before him were Rabbi and Mrs. Postofsky. His knees buckled and he felt faint of breath.

He just didn't know what to say. Were they going to scream at him and tell him how he had ruined their life? Would they shout at him for not having been more careful when Shlomele was crossing the street? Regardless, he had determined that he would accept their admonishments, come what may. He waited — but none came.

Rabbi Postofsky spoke softly and suggested that they sit down and talk for a short while. Luzer nervously invited them into his simple home. Luzer would have offered them drinks but he was simply overwhelmed.

"We've come to tell you, Luzer, that we know this tragedy had nothing to do with you. Many are the thoughts in the heart of a man— , but it is only the Creator of the world who has the power to be '*gozer umekayeim* — decree and implement.' Our Shlomele being taken from us is an edict from Hashem, thus we accept it lovingly. And we recognize that there was nothing you could have done."

Luzer could hardly believe what he was hearing. He had expected the Postofskys to vent their justified anger and not only were they not infuriated but *they* were comforting *him*!

Luzer shifted uneasily as Rabbi Postofsky continued, "Luzer, Chana Leah and I would like to express our thanks for the years of bus service you provided for our Shlomele." Luzer began to weep softly. "And we would be honored to have you continue driving our other children to *cheder*."

Luzer, who up until this point had kept his emotions in check, now embraced Rabbi Postofsky and, clutching his broad shoulders, begged this angelic couple for their forgiveness.

The very next morning Luzer pulled up warily to the intersection of Rechov Lapid and Hapisgah and hesitantly opened the bus door. There stood the Postofskys, parents and children, smiling.

And Luzer could not help but wonder, "*Mi K'amcha Yisrael!*"

Of Hugs and Kisses

SYMPATHY AND EMPATHY. BOTH TERMS DESCRIBE AN expression of feeling someone else's pain, being *nosei b'ol im chaveiro*. However, a fine line exists between the two. We all sympathize with another Jew's suffering but very few are able to empathize and join in the suffering of another as if it is his very own. One person who was able to do so was Reb Isser Zalman Meltzer.

War was on the horizon and the yeshivah of Kletzk, under the leadership of Reb Aharon Kotler, was forced to leave its home and move to America. With the future uncertain, Reb Aharon felt that his teenage son Shneur needed a more stable environment, and sent him to live with his grandparents, Reb Isser Zalman Meltzer and his wife, in Yerushalayim. Shneur would be able to learn and grow in his grandfather's yeshivah.

While Shneur developed into a young man under the watchful eye of his exalted grandfather, war-ravaged Europe experienced uncountable deaths for the next few years. All tolled, over six million Jews perished in the genocide. Few families remained intact. The majority of the Jewish people had suffered the loss of at least one close relative. Few parents had children and even fewer grandparents had grandchildren.

In Yerushalayim, Reb Isser Zalman cherished every moment he spent with his grandson. Each day he spent time learning with the young boy and cared for his every need. Having sensed his grandson's greatness even at a young age, he instilled in him a love for Torah and fellow Jews.

The war ended. Reb Aharon, who had worked tirelessly on behalf of European Jewry during all these years, knew it was time to call his son back to live with his parents, in America. The telegram reached the Meltzers and was met with a bittersweet reaction. On the one hand, they were happy that their grandson would now be able to rejoin his family in America and begin the next chapter of his life. However, the news brought with it some sadness, as they would miss their grandson dearly. He had been such an integral part of their lives over the past five years and now there would be such a void.

Arrangements were made for Shneur to travel by boat to America. He packed a few of his belongings the day before he was to leave and prepared himself for his voyage. The day finally arrived and a still quiet pervaded the morning. The taxi that would bring him to the boat had been scheduled to arrive shortly and Reb Isser Zalman and his rebbetzin waited outside their apartment building for the cab to come.

Finally it arrived. It pulled up alongside the curb and a hefty-looking man got out and opened the trunk. Shneur picked up his small suitcase and placed it in the car. His grandmother hugged him tightly and *bentched* him one last time before he left. Now the time had come for him to say good-bye to his grandfather. Reb Isser Zalman, normally a very emotional man, held out his hand to wish his grandson a *tzeischem leshalom*.

As his students watched, Reb Isser Zalman shook Shneur's hand and wished him well. Shneur got into the taxi, closed the door and waved good-bye one last time.

The farewell had surprised the students. They knew their rebbi as a warm caring sensitive man and now he had appeared to be stoic in parting from his beloved grandson. He had not even hugged his grandson good-bye.

The young men approached their rebbi as he and his wife walked slowly back to their home and asked him why he had not hugged his grandson good-bye. Didn't he feel emotional about his leaving?

Reb Isser Zalman smiled as he wiped his eyes with a handkerchief. "My dear students, I will tell you why I did not hug my grandson good-bye. Believe me, it was quite difficult. My Shneur feels more like a son than a grandson to me. After all, he has spent the last five years living in my home. Regardless, I felt that I would not be justified in expressing my true emotions.

"Think for a moment," Reb Isser Zalman's sincerity could be sensed by the impressionable young men. "How many grandfathers no longer have a grandson to hold close to them? How many grandchildren will never have the opportunity to walk and talk and feel their grandfather's loving embrace? I felt in some way that I had to share that pain. If I hold back from hugging my beloved grandson, perhaps I can understand, just a little, what these poor Jews are going through."

Their rebbi's empathy taught them a lifelong lesson about the sensitivity one must have for another Jew.

Last Moments

Often people are defined by the manner in which they conduct themselves toward the end of their life. The following incidents allow us a glimpse into the greatness of three gedolim.

*T*OWARD THE END OF HIS LIFE RAV YISROEL LIPKIN, BETTER known as Reb Yisroel Salanter, traveled around Europe to visit his children and grandchildren one last time. He left Paris and moved temporarily to Koenigsburg to replace the Malbim who had vacated the position as Rav of the town. While Reb Yisroel was there, his health deteriorated and he was confined to bed. One would have imagined that prior to his passing he would have been surrounded by scores of his disciples. But that was not the case. Instead he was together with only one other person, a simple unlearned man who tended to him as his nurse. The man sensed that Rav Yisroel's strength was ebbing away and that he was dying, and this terrified the caretaker. For many reasons, this man was very frightened of being near the dying or dead.

Reb Yisroel sensed that this fellow was uneasy and he began to assuage his fears. He explained to him that there was nothing to fear and that he would be all right. The man continued to question Reb Yisroel about the demons he had heard about, who surround a dead person, and again Reb Yisroel reassured him that he would be all right. The great sage patiently addressed every question the fellow had. And then, finally, Reb Yisroel was quietly *niftar*.

The caretaker did as Reb Yisroel had instructed him. But he was no longer afraid. He had come to terms with his fears and incredibly Reb Yisroel had convinced him that being a *shomer* for a deceased was nothing to be afraid of.

Eventually the *chevrah kadisha* came and with great respect and caution removed the body of this sacred individual. They spoke to the man and wanted him to relate every last word that Reb Yisroel had spoken prior to his passing. He repeated to the members of the *chevrah* his conversation with Reb Yisroel and how he had alleviated his fears, both of death and of the responsibility of being a *shomer* for a *niftar*. The men were shocked. They hadn't expected Reb Yisroel to be engaged in this type of last-minute preparation before ascending to Heaven. They had envisioned a heartfelt *Vidui* and meditation, not a mundane conversation with a man who had phobias and anxieties about being in the company of a dead person.

But then they realized that this was vintage Reb Yisroel. Perhaps he too had imagined his final moments as they did. But the opportunity to help another Jew had presented itself and what greater *zechus* could one have than spending one's last moments on this earth helping relieve the fears of another Jew.

A similar episode is told regarding the Alter of Novardik, Rav Yosef Yoizel Horowitz. Typhus, a terrible plague, had swept through the town. The townspeople of Kiev and the young men in the yeshivah who had contracted the dreaded disease were quarantined in a special area so that they could not contaminate anyone else. Those who contracted the illness knew their end had come and, though terrified and helpless, had no choice but to enter the designated area for the sick and infected.

And there was the Alter — walking around within the quarantined unit, reassuring and comforting the patients. Everyone marveled at the sight of this saintly aged man, calmly walking around the ward reassuring all those who needed help. Everyone tried to warn him of the danger of becoming infected, but the Alter would simply not listen. He could be seen holding and hugging those whose eyes were filled with fear and apprehension. And later that week the Alter himself was taken away from this world, having accomplished on his last day precisely what he had preached throughout his lifetime.

In 1929 the Jewish people suffered one of the most horrifying massacres of the 20th century. In the middle of the day blood-crazed Arabs ran wildly through the streets of Chevron murdering innocent men, women and children. All told, sixty-nine *korbanos,* including twenty-five boys from the Chevron Yeshivah, lost their lives. Rav Moshe Mordechai Epstein, the Chevroner Rosh Yeshivah, became both physically ill and emotionally disheartened after the tragedy. He held himself personally responsible for the deaths of his students and never recovered from the disaster.

Toward the end of his life he lay in bed unable to move, surrounded by his disciples and his children. He asked to speak to his son privately and requested that everyone else leave the room. As the room emptied, Rav Moshe Mordechai turned to his son and spoke slowly. "My dear son, I am about to leave this world. However this evening one of the young men in the yeshivah is getting married." I want you to give your word to me that tonight, regardless of what happens today, you will encourage the rest of the boys to go to the wedding. An hour later Rav Moshe Mordechai returned his soul to its Maker. The heartrending *levayah* was attended by thousands of Jews. It ended near sunset, at which point the last wish of the Rosh Yeshivah was announced. And that evening the broken young men from the yeshivah, with tears in their eyes and the pain fresh in their hearts, rejoiced at their friend's wedding.

Yehi zichro baruch!

Friendly Fighting

REB LEIBUSH VIEWED IT AS HIS MISSION IN LIFE. IT WAS not that he did not enjoy being the *gabbai* for the Sfas Emes, the first Gerrer Rebbe. But there were parts of the job that he did not enjoy — namely, being in charge of admitting the Chassidim to see the Rebbe. People came from all over to spend a few moments with the Rebbe. His sagely advice and sacred blessings were only part of the reason they came. Perhaps most important to them was the encouraging word and unbridled warmth that he displayed. There were husbands and wives in need of a blessing for children, unsuccessful businessmen who needed advice on how to begin a new business venture and broken families who just needed to hear from the Rebbe that everything would be all right. Balancing all these people's needs was Reb Leibush's job.

He had asked the Rebbe on a number of occasions if it would be possible to hand over this particular task to someone else. He had "served his time" and his soft demeanor was not conducive to the sometimes forceful responses necessary to those who tried to push their way into the Rebbe's office. Generally, those who arrived first were able to be seen first. However, if another Rebbe arrived or if there was some kind of an emergency, then the usual protocol was changed and that person took precedence. All in all, trying to juggle all the variables was a very difficult job.

On most days, the flow of visitors would move forward uneventfully. But it was on the days when an unexpected visitor would come that the Rebbe relied on Reb Leibush's expertise in dealing with people. His forthright honesty and ability to appease those who were growing impatient assured the Rebbe that his Chassidim would not lose patience. And that is precisely the reason that he refused to accept Reb Leibush's daily resignation pleas.

One Sunday afternoon the overflow of people who had come caused the line to extend past the waiting room and out the door. All types of people had come that day to share their worries and concerns with their Rebbe. One by one they entered the inner chamber to spend a few moments with him. To the many Chassidim who had assembled, the two- to three-hour wait was clearly well worth it.

One of those who came was Reb Chaim Grossman, a wealthy well-respected man from a town approximately twenty kilometers from Ger. His fur-lined coat and aristocratic appearance lent him an aura of great importance; however, even he had to wait. And today there was quite a long line. Slowly they all had their turn — husbands and wives, the unfortunate, the needy. And along with them waited Reb Chaim Grossman. With each passing hour one could see the frustration growing on his face. He was obviously not a person who was used to waiting. When Reb Chaim wanted something, he expected to get it quickly.

Many people, upon their departure, left a small donation for the Rebbe to distribute to the poor. Seeing this, Reb Chaim was struck with an idea. He removed his gold money clip which was overflowing with bills and counted out a hefty sum. Though his turn was approaching, he had waited long enough. He moved toward the *gabbai* and placed the money into the palm of his hand. "This is a little gift to move me to the front of the line."

Reb Leibush looked at the money in his hand and looked back at the man who had given it to him. "I'm sorry, that's not how things work here. You're more than welcome to leave a donation after you leave and the Rebbe will see to it that the funds are distributed appropriately. But we don't accept bribes." Reb Leibush spoke with firmness and it clearly surprised Reb Chaim. He was not used to that type of response.

Three and a half hours had passed since Reb Chaim had arrived. There were now only two people in front of him but his patience had worn thin. He had not expected to wait that long and the delay had taken its toll. "How much longer will it be?" Reb Chaim asked, exhibiting great restraint.

"It shouldn't be more than another half-hour." Leibush noticed that Reb Chaim was on the verge of losing his cool. But, he figured, as long as Reb Chaim remains calm everything will be all right.

Another half-hour passed and the last person in line before Reb Chaim stepped out of the Rebbe's inner chamber. But just as Reb Chaim's name was being called, in rushed a messenger from the local doctor. A little girl was hurt and needed an operation immediately. The operation had already begun and the little girl needed the Rebbe's *berachah*. Everyone waiting understood that this emergency took precedence and that the messenger needed to be seen immediately. However, Reb Chaim was not so understanding. He stood up in a huff and ran over to the *gabbai*. "I hope you're not planning to let this person in before me. I have been waiting close to four hours and it's my turn right now." Chaim's ranting scared some of those in the waiting room but Leibush was not in the least bit intimidated. "I'm very sorry but there are rules here. If there is an emergency then it takes precedence."

"I'm warning you. If you do not admit me immediately then I will never give money to the Gerrer institutions again." The threat seemed real but Leibush, although sympathetic, stood his ground. "I'm sorry but my position remains the same. You can go in after the messenger."

Leibush turned away from Chaim and moved toward the door of the Rebbe's room. He placed his hand on the doorknob and began to turn it when suddenly he felt an arm on his shoulder. Chaim, in a rage, grabbed the *gabbai* and turned him around. His face red with fury and his blood pumping feverishly, he clenched his fists, reached back and, to the shock of all those present, punched Leibush in the face, hitting him squarely in the jaw. Leibush's head snapped back and the force of the blow sent him reeling to the ground. The crowd was stunned. Never before had such an incident taken place. Leibush's nose was bleeding and his face was red and sore where he had been hit. All of this commotion caused the Rebbe to come out of his chamber. Bewildered, looking at his *gabbai* lying on the floor, the Rebbe asked Leibush what had happened.

Leibush did not say a word. He stood up shakily, placed a handkerchief on his nose and looked at Chaim, while the rest of those around helped him dust off his coat. Finally one person spoke. "Rebbe, this man hit Leibush for no reason. He wanted to see you and had been waiting a while and finally lost his patience when he would not be moved ahead."

The Rebbe stared at Chaim, who was still shaking and scowling. The Rebbe's face grew angry, "Is it true what they're saying? Did you really hit Reb Leibush?" The Rebbe did not want to believe what he had heard about Chaim, though he had to get to the bottom of this incident.

"Yes it is," Reb Chaim murmured in a barely audible tone. "I came from miles away to spend a few moments with the Rebbe. I've been married for fifteen years and have not been privileged to have children. For many years my wife has encouraged me to come for a *berachah* but I was always ashamed and embarrassed." Chaim, though the aggressor, now looked and sounded pitiful as he spoke with tears streaming from his eyes. "All I wanted was a *berachah* from the Rebbe."

The Rebbe glared at Chaim and then announced, "Well, I promise that I will not see you until Leibush grants you forgiveness." The Rebbe turned abruptly and walked back inside his chamber. The door closed and no one dared to speak. All eyes were fixed on the two combatants: Leibush, who clearly had the sympathy of those standing around, and Chaim, who stood there embarrassed, angry and ashamed.

Without saying a word Chaim turned to leave. He walked toward the door and placed his hand on the doorknob. But as he turned the handle, Leibush sprung up from his position and pounced on him like a barracuda. He grabbed both shoulders and with all his might pulled him back toward the Rebbe's chamber. In an unheard of move he burst into the Rebbe's office and shouted, "Rebbe!" The Rebbe turned around, shocked at what he saw.

"Rebbe, you say that you won't give Chaim a *berachah* until I forgive him. Well, I refuse to forgive him unless you promise him that he will be blessed with a child!"

Chaim was shocked and did not know what to say. The towering *gevurah* and self-control that Leibush had displayed after being struck in the face was astonishing. The Rebbe, knowing the greatness of his *gabbai*, nodded and placed his hands on Chaim's head. Recalling the years of pain and frustration he had endured, Chaim cried bitterly. The Rebbe whispered to himself for a moment and tears trickled from his eyes. Leibush watched and tears welled up in his eyes as well, though he was still quite shaken from the punch he had taken. The Rebbe completed his *berachah* and Chaim, not knowing what to say, quietly managed a thank-you to this angel of a man.

Nine months later a baby boy was born to Reb Chaim and his wife. When the Rebbe received the good news he made a *l'chaim* with his *gabbai*, who had been the first to receive word of the mazal tov. And at least for one more day Leibush agreed to remain the *gabbai* of the Gerrer Rebbe.

A Little White Lie

*T*HE FRUSTRATION WAS MOUNTING. NOT ONLY WAS DANNY upset, but his whole family, especially the childlren, had grown irritated with their difficult living arrangements. Though only 12 years old, he had already moved six times. His father, a congregational rabbi who had served in many small towns, always tried his best but the right job and the ability to support his family seemed to elude him. Danny, his sisters and brother suffered from the lack of stability and lack of long term friendships that other families enjoyed.

At the end of seventh grade, Danny was further frustrated with his family's situation and was becoming, as a result, bored and uninterested in his yeshivah studies. Noting this change, he and his parents decided he might do well in a yeshivah high school that allowed students to board with families in town, and that could accommodate his needs for a structured program. They felt that the benefits of living with a family would be perfect for Danny at this time in his life. After much research, they settled on a school where Danny's parents hoped that the warmth of the Rebbeim would spill over and help reinvigorate Danny's *Yiddishkeit*. Unfortunately things did not work out that way.

That year, Danny's mother was diagnosed with cancer. Danny's response to this turn of events was to become angry with the A-mighty. His Torah observance fell by the wayside and the resentment toward anything religious built up inside of him. By the time he was in ninth grade, 14 years old, he was a full-fledged *mechallel Shabbos*. He openly challenged accepted Jewish practices and customs, arguing vehemently with his rebbeim and boarder family. His relationship with his parents, strained from years of tension, got even worse. They barely spoke except for the occasional phone call when he would ask his father for more money.

As his mother's health deteriorated, Danny dreaded going back home but feelings of guilt got the better of him and he decided to return home for Pesach vacation, turning down an opportunity to become a waiter at a hotel in Miami. The doctors felt that there was no longer anything that could be done to help Danny's mother and so she was sent home. The living room became a hospital, with nurses and IV poles, and various machines that made it difficult for anyone to move around. As her breathing slowed and the family braced for the worst, Danny's bitterness added stress to an already horrific situation. And then, in middle of the night, on Erev Yom Tov, she passed away. The funeral was attended by a large crowd who came to pay their last respects to a warm caring woman. Danny, together with his older brother, recited the *Kaddish* and went home, broken and lost.

Danny's brother Yosi had unfortunately also become disenchanted with Torah and was now known as Joey. Danny and Joey tried to talk about their mutual estrangement from tradition, but ironically Danny found himself not only being a reticent debater, but actually trying to defend Jewish traditions. There was something deep inside of him that prevented him from just spewing forth his usual rhetoric against Orthodoxy. In fact, the Pesach Seder that night was strangely soothing. Their mother's sickness had dominated their lives for the past few years and now with the silencing of the beeping machines the quiet serenity that filled the sad home was a much-needed rest for a family so torn and splintered.

The next few years passed and Danny, who had recited the *Kaddish* when he was in shul, and had been pretty careful about attending *minyan* during his year of mourning, continued slipping. Shabbos was an afterthought and although he went through the motions of what he had to do in yeshivah, his anger at G-d for what had happened to his family continued to grow. His rebbi, Reb Tzvi, bestowed upon Danny much patience and love to prevent him from straying even further.

His disillusionment notwithstanding, somehow Danny was moved by Reb Tzvi's caring concern and that of his peers and decided to attend a yeshivah in Eretz Yisrael after high school. There, Danny nurtured relationships with kind caring rebbeim and though he was still unable to get along with his father and could not come to terms with his mother's passing, he began, ever so slowly, to grow in his Torah observance. His *Shemoneh Esrei* was time that he treasured, a time when he could speak to G-d and share with Him what was on his mind. And though he occasionally would slip here and there in his observance, he was headed — finally — in the right direction.

After his stay in Eretz Yisrael he moved back to America and was admitted to a fine yeshivah where he could continue to grow. He also began to learn a trade and worked part-time for a contractor. The arrangement went well and Danny felt happier than he could ever remember.

At some point, Danny was convinced by friends to become involved in NCSY, and he began to attend their Shabbatons. He would help out kids from secular backgrounds and teach then about the beauty of Torah and Judaism. He was well liked and respected by both the children and the staff.

One Friday night, Danny walked past a group of young teenagers who had just finished an inspiring workshop. Their group leader had spoken to them about overcoming *nisyonos* and how more often than not things would work out for the best. As Danny passed by, he could not help but hear the conversation going on. He heard a young boy, perhaps 12 or 13 years old, declare that his mother had cancer. Without thinking, and just as a manner of relating, Danny chimed in, "Really? My mother had cancer too."

The conversation stopped and immediately the young boy looked up. His eyes were intently focused on Danny and he was so happy that he had found someone to whom he could relate. "Your mother also had cancer?" It sounded strange but he was excited that someone else had been in the same predicament as he was. "So then what happened to her?"

The question stopped Danny in his tracks. He blew it. Why did he have to say anything. In a split second the pain and loneliness of not having a mother rushed into his heart. The bitterness that he always tried to keep locked up inside of him threatened to rear its ugly head at the expense of an unsuspecting, vulnerable little boy. He wanted to tell him that she died and that he still hadn't forgiven Hashem for making him have such a miserable life. He wanted to tell this kid that he was in for a miserable next few years and that when he needed his mother most she wouldn't be there for him. He wanted to unleash the anger and rage that he had been certain had left him — and which, he now realized, was still very much part of him.

But he didn't.

He looked at the young boy and put his arm around him. "You know what? She's doing great now. Really." The smile that formed on his little friend's mouth could not be contained. He spoke to the boy and encouraged him to always focus on the positive.

He had lied. But he finally knew that he would be all right. One day he would be able to transform the pain and anguish of the years of his suffering into happiness and joy.

Glossary

aishes chayil — a woman of valor

aleph-beis — the twenty-two letters of the Hebrew alphabet

aliyah — being called to the Torah

almanah (pl. *almanos*) — widow

amud — podium

aron — coffin

aveiros — transgressions

avodah — service in the Temple

avodas Hashem — the service of G-d

baal Mussaf — the one who leads the Mussaf prayer service

baal teshuvah — a penitent returnee to Jewish life

baalebatim — householders

baalei tefillah — those who lead the prayer services

Beis HaMikdash — the Holy Temple

beis medrash — study hall

bentching — saying Grace After Meals

berachah — blessing

bimah — table in synagogue from which the Torah is read

bircas habanim — parental blessings

Bircas HaGomel — blessing said by one who has been saved

Bircas HaMazon — Grace After Meals

bircas hedyot — layman's blessing

Birchos HaShachar — blessings said at the beginning of the morning prayers

blatt — folio page

Bnei Yisrael — the Children of Israel

bochur (pl. *bochurim*) — young man

Borei Olam — the Creator of the World; i.e. G-d

bris — circumcision

bubby — grandmother

chaburah — group

challah — braided bread used at Shabbos or festive meals

chashivus — importance

chavrusa — study partner

chayal (pl. *chayalim*) — soldier

chazzan — leader of prayer services

cheder — elementary school

chein — grace

chesed — kindness; acts of beneficence

chevrah kadisha — burial society

chiddushim — Torah novellae

chillul Hashem — desecration of the Divine Name

chinuch — education

chizuk — encouragement

choson — bridegroom

Choson Bereishis — the person called to the Torah to begin the new cycle of Torah reading on Simchas Torah

Choson Torah — the person called to the Torah to complete the annual cycle of Torah reading on Simchas Torah

Chumash — Five Books of Moses

chuppah — canopy under which the marriage ceremony takes place

d'veikus baHashem — the ecstatic state of cleaving to G-d

daf — page (of Talmud)

Daf Yomi — worldwide Torah study project in which all Jews study the same folio page of Talmud every day

derashah — sermon or discourse

doar — post office

emunah — faith

esrog — citrus fruit, one of the four species taken on Succos

gabbai — synagogue sexton; attendant of a Rebbe

gadol b'Torah — great in Torah

gadol (pl. *gedolei*) *hador* — Torah giant of the generation

gaon — genius

gedolim — Torah leaders

gevurah — inner strength

hadran — prayer recited at the conclusion of a tractate of Talmud

Hakafos — the dancing around the *bimah* in the synagogue on Simchas Torah

hashgachah pratis — Divine providence

hasmadah — consistency in Torah learning

Havdalah — ceremony marking the end of Shabbos and festivals

heiliga — holy

heimish — with an old-world flavor

hesped (pl. *hespedim*) — eulogy

illuy — genius

Ivrit — Hebrew

kabbalas panim — groom's reception before the wedding ceremony

Kabbalas Shabbos — Shabbos eve prayers

Kaddish — prayer sanctifying G-d's Name, often recited by mourners

Kaddish Yasom — *Kaddish* said by an orphan

kallah — bride

kasha — question

kavanah — concentration

kavod acharon — final honor

kedushah — holiness

kefirah — heresy

kehillah — congregation

kezayis — halachic unit of measure equivalent to the volume of an olive

kibbudim — honors

Kiddush — blessing recited over wine expressing the sanctity of Sabbath and festivals

kiddush Hashem — sanctification of G-d's Name

kiruv rechokim — teaching non-observant Jews about Judaism

kitel — shroud-like garment worn on certain solemn occasions

Klal Yisrael — Jewish people in general

Kol HaNe'arim — all the children ; when all the young children, as a group, are called to the Torah on Simchas Torah

Kol Nidrei — prayer which begins the Yom Kippur service

kollel — academy of higher Jewish learning, whose students are mostly married men

korban (pl. *korbanos*) — sacrifice

krechtz — moan, sigh

l'chaim — "To Life!"; traditional toast

lama lo — why not?

lamed vovnik — hidden saintly righteous man

landsmen — people from one's hometown

levayah — funeral

levayat hameit — escorting the dead

lulav — palm branch; one of the four species taken on Succos

machlokes — difference of opinion; dissention

Maftir — the last person called up to the Torah reading

maggid shiur — Torah lecturer

malkus — lashes

maseches — tractate

mashgiach — spiritual guide in a yeshivah

maspidim — eulogizers

matanos l'evyonim — charity to the poor, distributed on Purim

mayim acharonim — water used for rinsing the fingers at the end of a meal

mechallel Shabbos — person who does not observe Shabbos

Megillah — lit. scroll; commonly applied to the Book of Esther

mekubal (pl. *mekubalim*) — mystic; one who is well-versed in Kabbalah

melamed (pl. *melamdim*) — teacher

mesechta — tractate

meshulach (pl. *meshulachim*) — solicitor for charity

mesiras nefesh — self-sacrifice

mesorah — tradition

Mi She'beirach — prayer recited at public Torah reading (for the welfare of a particular person)

miklat — bomb shelter

mikveh — pool for ritual immersion

minhag — custom

minyan — quorum of ten men for prayer service

mishloach mannos — gifts of food sent on Purim

Mishnayos Moed — Tractate Moed in Mishnah

Modeh Ani — prayer said upon awakening

mohel — one who performs circumcision

Motza'ei Shabbos — Saturday night

mussar sefer — book on self-improvement

nachas — satisfaction, pleasure

nechamah — comfort

Ne'ilah — concluding prayer service on Yom Kippur

nekudos — vowel marks

neshamah — soul

netz — sunrise

niftar — passed away; one who passed away

niggun (pl. *niggunim*) — tune, melody

Olam Haba — the World to Come

oleh — one who is called to the Torah

parshah — portion of the Torah read each Shabbos

pasuk — verse

payos — sidelocks

peirush — explanation

posek (pl. *poskim*) — halachic decisor

rabbosai — gentlemen

rayah — proof

Ribbono Shel Olam — Master of the World, i.e. G-d

rosh kollel — the head of a *kollel*

sandek — one who holds the baby during circumcision

sefer (pl. *sefarim*) — book

shaliach tzibbur — one who leads the prayers

shalosh seudos — third meal on the Sabbath

Shamayim — Heaven

Shas — the six orders of the Talmud

Shas mentch — one who is well-versed in the entire Talmud

she'eilah — question of a halachic nature

Shechinah — Divine Presence

Shehecheyanu — blessing said on a holiday, new garment, new fruit, etc.

sheitel — wig

shekel (pl. *shekalim*) — Israeli currency, like dollars

shelichim — messengers

Shema Yisrael — prayer recited twice a day, affirming one's faith in G-d

shemirah — guard duty

Shemittah — the Sabbatical year when agricultural work is forbidden in Israel

Sheva Berachos — the seven blessings recited at weddings and the ensuing series of celebrations; the celebrations themselves

shidduch — marriage match

shiur (pl. *shiurim*) — lecture; lesson

shivah — seven—day period of mourning

shmuess (pl. *shmuessen*) — ethical discourse

shomer — watchman

shomer mitzvos — one who is observant of mitzvos

Shomer Shabbos — one who observes the Sabbath

shtender — lectern

shtetl — town, village

shtiebel (pl. *shtieblach*) — lit. room; shul, usually used by Chassidim

shtikel Torah — a Torah thought

shtreimel — fur hat worn by Chassidim on Sabbath and festivals

shvere — difficult

siddur — prayer book

sippur — story

siyata d'Shmaya — Heavenly assistance

siyum — celebration marking the completion of a course of study

succah — booth in which a Jew dwells on Succos

sugya — topic; conceptual unit in Talmud

tafkid — job, calling

taharah — ritual cleansing of the dead

tallis — prayer shawl

talmid (pl. *talmidim*) — student

talmid chacham — Torah scholar

tefillah (pl. *tefillos*) — prayer

tefillin — phylacteries

terutz — answer

teshuvah — repentance

tzaddik — righteous person

tzedakah — charity

tzeischem leshalom — a parting wish to one setting out on a journey

tzibbur — congregation

tzitzis — fringed four-cornered garment; the fringes themselves

Ulpan — Hebrew study program

upshlug — disproof

Vidui — confession said before death

vort — Torah thought

Yahrtzeit — the anniversary of a person's passing

Yamim Noraim — High Holy Days

yasher koach — lit. may your strength be renewed; thank you

yasom (pl. *yesomim*; f. *yesomah*) — orphan

yeshivah gedolah — yeshivah for older students

yeshivah ketanah — elementary school

yeshuah — salvation

Yetzias Mitzrayim — the Exodus from Egypt

Yiddishe treren — tears shed by a Jew

Yiddishkeit — Judaism

Yiras Hashem — fear of G-d

Yizkor — prayer recited in memory of departed relatives

yungerman (pl. *yungerleit*) — young married man

zaidy — grandfather

zechus (pl. *zechusim*) — privilege; merit

zemiros — songs sung at Shabbos and festival meals

z'man — semester

zocheh — worthy

This volume is part of
THE ARTSCROLL SERIES
an ongoing project of
translations, commentaries and expositions on
Scripture, Mishnah, Talmud, Midrash, Halachah,
liturgy, history, the classic Rabbinic writings,
biographies and thought.

For a brochure of current publications
visit your local Hebrew bookseller
or contact the publisher:

Mesorah Publications, ltd

4401 Second Avenue
Brooklyn, New York 11232
(718) 921-9000
www.artscroll.com